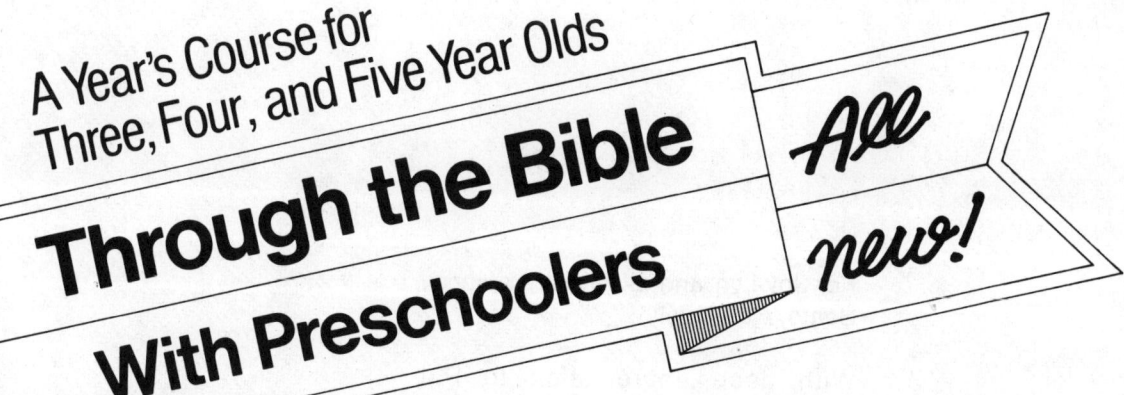

A Year's Course for Three, Four, and Five Year Olds

Through the Bible With Preschoolers

All new!

by Carole S. Matthews
Illustrated by Richard Briggs

Order a copy of *Through the Bible Activities for Preschoolers* for each child, plus two for the teacher. *Book One* (#3331) will be used with lessons 1-13. *Book Two* (#3332) will be used with lessons 14-26. *Book Three* (#3333) will be used with lessons 27-39, and *Book Four* (#3334) will be needed for lessons 40-52.

The book, *A Child's First Book of Bible Stories,* by Wanda Hayes (#2949), is used for its stories and pictures.

All music suggested in the lessons is taken from *Songs for Preschool Children* (#5754).

STANDARD PUBLISHING
Cincinnati, Ohio
3330

For Joy-Lyn and all my other Honey Bears, with love!

With deep appreciation to Pat Stansell, Laverne Kremer, and the many other friends whose "gift of helps" made this curriculum possible.

Scripture quotations marked (NIV) are from the Holy Bible, New International Version. Copyright © 1973, 1978, 1984 International Bible Society. Used by permission of Zondervan Bible Publishers.

Other Scripture quotations are from the International Children's Version, New Testament. Copyright © 1978, 1981, 1983 by World Bible Translation Center, Inc. Used by permission of Sweet Publishing Company, Inc.

Library of Congress Catalog Card No. 85-50191

ISBN 0-87239-945-1

Copyright © 1985 by The STANDARD PUBLISHING Company, Cincinnati, Ohio
Division of STANDEX INTERNATIONAL Corporation
Printed in the U.S.A.

TABLE OF CONTENTS

CR = Bible in Pictures for Little Eyes.

* For Joys, see p. 8.

Helps for the Teacher 5

Unit 1: God Made Everything Special
Getting Ready for Unit One 11
   1. God's Beautiful World . . . . *Gen. 1:1-25* 12
   2. The First People . . . . *Gen. 1:26-28* 14
   3. Adam and Eve Leave the Garden . *Gen. 3:1-14* 17

Unit 2: God's Special People
Getting Ready for Unit Two 20
   4. A Boat, a Flood, and a Promise. *Gen. 6:1 - 9:16* . . . 21
   5. God Blesses Abraham . . . *Gen. 12:1-9; 15:4-5; 17:1-8; 21:1-3* . . 24
   6. A Wife for Isaac . . . . *Gen. 24* 26
   7. A Stone Pillow and a Special Dream. *Gen. 27:41 - 28:19* . . 28
   8. Joseph and His Brothers . . . *Gen. 37; 39:1-6; 41-46* . . 30

Unit 3: God's Special Man—Moses
Getting Ready for Unit Three 33
   9. A Baby in the Bulrushes . . . *Ex. 2:1-10* . . . 34
   10. Moses Leads God's People . . *Ex. 3; 4:1-12* . . 36
   11. Crossing the Red Sea . . . *Ex. 13:17-22* . . 38
   12. Rules for God's People . . . *Ex. 19; 20:1-17* . . 40

Unit 4: God's Special People
Getting Ready for Unit Four 43
   13. The Promised Land . . . *Numbers 13-14* . . . 44
   14. The Walls of Jericho . . . *Joshua 1:1-9; 2; 5:13 - 6:21* . . 46
   15. Hannah Trusted God . . . *1 Samuel 1* . . . 49
   16. Choosing a King . . . . *1 Samuel 8-10* . . . 51

Unit 5: God's Special Man—David
Getting Ready for Unit Five 53
   17. A Boy Meets a Giant . . . *1 Samuel 17:1-54* . . 54
   18. Good Friends . . . . . . *1 Samuel 20* . . 56
   19. A Song of David . . . . *Psalm 8* . . . 58

Unit 6: God's People Obey Him
Getting Ready for Unit Six 62
   20. Building God's Temple . . . *1 Kings 5 & 6* . . 63
   21. A Young Girl Helps Naaman . . *2 Kings 5:1-16* . . 65
   22. Daniel in the Lion's Den . . . *Daniel 6* . . . 67

Unit 7: God's Special Son
Getting Ready for Unit Seven* 70
   23. Good News! . . . . . . *Luke 1:5-25, 57-66* . . 71
   24. An Angel Visits Mary . . . *Luke 1:26-45* . . 73
   25. Jesus Is Born . . . . . *Luke 2:1-20* . . . 75
   26. Wise-men Worship Jesus . . . *Matt. 2:1-12* . . 78

Unit 8: Jesus Prepares for His Special Work
Getting Ready for Unit Eight 80
27. A Special Trip .... *Luke 2:41-51* 81
28. John Baptizes Jesus .... *Matt. 3:13-17* 83
29. Jesus Says No .... *Matt. 4:1-11* 85
30. Jesus Chooses Helpers .... *Luke 6:12-16* 88

Unit 9: Jesus' Special Work
Getting Ready for Unit Nine 91
31. A Crippled Man .... *Mark 2:1-12* 92
32. Jesus Feeds a Big Crowd .... *John 6:1-15* 93
33. The Lost Son .... *Luke 15:11-32* 96
34. Jesus Finds a Friend in a Tree .... *Luke 19:1-10* 99

Unit 10: Jesus Shows God's Love
Getting Ready for Unit Ten* 101
35. Jesus and the Children .... *Luke 18:15-17* 102
36. Children Praise Jesus .... *Matt. 21:1-17* 104
37. A Special Supper .... *John 13:1-17* 106
38. The Saddest Day .... *Luke 22:39-23:56* 108
39. The Happiest Day .... *Luke 24:1-12 & John 20:1-18* 110

Unit 11: Jesus' Special Friends Do His Special Work
Getting Ready for Unit Eleven 113
40. Breakfast With Jesus .... *John 21:1-14* 114
41. Jesus Returns to Heaven and His Church Begins .... *Acts 1+2* 116
42. Cornelius Understands .... *Acts 10* 118
43. A Prayer Meeting .... *Acts 12:1-17* 120

Unit 12: New Friends Become Jesus' Followers
Getting Ready for Unit Twelve 122
44. An Ethiopian Reads God's Word .... *Acts 8:26-38* 123
45. Saul Becomes a Friend .... *Acts 9:1-22* 125
46. Dorcas Helps Others .... *Acts 9:36-43* 128
47. Paul the Missionary .... *Acts 18:1-6* 130

Unit 13: More Friends Tell the Good News
Getting Ready for Unit Thirteen 132
48. Barnabas, a Kind Helper .... *Acts 9:27, 11:19-26, 13:1-3* 133
49. A Young Helper .... *Acts 16:1-5* 135
50. Lydia Tells Others .... *Acts 16:11-15* 137
51. A Terrible Shipwreck .... *Acts 27* 139

Unit 14: Heaven: Our Special Home
Getting Ready for Unit Fourteen 141
52. John Sees the Heavenly City .... *Rev. 21* 142

*These units may be more effective if they are used at the appropriate time of the year. To maintain continuity, however, use an entire unit out of order rather than just one or two lessons.

HELPS FOR TEACHERS

Through the Bible With Preschoolers is a learning experience for young children. Through books, games, stories, songs, action games, role playing, and crafts, preschool children learn the truths of God's Word.

Each session is divided into six time segments.

1. **AS THE CHILDREN ARRIVE:** (15 minutes) a time for learning centers which correlate with the lesson. This time begins ten minutes before the class and extends to five minutes after the class begins. Be sure there is an adult at each center and no more than five children to a center.
2. **SINGING AND TALKING TO GOD:** (10 minutes) a time for singing, prayer, and exercise.
3. **READING ABOUT GOD'S WORD:** (10 minutes) a time for reading or telling a Bible story and reading Bible verses from the Scriptures.
4. **REMEMBERING GOD'S TRUTHS:** (5 minutes) a time for committing four Biblical concepts to memory. A total of thirty concepts are taught and retaught throughout the curriculum. These concepts are the essence of the Christian faith stated very simply in question and answer form.
5. **EXPERIENCING GOD'S TRUTHS:** (20 minutes) a time for role playing, games, or doing activities which correlate with the Bible lesson. An activity paper or project further teaches one of the concepts in the lesson.
6. **REVIEWING GOD'S TRUTHS:** (10 minutes) a time for reviewing the lesson concepts and other optional activities.

This curriculum can be used for worship time by combining the *Singing and Talking to God* segment with the *Reading About God's Word* segment. Have the children sit on chairs facing a worship table on which are placed an open Bible and flowers or a picture. This is the suggested order of service:

Song
Prayer by teacher
Active Song
Bible Verse
Quiet Song
Prayer by children
Songs—one active, one quiet
Story from Bible as suggested in each lesson
Song
Dismiss to small groups for the remainder of the lesson.

Through the Bible With Preschoolers can be used also as a Sunday night, Wednesday night, or week-day club curriculum. For class sessions running more than an hour consult page 10 under **Extended Sessions** for additional activities.

GETTING STARTED

Make the entire year easier by doing the following things before you start to prepare the first lesson.

1. Prepare a picture card file. It is essential that you use these picture cards in every lesson. You will need thirty brightly colored 8½" x 11" cards, each containing an appropriate picture on the front and questions and answers on the back. Copy the questions and answers from the next section of the book called, **PICTURE CARDS.** You should cut bright, appropriate pictures from magazines or extra Bible-teaching pictures; or, if you buy an extra copy of each of the four activity books, they could be cut up to provide many of the pictures. Adding some color with a magic marker would make them attractive. When you write the concept question and answer on the back of the card, include the name of the section of the file (Ex., Heavenly Father) where the card should be filed. Cover each card with clear contact paper (available in hardware stores), and file it in the proper section of a 9" x 12" cardboard accordion file (available at stationery or office supply stores). Remove the appropriate cards at home in preparation for each lesson. Replace them after each meeting. Divide the file into these sections:

    The Church
    God's Care
    I Pray

PICTURE CARDS

Concept	Suggested Pictures From Activity Books 1-4	Concept	Suggested Pictures From Activity Books 1-4	Concept	Suggested Pictures From Activity Books 1-4
The Church Pictures:		**I Pray Pictures:**		What can God do? God can do anything.	Book 4, page 11
Who are the church? All people who love and trust Jesus are the church.	Book 3, page 8	When you pray, what are you doing? When I pray, I am talking to God.	Book 1, page 6	**Jesus Pictures:**	
Be sure to explain to the children what it means to love and trust Jesus.		Does God hear you when you talk to Him? Yes, God always hears me when I talk to Him.	Book 1, page 6	Who is Jesus? Jesus is the Son of God.	Cover of Book 4
Who are in God's family? All people who love, and trust Jesus are in God's family.	Book 4, page 4			Who is your best friend? Jesus is my best friend.	Book 3, page 2
Be sure to explain to the children what it means to love and trust Jesus.		When can you talk to God? I can talk to God any time.	Book 1, page 6	Is Jesus alive today? Yes, Jesus is alive today.	Book 4, page 2
What is the Bible? The Bible is the Word of God.	Book 4, page 6	When you have a problem, what should you do? I should pray and ask God to help me.	Book 1, page 8	Will Jesus ever die again? No, Jesus will live forever.	Book 4, page 2
		When you are very happy, what should you do? I should thank God for making me happy.	Cover of Book 3	How did Jesus show you that He loved you? Jesus died for me.	Book 3, page 12
God's Care Pictures:				What is the best gift God has given you? Jesus is the best gift God has given me.	Book 2, page 1
Who takes care of you when you sleep? God takes care of me when I sleep.	Book 1, page 7	When you do something wrong and then say, "I'm sorry, God," what does God say? I forgive you.	Book 4, page 7	What is Christmas? Christmas is the time we celebrate Jesus' birthday.	Book 2, page 12
Who can help you when you are afraid? God can help me when I am afraid?	Book 1, page 10	**Heavenly Father Pictures:**		Why did Jesus come to earth? Jesus came to show us that God loves us.	Book 3, page 2
If you go far away, who will take care of you? God will take care of me.	Book 1, page 5	Who is God? God is our Heavenly Father.	Cover of Book 2	**About Me Pictures:**	
Who gives you food? God makes food grow for me.	Magazine pictures of food	Where is God? God is everywhere.	Cover of Book 1	Who made you? God made me.	Book 3, page 9
		Who made the world? God made the world.	Book 1, page 1	Who helps you to obey? God helps me to obey.	Book 1, page 3
When you are alone and sad, what should you do? I should ask God to help me.	Child praying	Who can go to Heaven? All people who love and trust Jesus can go to Heaven. Be sure to explain to the children what it means to love and trust Jesus.	Book 4, page 2	Does Jesus love children who have problems? Yes, Jesus loves everyone.	Book 1, page 2

Heavenly Father
Jesus
About Me

2. Using tabs, mark the following sections in this book so that you can refer to them easily:

   Singing (S)
   Talking to God (T to G)
   Act It Out (A I O)
   Games (G)
   Add Variety (V)
   Extended Session Suggestions (E S)

3. Secure a list of all the children in your church family who are eligible to attend. Write an invitation to each.

4. Using your copy of *Songs for Preschool Children,* learn the songs suggested and make the additions recommended in each lesson.

5. Using a tape recorder and a pianist, make a recording of all the songs listed in each lesson and play them as you do household tasks or travel in your car. It would also be wise to read the thirty questions and answers, and the ten questions and Bible verses (see **GOD'S WORD** p. 8) into the tape so that you can be familiar with the memory work found in this course. Be sure to include the question each time and include the reference for the Scripture verses.

6. Seek the help of two or three additional teachers. Stress the importance of commitment and dependability. Include them in the planning of each lesson. Plan monthly meetings to inform each teacher of his or her expected duties for each lesson.

YOUR CLASS

Preschool children learn best in a structured, loving atmosphere where the teacher clearly has control and the children are free to express themselves within limits.

Here are a few suggestions as to how to achieve this goal:
1. Be well prepared so that you can give the children your full attention.
2. Greet the children warmly at the door and direct them to constructive activities immediately.
3. Do not allow *any* running around, gun play, loud noises, hitting or nastiness in your classroom. If you establish these rules in the beginning and apply them consistently, your class sessions will be much more constructive.
4. Be prepared to do all the activities in each lesson each week so that the children are never left with time on their hands for getting into mischief, but be flexible.
5. Teach your class to respect each other by listening to each other and expressing concern for each other's needs. Model this behavior yourself.
6. Allow movement from one area of the room to another for various activities. Do not expect preschoolers to sit for long periods of time. One minute per year of age is the length of their attention span.
7. Place an attractive box at the door of your classroom. Call it the "Safe Keeping Box" and ask the children to put toys brought from home into the box for safe keeping during class.
8. Give each child personal attention whenever possible. Kneel on the floor or sit on a small chair to get on the child's level.
9. Send cards to your students during the week to remind them of your love for them.
10. Give each child esteem-building compliments. Example, "God gave you such pretty blue eyes. I like the way you share. It makes me happy to see you being so polite. I'm glad you chose the color red."

AS THE CHILDREN ARRIVE

Three learning centers are suggested in each lesson. They should be set up and ready for use 10 minutes before the class is scheduled to begin. A teacher or mature teen helper should be waiting at each learning center to help the children as soon as they arrive.

The first center is the **Attendance Check Center.** An attendance chart with each child's name carefully printed on it or attendance cards for each child will be needed. Example:

Kristen Carver

Provide stickers or stars for the child to place on the appropriate date after his name or on his card. Every child present should spend a minute or so at this center. Talk to each child about how happy you are that he has come. Congratulate children who come faithfully.

The second learning center is the **Bible Word Center.** Here the children will learn a Bible verse. The introductory sections, *Remembering God's Word* and *God's Word,* will further explain the memorizing of Bible verses (see p. 9). At the **Bible Word Center** you will use materials you make at home. Keep these materials because they are to be reused throughout the curriculum. Clear contact paper, applied to paper or cardboard items, will enable you to use them for years. Keep in mind that preschoolers do not read; be careful never to imply that they should. When words are used at this center, they are for the teacher to read to the child. The child may learn to read the words in the process, but memorizing the verse and reference is more important.

The third learning center changes weekly, and often involves bringing items from home.

SINGING

Preschoolers love to sing. A guitar, autoharp, or piano adds to the enjoyment. If you do not play an instrument, you might ask a musician in your congregation to come to your class to lead the singing. Choose a person who relates well to small children, and ask all the teachers to be present to sing with the children.

Appropriate songs are suggested in each lesson. SPC indicates that the song is found in *Songs for Preschool Children,* (order #5754) Standard Publishing. Additional songs are printed in this book, pages 23, 42, 61, 69, and 90.

TALKING TO GOD

For the preschool child, prayer is natural and spontaneous. If the teacher is uninhibited, the

children will usually follow his/her example.
Here are some hints to help you as you pray with your preschoolers:
1. Use simple words and short sentences.
2. Pray with the children at any time during the lesson that seems appropriate in addition to the times suggested in the lesson.
3. Pray with enthusiasm in your voice.
4. Remember to balance praise and thanksgiving and petitions.
5. Pray about things that the children are interested in.
6. Whenever possible, use the words of one of the concepts you are teaching. Example, "Thank You, God, that You always hear me when I talk to You," or "I thank You that Jesus is alive today."
7. Always introduce prayer by telling the children that we are going to talk to God. Remind them to fold their hands and close their eyes.

Six Ways to Pray With Preschoolers:
1. **Individually**—When one child has a private need or problem, pray with him alone in a quiet place.
2. **Teacher directed**—Sometimes the teacher can pray, and the children listen.
3. **Individual child**—Sometimes one child (usually one of the older ones) will pray out loud while the others listen.
4. **Repetition**—This is a simple way of introducing individual prayer. The teacher tells the students one sentence, and each child prays that sentence as the teacher touches him to indicate it is his turn to pray.
5. **Children's ideas**—The group talks about a subject and each child gives his ideas. Example, "Thank you God for (child's name)." Then the teacher asks each child to fold his hands and close his eyes. The teacher walks around and touches each child when it is his turn to pray his sentence prayer.
6. **Group repetition**—In this type of praying, the teacher asks the children to close their eyes, fold their hands, and say the words after the teacher. The teacher prays by saying only two or three words at a time.

GOD'S WORD
The most important book in this curriculum is the Bible. *The International Children's Version* (Sweet Publishing, Fort Worth, Texas) is used for reading because the vocabulary is chosen from words appropriate to a third grade reading level. It is one of the few versions intelligible by preschoolers. *Open* it, *read* from it *each* session, and teach your children to love God's Word.

All Bible verses to be memorized are quoted from the *New International Version* (Zondervan Bible Publishers, Grand Rapids, Michigan).

The stories are taken from Wanda Hayes' book, *A Child's First Book of Bible Stories*. This book contains pictures to accompany most stories. Preschoolers need visuals! So use the pictures in the storybook or from your church picture files.

The following Bible verses are the suggested memory work. Quote, sing, talk about, and ask questions about these verses frequently during each class session.
1. What does the Bible tell us about God?
   God is good. (Psalm 73:1, NIV) 12, 34, 44, 63, 81, 142
2. Why do we love Jesus?
   We love (Him) because he first loved us. (1 John 4:19, NIV) 58, 88, 92, 93, 108
3. What is a Bible verse that tells us that God loved the world?
   For God so loved the world that he gave his one and only Son. (John 3:16, NIV) 28, 71, 73, 75, 78
4. What should you do when you are afraid?
   I will trust and not be afraid. (Isaiah 12:2, NIV) 30, 36, 38, 46, 54, 106
5. Who should you love?
   Love one another. (I John 4:7, NIV) 56, 133
6. What does the Bible say about obeying?
   Children, obey your parents. (Ephesians 6:1, NIV) 17, 24, 40, 96, 125
7. What does the Bible say about doing what is right?
   Do what is right and good. (Deuteronomy 6:18, NIV) 51, 65, 67, 85
8. What does the Bible say about being kind?
   Be kind ... to one another. (Ephesians 4:32, NIV) 14, 120, 128
9. What does the Bible say about giving thanks?
   Give thanks to him and praise his name. (Psalm 100:4, NIV) 21, 26, 49, 104, 114, 139
10. What people can be children of God?
    To those who believed in his name, he gave

Unit 7 = Christmas - see also Scripture #3 above
Unit 10 = Easter

the right to become children of God. (John 1:12, NIV) 83, 99, 102, 110, 116, 118, 123, 130, 135, 137

Each of these ten Bible verses will be used in the **Bible Word Center** throughout the year. Be sure to keep the word cards, puzzles, etc., that are made for this center and use them often for review.

Remembering God's Word

The purpose of memory work is to implant certain verses and facts in the child's mind and heart so that when he is old he will not depart from the faith.

Learning is natural and fun for preschoolers. Therefore, a game-like, positive, consistent approach is used, with repetition as its key.

Some Do's and Don't's

1. Don't ever use the word "memorize" with the children. Don't ever say "You have to learn this."
2. Read the picture card several times, and then say, "Let's pretend you can read the words," or "Let's see if you can do it," or "Who knows this one?" You read the question, and then see if the children can give the answer.
3. Repeat the same material at several different times each meeting. Give lots of praise, and **be positive.**
4. Act pleased and surprised when the children do know something. Never expect them to know it.
5. If one child gives a correct answer, ask the whole class to say the sentence in unison. Use words like, "That's good. Let's all say the answer now."
6. Make use of rhythm by clapping, chanting, or marching while saying the verse or the answer to the question. Once you decide on a rhythm of a verse or answer, use that same rhythm every time you say those words.

ACT IT OUT

Role playing a story or a situation is frequently used in this curriculum, so the teacher should become very familiar with these guidelines. The teacher's best preparation is observing children at play—either in a home or a preschool. Watch how uninhibited they are, and how freely they play out situations. If the teacher can forget his or her self-consciousness, then pretending will be a delightful part of the lesson.

Here are some guidelines:
a. Let the children express themselves without adult criticism.
b. Never force a child to be part of the role playing. Always make it a privilege to be chosen as an actor.
c. Teach the "freeze" command so that when you need the action to stop, you can say "freeze" and all actors will be perfectly still and quiet—the way real TV actors do it!
d. Always be willing to do it first if the children are hesitant.
e. Always clap after a performance!!
f. Make sure the children understand the story before they act it out.

GAMES

Going on a Trip: Bring a small suitcase from home, and put the lesson's picture cards in the case. Let one child carry the case as everyone walks around the room pretending to go on a trip. Stop occasionally for children to sit as you let a child take one picture card from the case. Ask the question, and let the children state the answer. Then repeat. If you wish, you can pretend to be traveling by plane, train, or car.

Pop-Up Game: You will need a small sheet or baby receiving blanket to cover each child. These covers are also used for the "It's a New Day" game. Use the picture cards described in the lesson plus possibly other cards from other lessons. Let each child curl up on the floor, and cover him with the cover. Ask a question from the picture card. Tell the children that if they know the answer, they can pop up from their covers to answer the question. After one child answers the question, let all the children pop up to answer, too. Repeat for other cards.

Hide the Picture Cards: Have the children hide their eyes while the teacher hides four picture cards in different locations around the room. Tell the children to uncover their eyes and search for the four cards. When one card is found, have the children sit while you ask the question and help them answer. Teach the answers as printed—whole sentence. When the answer is learned, let the children search for another card and learn its answer. Repeat with the other cards.

It's a New Day: Provide small blankets (baby receiving blankets, pieces of sheet, etc.) for each child. Let the children scatter around the room and pretend to be sleeping. Use a bell, or a ringing noise you make with your mouth to awaken the children. Let them pretend to get up when they hear the sound, come over to you, and sit while you ask them one of the questions on the picture cards used in this lesson. Help them answer in complete sentences as written on the card. Then they go back to their pretend sleeping, and you repeat the game with other cards.

Musical Picture Cards: Set up chairs like for the "musical chairs" game with enough chairs for each child. Children march around chairs while the music plays and sit when the music stops. While sitting, ask one question from the picture cards suggested in the lesson. Let the children answer in unison.

EXTENDED SESSIONS

If your class is more than one hour, choose some of the following activities to add to the lesson:

1. Tell the Bible story in a more elaborate way, using flannelgraphs, acting out the story, or using puppets to tell the story.
2. Repeat the songs at the end of the lesson. Preschoolers love to sing.
3. Play games suggested in the **Games** section of this book.
4. Review the Bible verses from the last few lessons.
5. Read one of the books suggested in the supplementary reading list.
6. Let the children act out the Bible story, an incident from the supplementary book, or an idea suggested in the *Experiencing God's Truths* section of the lesson.
7. Add painting and Play-Doh to your activities.
8. Serve a nutritious snack.

ADD VARIETY

In addition to the weekly lesson described in this book, you can spice up your session with the children by writing them a letter and telling them of the special event taking place at the next meeting. Here are some ideas for special events:

Puppet Show—Invite a puppet group from your church or outside your church to tell the Bible story with puppets.

Popcorn Night—Serve popcorn at the end of the session.

Red Night—Everyone wears something red.

Barefoot Night—(summer, of course) Tell the children, "Come to class, but leave your shoes at home." (House-slipper Night can be used in the winter.)

Hat Night—Everyone wears his favorite hat or cap.

Pretend Birthday Party—Have a short birthday party, complete with cake and decorations. (Do not serve anything with red artificial food coloring or chocolate in it. Many children have allergies).

Ice Cream Night—Serve ice-cream cones at the end of the class hour.

Summer Fun—Tell parents to bring a 3-wheeled riding toy for each child and to dress the children in swimsuits. Teacher brings several garden hoses and sprayers. Set up a riding track complete with occasional spray. This special event would need to be held at the end of the class session so that dripping children could go right home after the fun.

Balloon Night—Have a large helium-filled balloon for each child to take home, tied to his arm.

Costume Night—Tell parents to bring the children dressed as a *Biblical* character.

Friend Night—Tell each child he may bring a friend (plan extra teacher help).

Parent Night—Invite parents to attend class with their children.

Lollipop Night—Give each child a large lollipop—avoid red and orange to help children with allergies.

Pajama Night—Teachers and children come clad in pajamas.

Tent Night—Bring a camping tent and set it up (outside if weather permits). Let the children sit in the tent to hear the story.

Gum Night—Everyone is given a piece of gum (avoid pink or red gum) to chew during class. Make sure the children know that this is a special time when they are allowed to have gum and that gum is usually not permitted in class.

Picture Night—Take a picture of each child.

Baby-Picture Night—Each child brings a baby picture of himself with his name on the back. The children have fun guessing who is in the picture.

Unit 1—God Made Everything Special

GETTING READY FOR UNIT ONE

Getting to know the Bible can be a happy experience for preschoolers. Use the Bible in each lesson and help the children know that God's Word is special.

The theme of this unit will be that God made everything special. The Bible stories deal with God's love and power revealed in creating the world and people in His image, and in providing for our salvation. The children should begin to understand that God takes an active role in the world, and that He cares about all that happens. His creation is special to Him. Each child is special to Him.

Learning Objectives: Some things you should expect your children to accomplish in this unit:

The children should know (1) God made the world; (2) God is our Heavenly Father; (3) God loves them.

The children should feel (1) Thankful to God; (2) Love for God; (3) A desire to obey God.

The children should be able to: (1) Tell the highlights of the Bible stories; (2) Say the Bible verses and state simple answers to concept questions; (3) Relate to a handicapped person; (4) Be aware of the need to obey.

Remember, because of the differences in age and maturity, some children will meet more of these objectives than others will.

Bible Verses: Three Bible verses will be introduced in this unit and will be reviewed in later units. There will be a **Bible Words Center** which will help the children understand the memory verse for each lesson. Follow the suggestions in each lesson. Use the words, help the children "read" them in the Bible and say them, and sing them at every opportunity. Be sure to keep the teaching aids used at this Center for use in later lessons.

Books: Several books are suggested for reading at the end of each lesson, if time permits. These books may be placed in the quiet, book corner of your room. *Thank You, God for Wonderful Things; Thank You, Lord, for Me; God Made Everything; Choosing Is Fun;* and *My Sister Is Special* are suitable for the ages of the children and for the subjects being studied. Check your church library, your local bookstore, or order from Standard Publishing.

Bulletin Board: You will need a bulletin board or wall space near the story circle to display words, numbers, and pictures made in class for each lesson, at the eye level of the children. Arrange these items attractively on the board or wall and refer to them during the three lessons of this unit. Use the heading, *God Made Everything Special.*

THINGS TO DO:

Lesson 1: Make or purchase attendance cards or chart, and purchase seals or stars to use with them. Make word cards on 3" x 5" index cards for the **Bible Word Center** (see p. 12). Make number cards from 1-7 (see p. 12).
You will need to gather items needed for *Experiencing God's Truths* suggested on page 13.

Lesson 2: Make a Bible word jigsaw puzzle (see p. 14). Make the "Body" puzzle needed for the **God Made Me Center** (see p. 14). Check library for books about handicapped people. Be sure these books have pictures suitable for showing preschoolers.

Lesson 3: Make Bible word cards (see p. 17). Get a strip of shelf or butcher paper, five feet long, for a mural. Bring items needed for the *Experiencing God's Truths* section (see p. 18).

Unit One: God Made Everything Special
Bible Verse: God is good. (Psalm 73:1, NIV)

Genesis 1:1-25
Lesson 1

GOD'S BEAUTIFUL WORLD

AS THE CHILDREN ARRIVE: Welcome each child. Direct each one to a learning center. It is best not to have more than five children at a table, and it is not necessary for each child to go to all three centers.

Attendance Check Center: Have attendance cards for each child, or write each child's name on a large attendance chart. Display the cards or chart on a wall or bulletin board where each child can easily see and reach it. Be sure to have seals or stars available for each child to place one in the space provided. Let each child know you are glad he or she is present.

Bible Word Center: Have a Bible open to Psalm 73:1. Make a construction-paper arrow, and place it on the open Bible, pointing to the Bible Words, *"God is good."* Show these words to the children. Have each word written on a 3" x 5" card. Let the children see the words in order. Scramble the word cards, and let each child have an opportunity to put them back in order. Ask each child, "What good thing has God done for you today?"

Numbers Center: Write the numbers 1-7 on 3" x 5" cards, using different colored marking pens. Hold up each number, and ask a child to identify it. Let the children put the numbers in correct order. You might say, "We will talk about seven days that are important to us. God did something very special in seven days." Encourage them to listen carefully to find out what happened. You will want to use the numbers when you are reading or telling the Bible story.

At the sound of music from the piano or a cassette tape, have the children go to the story area of the room for singing.

SINGING AND TALKING TO GOD: Sing these songs: "Sing, Little Children, Sing" (p. 37, *Songs for Preschool Children*); "God Is Good" (p. 38, SPC, add a second verse, "Psalm 73, verse 1, God is Good."); "All Things Were Made by Him" (p. 49, SPC); and "Please Him, Please Him" (p. 39, SPC).

Then pray, "Father, thank You for making our beautiful world for us to take care of and enjoy. In Jesus' name, amen."

READING ABOUT GOD'S WORD: Read John 1:3, from the *International Children's Version*. "All things were made through him. Nothing was made without him."

Read the Bible story to the children, using the numbers from the **Numbers Center** to emphasize the number of days. The story is taken from Genesis 1:1-25. CR p. 7,8

God's Beautiful World

At the very start of our world, there was no light at all. It was very dark. Then God's Spirit moved over the dark, wet earth, and He said, "Let light start to shine." And it did because when God tells something to happen, it happens.

God said, "The light is good." Then He divided the light from the darkness. God also said, "I will call the light 'day' and the darkness 'night.'" And that evening, and that morning were the very first day.

On the second day of the world, God made the sky above the wet, shapeless earth.

On the third day, God said, "Let all of the water on the earth come together so I can see dry land." And that is what happened. God watched the waters run together and called them seas.

When the water ran together into seas, it left big, big patches of dry land—hills, valleys, mountains, rocks, and sand. God looked at them and said, "I will call the dry land earth." Then He said, "The earth and the seas that I have made are good."

God looked again at the dry land and said, "I will make all kinds of plants and fruit trees to grow on the earth. And I will put seeds in them so there will be more and more plants and trees on the earth I have made." Then all kinds of plants and fruit trees began to grow just as God told them to. And there was evening and morning one more day.

On the fourth day, God looked at the sky above His earth and said, "I need big lights to shine on my earth to rule the day and the night." So He made the big, bright sun and put it in the sky to shine on the earth in the daytime. And He made the big, round moon and put it in the sky to shine on the earth in the nighttime. Then God filled the wide heavens with millions of bright, shiny stars. When He was through, God looked at the sun, the moon, and the millions of stars He had made and placed in the sky. God said, "They are all very good."

On the fifth day, God filled the seas and rivers with every kind of fish and sea creature that could live in them. He made them so there would be more and more. The whales would make more whales, the frogs would make more frogs, and the fish would make more fish.

After God made all kinds of fish, He filled the skies with beautiful and interesting birds. He made some that fly in the sky and some that just walk around on the earth. He made birds with different shapes like ducks and swans. He made them with feathers every color of the rainbow. The earth and sky were even more beautiful with all of the pretty birds.

God must have been very happy and excited about His new creations. The seas and skies were full of them. But He was not finished. On the sixth day, God made animals to live on His earth. He made cows and pigs and wild animals like tigers and lions. He made small animals like squirrels and tall ones like giraffes. And He made sure there would be more and more animals to fill His beautiful earth. God looked at His creatures and said, "They are good. I like them all."

In six days, God made a beautiful world and filled it with all kinds of plants and animals, but He was not finished yet. Before the sun went down on the sixth day, God said, "Now, I will make the most important creation of all."

From *A Child's First Book of Bible Stories* by Wanda Hayes. Standard Publishing, pp. 10, 11.

REMEMBERING GOD'S TRUTHS: You will need four picture cards from your picture file for today's lesson. The first three are from the *Heavenly Father* section and the last is from the *I Pray* section of your file.

- In our story we learned about our great God. Who made the world?
  God made the world.
- Yes, God made the world.
  Who is God?
  God is our Heavenly Father.
- Yes, God is our Heavenly Father.
  What can God do?
  God can do anything.
- When we look at the beautiful world God made, we feel very happy.
  When you are very happy, what should you do? [*I pray*]
  I should thank God for making me happy.

EXPERIENCING GOD'S TRUTHS: Bring from home a bag containing ten or more objects that God made (Example, a leaf, apple, stone, carrot, piece of wood, potato, feather, shell, etc.). Use the following six statements, and allow one child at a time to answer, "Right" or "Wrong." Encourage the children to explain the wrong answers.

1. At the start of the world, there was no light. (Right)
2. God said, "Let light start to shine." (Right)
3. When God tells something to happen, it happens. (Right)
4. God made the earth and the seas. He looked at them and said, "They are bad." (Wrong; God said the things He made were good.)
5. God filled the earth with fish and the ocean with animals. (Wrong; God put fish in the ocean and animals on the land.)
6. It took God 100 days to make the world. (Wrong; God made the world in six days—hold up six fingers and refer to the numbers used earlier). Say, "Next week we'll find out what else He made on Day Six."

The child who answers the question may reach into the bag (without looking into the bag) and feel one of the objects. The child tries to guess what the object is. If he guesses correctly, he then removes the object from the bag and places it on the worship table.

After each child has had an opportunity to feel and identify an object, play Follow the Leader around the room, pretending to be various animals that God made. After several times around the room, lead the children to the tables.

Give each child an activity sheet, "Things God

Made," (p. 1, *Through the Bible Activities for Preschoolers, Book 1*) and a gift-box or piece of cardboard that is the size of the activity sheet. Let each child glue his activity sheet to the cardboard or box. Place at least six small objects per child on the table. These are objects that God has made (Example, kernel of corn, leaf, small stone, feather, sprig of evergreen, flower, etc.). Help the children match the object to the picture on the activity sheet and glue the object on the picture. Say, "God made this (object) for us to use and enjoy."

Be sure the child's name is printed on the box.

REVIEWING GOD'S TRUTHS: Leave the activity sheets on the table to dry, and have the children return to the story circle. Read, *Thank You, God for Wonderful Things,* by Ruth Odor, Standard Publishing (#4921), if it is available.

Pretend to be seeds. Act out the planting and sprouting of seeds with the children. Demonstrate with one child and then let everyone in the group have a turn. Use pieces of sheet or blankets to cover each child. Talk about the seed being put into the ground and covered with soil. Say, "God sends the rain and sun and makes the seed slowly grow." Each child is to slowly stand up and stretch.

If you have pictures of seeds sprouting, show them to the children to add to their understanding.

Review the statements in *Remembering God's Truths*. Ask the children this question, "What does the Bible tell us about God?" Encourage them to answer, *"God is good."* Have a closing prayer. Let the children express their thanks to God.

UNIT ONE: God Made Everything Special Genesis 1:26-28

Bible Verse: Be kind ... to one another. (Ephesians 4:32, NIV) Lesson 2

THE FIRST PEOPLE

AS THE CHILDREN ARRIVE: Greet each child and direct each one to a learning center. It is best to have no more than five children at a table. It is not necessary for each child to go to each of the three centers.

Attendance Check Center: Help each child find his or her name on the chart or the attendance card and place a star or sticker in the appropriate place. Let each child know you are glad he or she is there.

Bible Word Center: Provide a large jigsaw puzzle for the children to put together. Make the puzzle by purchasing a large piece of tagboard or poster board. Print today's verse and reference, **"Be kind ... to one another." Ephesians 4:32, NIV,** in large bold letters on the poster board. Cut out and glue on small pictures of people being kind to one another. For durability of the puzzle, cover the poster board with clear contact paper. Cut the poster into 7 or 8 pieces.

At the center, let the children enjoy putting the puzzle together on the floor and then read the words to them. Let them practice saying the words with you. Then mix up the pieces and let the children be kind to each other as they give others a turn putting the puzzle together.

God Made Me Center: At home, draw or cut from a magazine a large picture of a person.

Glue the picture to cardboard and cover with contact paper for durability. Cut out the pieces so that the head, trunk, arms, and legs are separate pieces.

In class, let the children put the puzzle-person together. Talk about each piece as the children put it together. Stress that God made each part of you. Say, "God made both the inside and outside of you. He made all your body parts grow together. Let us thank God, because He made each of us in such a wonderful way." Pause to thank God.

At the sound of music from the piano or a cassette tape, have the children go to the story area of the room for singing.

SINGING AND TALKING TO GOD: Sing, "Let Us Love One Another" (p. 29, *Songs for Preschool Children,* singing the Scripture reference for the last phrase, "John 4, verse 7"); "God Loves Me" (p. 36, vs. 1, SPC); and "Please Him, Please Him," (p. 39, SPC, change "God is love" to "God made me"); and "All Things Were Made by Him" (p. 49, SPC).

Use the Group Repetition suggestion (see p. 8) for praying this prayer: "Thank You, God, for making me special. Thank You for loving me. In Jesus' name, amen."

Lead the children in a march around the room for exercise, as you sing "The Marching Song" (p. 11, SPC). Return to the story circle.

READING ABOUT GOD'S WORD: Read 1 Timothy 2:13 from the *International Children's Version.* "For Adam was made first, Eve was made later."

Also Genesis 1:26-28

The First People

On the sixth day, God also made His last and best creation. God took some of the dirt from the ground and made a man. God breathed into him, and the man became a living soul. Then God made a beautiful garden for the man in a place called Eden. He put the man He had made in the garden and named him Adam.

Adam saw a beautiful sight when he looked at the garden. He saw all kinds of delicious fruit hanging from the trees.

God told Adam, "You may eat as much of the fruit from these trees as you want. But there is one tree in the garden that you must not touch. You cannot eat the fruit of that one tree."

Adam had lots of work to do every day. He took care of the trees in the garden. He named all of the animals and fish that God had made. But God said, "Adam should not be the only person here in the garden. He needs someone to be here with him."

Then God did a very wonderful thing. He made Adam go to sleep, and while he was sleeping, God took one of his ribs. Then He closed the place on Adam's body where He had removed it. And while Adam was still asleep, God took the rib and made a woman to be Adam's helper. God brought the woman to Adam, and she became his helper. Adam named her Eve. He liked her very much, and they lived together in the Garden of Eden. They were the very first people in the world. God had made the beautiful world for them—His best creation.

From *A Child's First Book of Bible Stories* by Wanda Hayes. Standard Publishing, pp. 12, 13.

REMEMBERING GOD'S TRUTHS: You will need four picture cards from your picture file for today's lesson. Be enthusiastic as you teach these concepts. Let the children clap when they give the correct answer.

- Here is a question. You learned the answer last week.
  Who made the world?
  God made the world. (*Heavenly Father* section)
- God, our Heavenly Father, made the world. Who made you?
  God made me. (*About Me* section)
- It makes us happy to think that God made us. When you are very happy, what should you do?
  I should thank God for making me happy. (*I Pray* section)
- Some of the people that God made have problems. Some cannot walk. Some cannot see.
  Does Jesus love children who have problems?
  Yes, Jesus loves everyone. (*About Me* section)

EXPERIENCING GOD'S TRUTHS: Allow the children to get some exercise for a few minutes by having them stand and point to various parts of the body as they imitate you. Say, "Thank You,

God, for my feet." etc., as you point to them.

Invite a child or an adult who has a handicap he or she was born with to come to the class to talk to the children. You might choose someone in a wheelchair or someone with a minor problem. Be sure this person is able to talk openly about his or her handicap. Inform the visitor that the children will ask questions. Be relaxed and at ease, yourself, as you talk to the visitor. At this time, emphasize the truth that God made everyone, regardless of appearance or handicap.

Before the visitor arrives, prepare the children by talking about these things: What is a handicap? Tell them who is coming, and what kind of handicap the person has. Describe what the visitor will look like and what will be different about him or her. Discuss being polite and kind to handicapped people.

Invite the visitor to come into the room. Give him or her a warm welcome. Talk with the visitor about some of the following ideas: What is a handicap? Were you born with this handicap? How is your life different from other people's? Do you need special equipment to help you? Have you ever had an operation to help make your problem better? When you were a child, how did you wish that other children had treated you? Are you ever sad because of your handicap? What can children like the children in our class do to help people like you?

Ask the children, "Who made *(visitor)?*" Yes, God made everyone. Ask, "Does Jesus love children who have problems?" Yes, Jesus loves everyone. Emphasize that God loves everyone regardless of what he or she looks like.

Thank the visitor for coming and ask the children to express their thanks by clapping or saying "thank you."

Have the children return to the tables. Give each child an activity sheet, "God Made Everyone", (p 2, *Through the Bible Activities for Preschoolers, Book 1*). Read the paper to the children. Have them point to the picture of the child in a wheelchair. Say, "How can you be kind to this child?" Have them point to the Downs Syndrome child. Ask the same question. Now look at the normal child. Ask the same question. Allow time for the children to tell about one of their friends who is handicapped. Direct the children to color one of the people in the picture who is different from himself or herself. Be sure the child's name is printed on the paper.

REVIEWING GOD'S TRUTHS: Borrow from your church or public library a book on handicapped people that contains good pictures for preschoolers to see. Read or look at the book with the children. Talk about all the different kinds of people God made. (Example, "God made some people with only eight fingers.... Some people have legs that do not work.... Some people have brains that do not work as well as yours.")

Once again state, "God made everyone." Ask the children, "What does the Bible say about being kind?" Encourage them to answer, "Be kind ... to one another." (Ephesians 4:32) God wants us to be especially kind to handicapped people.

If time permits, read *Thank You, Lord, for Me* by Jane Moncure, Standard Publishing (#4912). Say, "God made you special." Discuss how they like to be treated. Stress that we will be happy when we treat others the way we want them to treat us. Encourage them to "Be kind ... to one another" (Ephesians 4:32).

Let each child have an opportunity to pray a sentence prayer asking God to help him or her to be kind to others. Encourage them to name a person.

UNIT ONE: God Made Everything Special
Bible Verse: Children, obey your parents. (Ephesians 6:1, NIV)

Genesis 3:1-14
Lesson 3

ADAM AND EVE LEAVE THE GARDEN

AS THE CHILDREN ARRIVE: Greet each child warmly. Direct him or her to a learning center.

Attendance Check Center: Praise the child who has been present every meeting so far. Add to the attendance chart the name of any new child or prepare a card for any new child. Help each child to place the star or sticker on his attendance chart.

Bible Word Center: Find a picture of several children and a picture of a father, a mother, or both parents. Glue these two pictures on two 5" x 7" cards. Print each of the following words on a separate 5" x 7" card: "obey" and "your." Open your Bible to Ephesians 6:1, "Children, obey your parents." Show the printed verse to the children. Place the four picture and word cards in order on the floor. Point to the picture and word cards as you say the verse. Sing the verse (p. 26, *Songs for Preschool Children*). Then scramble the order of the cards and let the children put them back in the correct order as they sing or say the verse with you. Ask, "What does the Bible say about obeying?" Encourage the children to answer by stating the Bible verse and reference.

The Garden Mural: Cut a five foot strip of paper from a roll of shelf paper, brown paper, or butcher paper. Tape this paper to a table. Provide crayons or marking pens and have the children draw pictures of things they think would be found in the Garden of Eden. Give each child a designated space for his or her drawing. When drawings are complete, place cut-out figures of Adam and Eve in the garden. Hang this mural in the story-circle area for use during the Bible-story time.

At the sound of music from the cassette tape or piano, have the children leave the centers and go to the story-circle area of the room for singing.

SINGING AND TALKING TO GOD: Sing "Pleasing God" (p. 26, v. 2, *Songs for Preschool Children,* add a Scripture verse: "Ephesians 6, verse 1, is a very good verse for me; It's message tells me what to do; it's a very good verse for you. 'Children, obey your parents.' 'Children, obey your parents.' This is what you ought to do, 'Children, obey your parents.'"); "In His Bible Book" (p. 41, SPC, add "obey" and "choose right" to the verses.); "Praise Ye the Lord" (p. 28, SPC); and "God Is Good" (p. 38, SPC).

Have a special time of talking to God. For this lesson, it would be appropriate to have each child tell of one thing he does that he knows is disobeying. Then let each child ask God to help him to obey, and tell God he is sorry for disobeying.

Repeat one of the above songs as you lead the children in a march around the room. Return to the story area.

READING ABOUT GOD'S WORD: Read Romans 5:12 and 14b from your copy of the *International Children's Version.* "Sin came into the world because of what one man (Adam) did. And with sin came death. And this is why all men must die—because all men sinned. Adam died because he sinned by not obeying God's command."

Refer to the children's garden mural as you read or tell the Bible story. Remove Adam and Eve from the garden when you come to that part of the story.

Also Gen. 3:1-14 CR p.10

Adam and Eve Leave the Garden

Adam and Eve were very happy in the beautiful garden that God had made for them. They loved to take care of the trees. They enjoyed watching the animals walking through the garden. They enjoyed hearing the songs of the birds and seeing the fish swim in the rivers. They liked the sweet smell of the beautiful flowers and the good taste of the food God made for them. Adam and Eve had everything they needed. But they had something else too—they had God as their best friend. When they heard the leaves of the trees moving in a soft rustling sound, they knew that God was nearby.

One day when Eve was by herself, a snake came up to her and asked, "Has God told you not to eat the fruit from any of the trees in the garden?"

"Oh, Adam and I may eat the fruit from all the trees in the garden except one," Eve told the snake. "God told us not to touch the tree in the middle of the garden and not to eat any of its fruit. If we do, we will die."

"Oh, no!" said the snake. "You will not die. God does not want you to eat the fruit of that tree because He knows it will make you as smart as He is."

The snake said that God had lied to Adam and Eve, but God cannot lie. The snake had lied, and Eve believed the snake. She looked at the tree in the middle of the garden. The fruit looked good to her. Eve thought about how smart she would be. So she disobeyed God and ate some of the fruit. Then she gave some to Adam, and he ate it, too.

Adam and Eve did the one thing that God had told them not to do. And now they felt so bad. They tried to hide from God. But God called out to Adam, "Where are you?"

Adam said, "I was afraid for You to see me."

"Why were you afraid?" God asked. "Did you eat from the tree in the middle of the garden?"

Then Adam told God that Eve had caused him to eat the fruit. And Eve said the snake had told her to eat it. But it was no use. God knew the truth.

Now God had to punish Adam and Eve and the snake. He told the snake, "You will have to crawl on your belly in the dirt all of your life." And He told Adam and Eve, "You will have to leave this beautiful garden now, and your life won't be as happy as it was here."

Then God gave Adam and Eve coats of animal skins and sent them out of the garden. Their lives would never be the same. But God still loved Adam and Eve. He cared about them very much and gave them a special blessing—a baby boy. They named him Cain. Later God let them have another baby boy, and his name was Abel.

From *A Child's First Book of Bible Stories* by Wanda Hayes. Standard Publishing, pp. 14, 15.

REMEMBERING GOD'S TRUTHS: You will need four picture cards from your picture file for today's lesson. Be prepared to use these pictures in a fun way.
- Adam and Eve choose not to obey God.
  Who helps you obey?
  God helps me to obey. (*About Me* section)
  When you do something wrong and then say, "I'm sorry, God," what does God say?
  I forgive you. (*I Pray* section)
- But God has done something to help us handle our disobeying.
  Why did Jesus come to earth?
  Jesus came to show us that God loves us.
  How did Jesus show you that He loved you?
  Jesus died for me. (*Jesus* section)

EXPERIENCING GOD'S TRUTHS: Bring a ball, a baby stroller and doll (or ask a parent to 'lend' her real baby for a few minutes), a letter that you have received in the mail, and a big wheel riding toy. You will use these items when acting out the two stories which involve making the right choice.

Explain to the children that:
1. Every day each of us chooses whether we are going to obey or disobey.
2. Eve and Adam chose to disobey.
3. Sometimes parents choose to disobey, too.
4. We are not pleasing God when we choose to disobey Him.

Story One: Mother told John, "Never lay the mail down. Always bring it to me. It might be an important letter that we need." One day the postman gave a letter to John and said, "This is for your family." Just then, John's friend came riding down the sidewalk on his big wheel. Oh, oh, what will John choose to do?

After reading the story to the children, allow them to choose parts and act out the story. Four actors will be needed: a mother, a postman, John and John's friend. Give the postman the letter, and give the friend the big wheel. Encourage the children to role play the story as you read or tell it again. Let "John" choose whether he will lay the letter down outside and run off to play with his friend, or take time to go into the house to give the letter to his mother.

Story Two: Mandy's father told her she could take the baby for a walk if she obeyed two rules. She had to promise to keep her hands on the stroller and go no farther than three houses away from Mandy's house.

Mandy began pushing the stroller. She saw some of her friends 'way up the street.' She wanted to push the baby 'way up the street' to show her friends how important she was because she could push the stroller by herself. But, to go more than three houses up the street would be disobeying her father. What should Mandy choose to do? (Do not let the children verbally answer this question. Let them role play the story while you read it the second time, and act out the ending they choose.)

After discussing Mandy's choice, direct the children to go to the tables. Give each child an activity sheet, "Choosing to Obey", (p. 3, *Through the Bible Activities for Preschoolers, Book 1).* Read about the choice that Adamino had to make. Look at the two pictures of the boys playing ball. Adamino's father told him not to play ball near the street. Color the picture that shows Adamino made the right choice. Callie's mother told her to sit on the chair while her mother talked to the doctor. Look at the two pictures of Callie, and color the picture that shows that Callie chose to obey her mother.

REVIEWING GOD'S TRUTHS: Play the game, Musical Picture Cards (see p. 10). Use the pictures that you used earlier in *Remembering God's Truths.* Be sure to include also those pictures used in lessons one and two.

If time permits, read *Choosing Is Fun* by Mary Bachman, Standard Publishing (#3580).

Ask the children, "What does the Bible say about obeying?" Encourage them to answer, "Children obey your parents. Ephesians 6:1." Have a closing prayer: "Dear God, thank You for always listening to me when I talk with you. Please help me to make the right choices and to obey my parents. In Jesus' name, amen."

LOOKING AHEAD—Send a note home with the children, asking them to bring or wear their raincoats, hats, and boots to the next class meeting.

Unit 2—God's Special People

GETTING READY FOR UNIT TWO

The Bible stories in this unit will deal with Noah, Abraham, Isaac, Jacob, and Joseph who loved, served, and worshiped God. It is important to point out that these men were faithful even in difficult times. God cared for them, just as He does us.

Learning Objectives: Some things you should expect your children to accomplish in this unit:

The children should know (1) God can do anything; (2) He can talk to God; (3) God will take care of him; (4) God hears his prayer.

The children should feel (1) God's love; (2) The assurance that God is with him when he is afraid; (3) That he can pray anytime and anywhere; (4) Thankful to God.

The children should be able to (1) Tell the highlights of the Bible stories; (2) Say the Bible verses and state simple answers to concept questions; (3) Pray a simple prayer; (4) State a way to deal with fear.

Remember, because of the difference in age and maturity, some children will meet more of these objectives than others will.

Bible Verses: There will be three new verses and two review verses in this unit. Follow the suggestions in each lesson for ways to make learning the Bible verse fun. Be sure to keep the teaching aids used at the Bible Words center for use in other lessons.

Books: These books may be used in the quiet, book corner of your room. They will need to be read to the children, or the children may enjoy looking at the pictures. *Baby Moses in a Basket; God Is With Me; God Is in the Night; When I'm Afraid;* and *I Can Pray to God* are suitable for the subjects being studied.

Bulletin Board: Place the "Raindrop Mobile" on the board, and place the children's drawings under the heading, "Where I Pray", on the bulletin board or wall. Add the "Nighttime Reminders" picture.

THINGS TO DO:

Lesson 4: Be familiar with the actions used to teach the Bible verse. Gather small toy animals or pictures of animals and a shoe box (see p. 21). Bring extra rainwear for children who may forget theirs. Cut string or yarn 24" for mobile, and cut out raindrops for the three-year-olds (see p. 23). You will need a small suitcase for the game, "Going on a Trip" (see p. 9)

Lesson 5: You will need the Bible word cards from Lesson 3, a toy truck, doll house furniture, a small wagon, a suitcase (see p. 24). Cut out three construction-paper suitcases for each child. See page 25 for the pattern.

Lesson 6: You will need drawing paper and crayons, and these words cut-out or printed, "Where I Pray." Plan the route you will take on your "trip" (see p. 27).

Lesson 7: Learn the motions to be used with the Bible verse (see p. 28); purchase black paper, cut-out moon and stars (see p. 28). Provide small blankets or pieces of sheets for each child.

Lesson 8: You will need a large cardboard box (see p. 30), a tricycle, a long strip of paper, a candy bar or a $1 bill, a coat, or man's hat.

Unit Two: God's Special People
Bible Verse: Give thanks to him and praise his name. (Psalm 100:4, NIV)

Genesis 6:1 — 9:16
Lesson 4

A BOAT, A FLOOD, AND A PROMISE

AS THE CHILDREN ARRIVE: Greet each child warmly and make each one feel important. Direct each child to one of the learning centers.

Attendance Check Center: Have each child find his or her name on the chart or card and place a star or sticker on the space designated. When finished, have the child go to one of the other centers.

Bible Word Center: Today's verse will be presented with actions. Tell the children, "When you say this verse you are to fold your hands and bow your head as you say, 'Give thanks to Him.' You will clap your hands while you say 'Praise His name.' You will jump up and down in place as you say, 'Psalm 100:4.'" Demonstrate these actions as you state the instructions.

It is a fact that adding rhythm and movement to memorization fosters quicker learning and longer retention. So, have fun with your children by learning this verse as suggested. Ask this question first, "What does the Bible say about giving thanks?" Then open your Bible and read the verse, "Give thanks to him and praise his name." (Psalm 100:4, NIV) The children will quickly learn the verse as they fold, clap, and jump.

Animals Center: Bring to class small replicas of various animals, separate pictures of animals or a book containing animal pictures. Let the children point to and name as many animals as they can identify and possibly talk about what each animal eats. Make an ark out of a shoe box, and have the animals go into the "ark." Talk about how Noah and his family had to care for the animals while they were in the ark.

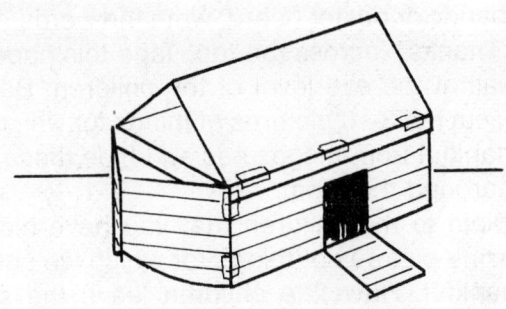

At the sound of music from the cassette tape or piano, have the children go to the story area of the room for singing.

SINGING AND TALKING TO GOD: Sing these songs: "Trust in the Lord" (p. 25, *Songs for Preschool Children*); "I Will Trust in God" (p. 38, SPC, add a second verse: "Psalm 73: 1, God is good."); "Please Him, Please Him" (p. 39, SPC); "God Loves Me" verse 3 (p. 36, SPC); and "Give Thanks" (p. 23, this book).

Ask the children, "What is a promise?" Discuss times when they have made promises and when others have made promises to them. Ask, "What is important to remember when making a promise?" Let each child have an opportunity to answer. Offer a prayer to God, thanking Him for keeping every promise He makes.

Let the children choose an animal they would like to pretend to be. Lead them on a walk around the room as they pretend to be that animal, and then to the story area.

READING ABOUT GOD'S WORD: Read Hebrews 11:7, from your copy of the *International Children's Version*. "It was by faith Noah heard God's warnings about things that he could not yet see. He obeyed God and built a large boat to save his family. By his faith, Noah showed that the world was wrong. And he became one of those who are made right with God through faith."

Read or tell the Bible story.
Genesis 6:1-9:16 CR p.12,13,14,15

A Boat, a Flood, and a Promise

God had made the earth just right for people, and He wanted people to love each other and be kind. But instead, people were hurting and killing each other.

God felt very sad. He said, "I am sorry I made people. I am going to destroy them and all my other creatures, and start all over."

But God found one good man. His name was

Noah. Noah was kind to other people and obeyed God.

God told Noah how he would be saved. He said, "Build a big boat of gopher wood. Make rooms in it. Make three decks, and cover it with pitch so water can't get in. Build a door in the side and make one window."

God told Noah, "I am going to flood the earth with water and destroy all living things. But I will make a special promise to you and your wife and your sons, Shem, Ham, and Japheth, and their wives. I promise that all of you will be saved." God planned to begin a new world of people with Noah's family.

God also had plans for the animals, birds, and fish. God told Noah to take pairs, which means two, of each kind of His creatures into the big boat. He said to take one pair of some kinds of animals and seven pairs of others. Then the animals would be saved, too.

Noah worked very hard to build the ark. It took a long time, and the wicked people made fun of Noah and laughed at him. But Noah kept building the ark. And when the boat was finished, Noah and his family took all of the animals and led them into the ark. Last of all, Noah and his family went inside, and God shut the door.

After seven days, everyone in the ark heard the sound of rain—hard rain. Day after day, the rain fell. The water rose and flooded the earth and made the ark float on top of it. The rain fell on the earth for forty days and forty nights without stopping. Every living thing died, and the water rose so high that it covered the mountains.

But God did not forget Noah and his family and the animals in the ark. God caused a strong wind to blow and begin drying the earth. The water began to go back into the lakes, seas, and rivers. Then Noah's ark stopped floating and came to rest on top of a tall mountain called Ararat.

Forty days after the ark stopped moving, Noah opened the window and no water came in. He took a raven and let it fly out. The raven did not come back. Then Noah let a dove fly out the window. The dove flew around but couldn't find a place to live because of the water, so she came back to the ark. She landed on Noah's hand.

After a week, Noah sent the dove out again. This time the dove brought an olive leaf back in her beak. Noah knew the water was lower. After seven more days, Noah sent the dove out again. This time, she did not return to the ark. She had found a home.

Then God told Noah, "You and your family may leave the ark. Take the animals and birds with you. I want the earth to have more people, more animals, and more birds. I want it to be beautiful and full of life again."

Then God promised never to destroy the earth with a big flood again. And to remind us of His promise, God put a rainbow in the sky.

From *A Child's First Book of Bible Stories* by Wanda Hayes. Standard Publishing, pp. 18, 19.

REMEMBERING GOD'S TRUTHS: Use the pictures from the picture files suggested on page 6. You will need four for today's lesson.

- In our story we learned about how God took care of Noah. God is very powerful.
  What can God do?
  <u>God can do anything.</u> (*Heavenly Father* section)
- God told Noah to build a big boat. Noah obeyed God.
  Who helps you to obey?
  <u>God helps me to obey.</u> (*About Me* section)
- When the flood was over and Noah got off the ark, he prayed. Can you answer two questions about praying?
  When you pray, what are you doing?
  <u>When I pray, I am talking to God.</u>
  When can you talk to God?
  <u>I can talk to God anytime.</u> (*I Pray* section)

EXPERIENCING GOD'S TRUTHS: Have the children put on the raincoats, umbrellas, boots, and rain hats that they brought and pretend they are walking in the rain. While they are dressed for rain, have them sit and thank God for rain. Then have them take off the rain gear and put it away.

On a large piece of shelf paper, brown wrapping paper, or poster board, write the words, "We Give Thanks," across the top. Tape this paper to the wall at the eye level of the children. Before class, cut out 8-10 pictures of things for which we are thankful from magazines and hide these pictures around the room.

Explain to the children that you have hidden magazine pictures of things for which we should be thankful. Have the children leave the story circle when you say, "Go," and look for the pictures.

When one picture is found, tell the children to stop their search and return to the story circle. Discuss the picture, and then have the children repeat after you a prayer of thanks. (Example, "Dear God, thank You for sending us rain to help our food grow. In Jesus' name, amen.")

Let the child who found the picture paste the picture to the paper. Repeat until all pictures are found.

Give each child an activity sheet, "Raindrop Mobile," (p. 4, *Through the Bible Activities for Preschoolers, Book 1*). Provide scissors for each child to cut out the raindrops. (You may have to cut the raindrops ahead of time for younger children. Place each set in a different envelope.) Cut a 24" piece of string for each child in your class.

Help each child tape the raindrops on to the string so that the top raindrop is one inch from the top of the string, and the last raindrop is at the bottom of the string. The other two raindrops are to be spaced evenly in the center of the string. Review with the children the statements on the raindrops. Place each finished mobile in

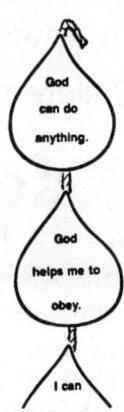

an envelope and print the child's name on the envelope. Encourage the children to hang the mobiles up in their rooms at home.

REVIEWING GOD'S TRUTHS: Play the game, "Going on a Trip." The directions for this game are found on page 9. Pretend your trip is on a boat.

Ask the children this question: "What does the Bible say about giving thanks?" Encourage them to answer, "Give thanks to him and praise his name. Psalm 100:4." Have a closing prayer.

Unit Two: God's Special People   Genesis 12:1-9; 15:4,5; 17:1-8; 21:1-3

Bible Verse: Children, obey your parents. (Ephesians 6:1, NIV)   Lesson 5

GOD BLESSES ABRAHAM

AS THE CHILDREN ARRIVE: Greet each child warmly. Say, "I am happy to see your smiling face. I am so glad you are here!" Direct each child to a learning center.

Attendance Check Center: Help each child to place a star or a seal on the attendance chart or card. Help them to find their names on the chart or card and then direct them to another learning center.

Bible Word Center: This is a review of Ephesians 6:1, which was taught in lesson 3 (p. 17). Use the cards and ideas in Lesson 3 to review the Bible verse, "Children, obey your parents." Turn the cards face down on the floor. Let a child turn one over. See if he can tell you what the word is. Be careful not to make a child feel bad because he or she cannot read the word. Help him with each word as he needs it. Act surprised if a child knows the word. Have the children put the words in correct order. Say the words together and be sure to give the reference.

Moving Center: You will need a toy truck and doll house furniture for this center. You may bring these from home or ask a parent to supply them for this lesson.

In class, allow the children to load the furniture on the truck. Introduce the idea that sometimes God tells people to move from one house, city, or country to another. Ask if any of them have ever moved before. Ask, "What did you like about moving?" Give the child an opportunity to tell how he felt. Then ask, "What did you not like about moving?" Allow time for the child to answer. Stress that sometimes we feel both good and bad about moving. Discuss these feelings.

At the sound of music from the cassette tape or piano, have the children go to the story area of the room for singing.

SINGING AND TALKING TO GOD: Sing these songs: "I Will Trust in God" (p. 38, *Songs for Preschool Children*, add a second verse: "Psalm 73, one, God is Good."); "Trust in the Lord" (p. 25, SPC); "He Careth for You" (p. 32, SPC, change "careth" to "cares"); "Pleasing God" (p. 26, v. 4, SPC); and "God Loves Me" (p. 36, v. 3, SPC).

Have a special time for talking to God. Pray, "Dear God, thank You for all You have done for us. Please help each of us to obey Your Word, and to obey our parents. In Jesus' name, amen."

Say, "We are talking today about moving. Let's pick up our chairs and pretend we are moving our furniture to another place." Walk around the room and stop at an appropriate place for the Bible story.

READING ABOUT GOD'S WORD: Read Acts 7:2, 3, from the *International Children's Version*. "Brothers and fathers, listen to me. Our glorious God appeared to Abraham, our father.... God said to Abraham, 'Leave your country and your relatives. Go to another country that I will show you.'"

Read or tell today's Bible story.

God Blesses Abraham

God loved His people, and He had special plans for them. One of the men God had special plans for was Abram. God told Abram, "I want you to leave your country and your father's family and go to a land that I will show you. And I will make you very happy. You will have a big family, and be a great person. Then someday, someone from your family will make all of the families in the world happy."

Abram loved God and did just what God told him to do. Abram took his wife, Sarah, and his nephew, Lot, and everything they owned and started to go to the land of Canaan.

God said, "I will give this land to your family." Abram was so thankful that he built an altar and thanked God.

Abram and Sarah and Lot and the people who worked for them traveled some more. Then they came to a place called Bethel and pitched their tents. There Abram built another altar and prayed to God, because God was helping him.

God had promised Abram that he would have a big family with many grandchildren, great-grandchildren, and great-great-grandchildren. More and more children would be born as the years passed. God said, "There will be as many people in your family as there are grains of sand on the seashore and stars in the sky. And from now on your name will be Abraham."

Abraham believed God, but he and Sarah were getting old, and they still didn't have a child. But God always keeps His promises. And soon Sarah had a son. They named him Isaac. Sarah and Abraham knew that God would bless Isaac. He would keep His promises to Isaac as He had to them.

<small>From *A Child's First Book of Bible Stories* by Wanda Hayes. Standard Publishing, pp. 20, 21.</small>

REMEMBERING GOD'S TRUTHS: Use the pictures from the picture files suggested on page 6. You will need four for today's lesson.

- Abraham obeyed God by doing what God told him to do. He moved to another place.
    Who helps you to obey?
    <u>God helps me to obey.</u> (*About Me* section)
- God told Abraham to move far away. God took care of Abraham and Sarah when they were awake and asleep.
    Who takes care of you when you sleep?
    <u>God takes care of me when I sleep.</u> (*God's Care* section)
- How about you?
    If you go far away, who will take care of you?
    <u>God will take care of me.</u> (*God's Care* section)
- Do you think Abraham and Sarah were a little sad when they left their home and their friends?
    When you are alone and sad, what should you do?
    <u>I should ask God to help me.</u> (*God's Care* section)

EXPERIENCING GOD'S TRUTHS: Provide an opportunity for the children to act out today's story. Bring to class a child's wagon, a suitcase filled with children's clothing and small toys, shirts for Abraham and Lot, and a robe or a dress for Sarah.

Tell the children that the class is going to act out the story as you read it again. Let the children volunteer to be Abraham, Sarah, Lot, and the servants. Dress Abraham, Sarah, and Lot in the clothing you brought. Let the children select the place where Abraham's old home (Haran) is and a place for Abraham's new home. You may want to select a location in another part of the church building for the new home.

Tell the children that the wagon is a pretend cart used for carrying the clothes. Be sure the children understand that in Abraham's day there were no cars, trains, or airplanes. Be sure to pack some pretend food.

With the children seated, begin reading the story. Let the children role play the story: packing the suitcase, saying good-bye, walking, stopping to eat, sleeping, walking some more, crossing the river, arriving at their new home, thanking God, etc. Have the children return to the tables.

Give each child an activity paper, "Sarah Obeys God" (p. 5, *Through the Bible Activities for Preschoolers, Book 1*). Cut from various colors of construction paper little suitcases, approximately 2" by 1". Be sure to put handles on them. Make three suitcases for each child in your class. Let each child glue the suitcases on the activity sheet near Sarah's feet.

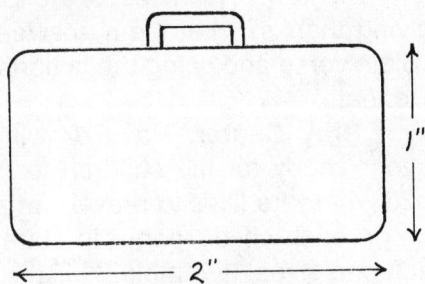

REVIEWING GOD'S TRUTHS: Let the children role play the story of Sarah and her family going to another country as missionaries.

The parent and children pack their suitcase (the same suitcase used earlier).

They tell their friends where they are going. The family prays to ask God to help them.

They go to the airport, and the child gets his ticket.

Everyone pretends to be flying to another country.

Closing prayer: "Dear God, please help us to obey You. Please help us, wherever we are, to tell others about Jesus, too. In Jesus' name, amen."

Unit Two: **God's Special People**

Bible Verse: Give thanks to him and praise his name. (Psalm 100:4, NIV)

Genesis 24

Lesson 6

A WIFE FOR ISAAC

AS THE CHILDREN ARRIVE: Be in the classroom when the children arrive and greet them warmly. Be aware of any child who needs special attention and encouragement. Direct each child to a learning center.

Attendance Check Center: Help the children to put stars and stickers on the attendance chart or cards. Talk with each child about what he or she has done this day. Encourage them to thank God for His goodness.

Bible Word Center: See Lesson 4, page 21, for suggestions for this center. Repeat the instructions for any child who may not have been present for that lesson. "You are to bow your heads and fold your hands when we say, 'Give thanks to him.' We will clap our hands when we say, 'And praise his name.' We will jump in place while we say, 'Psalm 100:4.'"

Ask the children, "What does the Bible say about giving thanks?" Let them answer by saying the Bible verse and doing the actions as they say it. Repeat.

Where I Pray Center: Have drawing paper and crayons ready for the children to use. Ask each child where he likes to pray. Print a simple sentence on each child's paper to state the answer each one gives. (Example: "I like to pray in my back yard.") Then have the child draw a picture of the place where he or she likes to pray. Display the drawings on the wall or bulletin board under the heading, "Where I Pray."

At the sound of music from the cassette tape or piano, have the children go to the story area of the room for singing.

SINGING AND TALKING TO GOD: Sing "Give Thanks," (p. 23, this book); "God Loves Me" (p. 36, v. 2, *Songs for Preschool Children*); "In His Bible Book" (p. 41, SPC, use the word "trust"); "Bible Song" (p. 41, SPC, use "Isaac"); and "I Can Talk to God" (p. 80, SPC).

Prayer: "Father, we thank You that we can talk to You any time and anywhere. Thanks for listening to us. In Jesus' name, amen."

Sing an active song to provide an opportunity for the children to move around. You may use "The Marching Song" (p. 11, SPC).

READING ABOUT GOD'S WORD: Read or tell the Bible story.

Genesis 24   CR p. 22, 23

A Wife for Isaac

Abraham was one of the happiest people on earth. God had given him everything he needed and wanted. God also had promised Abraham that he would have a large family with many grandchildren, great-grandchildren, great-great-grandchildren, and on and on through the years.

Abraham knew that it was time to choose a wife for his son, Isaac. So he told his oldest and best servant exactly how to choose a wife for Isaac. "Go back to the land where I used to live," Abraham said. "Take gifts and listen to God. He will help you know who will make a good wife for Isaac."

The good servant obeyed Abraham. He took ten camels and gold and silver jewelry and beautiful cloth. When he got to the city where Abraham's brother lived, he stopped and prayed, "Lord, God of Abraham, I am going to wait by this well of water until You show me the woman You want to be Isaac's wife. So I'll know which one she is, let her be the one who gives me a drink of water and then gives a drink to my camels also."

The servant waited until a pretty woman named Rebekah came to the spring to get water. When she had filled her jar, he said to her, "Will you please let me drink a little water from your jar?"

"Drink, Sir," Rebekah said. And she quickly gave him a drink of water. Then Rebekah said, "I will give your camels water, too, until they have had enough to drink."

The servant was excited. He gave Rebekah a gold ring and two gold bracelets. Then he asked her, "Who is your father? And does he have room for me and the people with me to stay at his house tonight?"

"I am Bethuel's daughter," Rebekah told him, "and we have plenty of room for you and your camels."

Then the servant knew that God had answered his prayer. "Thank You, God," he prayed, "for leading me to the house of Abraham's brothers."

Soon Rebekah and her servants started back with Abraham's servant to where Isaac lived. As they came near, Isaac was in a field watching them. He saw Rebekah riding a camel and came to meet them.

When Rebekah saw Isaac, she got off her camel and asked the servant, "Who is he?"

"He is my master, Isaac," the servant answered.

When Rebekah and Abraham's servant got to Isaac, the servant told him everything that had happened. Isaac was pleased. He married Rebekah and was very happy.

From *A Child's First Book of Bible Stories* by Wanda Hayes. Standard Publishing, pp. 22, 23.

After reading the Bible story, say to the children, "We can pray any place. Isaac's servant prayed outside near a well. God heard the servant's prayer and answered it exactly the way the servant asked. Jesus used to pray outside, too." Read Matthew 14:23 from the *International Children's Version*. "After he (Jesus) said good-bye to them (His followers), he went alone up into the hills to pray."

REMEMBERING GOD'S TRUTHS: You will need four picture cards for today's lesson from the *I Pray* section of your file.

- The servant had a problem. He needed to find the right girl to be the wife of Isaac.
    When you have a problem what should you do?
    <u>I should pray and ask God to help me.</u>
- The servant did not wait to go to a worship service to pray. He prayed immediately.
    When can you talk to God?
    <u>I can talk to God anytime.</u>
- You pray when you have a need, too.
    When you pray, what are you doing?
    <u>When I pray, I am talking to God.</u>
- God heard the servant's prayer and answered it right away.
    Does God hear you when you talk to Him?
    <u>Yes, God always hears me when I talk to Him.</u>

EXPERIENCING GOD'S TRUTHS: Decide on several unusual places in or near your church building where you can take your class. Some suggestions are the kitchen; bathrooms (if you have a man available to take the boys to the men's room and a woman to take the girls to the ladies' room); outside on the grass; in your car; in the furnace room (if it is safe); or in an office of one of the staff members (be sure to get permission and a key).

Ask the children, "Where can you pray?" Teach them that the place does not matter, for they can pray anywhere. Explain to the children that you are going to take them for a walk to see some unusual places where they can pray. If there is more than one teacher available, divide the children among the teachers and go in small groups.

Visit the first place you have chosen. Have the children sit down, if the area is clean. Spend a moment praying in that area. Make the prayer short and one of thanks.

Ask the children, "Where can you pray?" Encourage them to answer, "I can pray anywhere." Yes, even in the furnace room. Continue on to the other locations and repeat the activity.

When you get back to the classroom, have the children sit at the tables and give them each an activity sheet, "I Can Pray Anywhere" (p. 6, *Through the Bible Activities for Preschoolers, Book 1*). Read each statement. Give each child only one crayon—the color of his skin. Tell him to color only the face and hands of the child in each picture. Be sure the child's name is on his paper.

REVIEWING GOD'S TRUTHS: Play "Musical Picture Cards" as described in the Games section of this book, page. Read *I Can Pray to God*, by Sandra Brooks, Standard Publishing (#3586).

Ask the children this question, "What does the Bible say about giving thanks?" Encourage them to answer, "Give thanks to him and praise his name. Psalm 100:4." Let the children express their thanks to God for something they learned today.

Unit Two: God's Special People

Bible Verse: For God so loved the world that he gave his one and only Son. (John 3:16, NIV)

Genesis 27:41—28:19

Lesson 7

A STONE PILLOW AND A SPECIAL DREAM

AS THE CHILDREN ARRIVE: Greet each child with a loving welcome. "I love you and am glad you are here!" Direct the children to the learning centers.

Attendance Check Center: Have stars or stickers ready for the children to put on the attendance chart or cards. Help them find their names and let them know how glad you are that they have come to class.

Bible Word Center: Today's verse is one of two long verses to be taught in this curriculum. The verse is included in six different lessons, so don't be concerned if your class cannot learn it immediately. Practice the following actions at home so that you are comfortable doing them. Remember that rhythm and movement enhance memorization.

Tell the children, "When you say, 'God,' point one finger up to Heaven. When you say, 'love,' give yourself a hug. When you say, 'one,' hold up one finger. And when you say, 'John 3:16,' march in place to the rhythm of the words."

Ask the children, "What is a Bible verse that tells us that God loved the world?" Open your Bible and show the verse to the children as you read it. "For God so loved the world that he gave his one and only Son." (John 3:16, NIV)

Have fun teaching the verse and reference using the action, game-like approach.

Nighttime Reminders Center: You will need a piece of black paper, a paper moon cut from white paper, and stars for each pupil. As the children arrive at the learning center, let each one paste a moon and stick the stars on his black paper. Talk to them about nighttime. Tell them that the moon and stars are reminders in the sky that God cares for them while they sleep. Tape the sample picture made by the teacher on the wall near the Bible-story area, for the children to see as they listen to the Bible story. Let the children take their papers home with them.

At the sound of music from the cassette tape or piano, have the children go to the story area of the room for singing.

SINGING AND TALKING TO GOD: Sing "God So Loved," (p. 42, this book); "He Careth for You" (p. 32, *Songs for Preschool Children,* change to "cares"); "God Loves Me" (p. 36, v. 3, SPC); "Song of Praise" (p. 75, v. 2, SPC); and "Sing, Little Children, Sing" (p. 37, SPC).

Take time to talk to God. "Thank You, God, for always taking care of us. Amen."

Have the children march around the room singing, "Sing, Little Children, Sing" (p. 37, SPC).

READING ABOUT GOD'S WORD: Read Matthew 28:20, from the *International Children's Version.* Jesus says to us, "You can be sure that I will be with you always."

Read or tell the Bible story.

Genesis 27:41-28:19   CR p. 24, 25

A Stone Pillow and a Special Dream

Jacob was running away from home. But he wasn't a little boy; he was a grown man. Jacob was leaving his parents, Isaac and Rebekah, because his brother, Esau, was very angry with him. Esau was so angry at something Jacob had done to him, that he had said, "I want to kill Jacob."

Jacob's mother told him, "You must leave at once and go to the country where your uncle, Laban, lives. Stay there until your brother, Esau, isn't angry anymore. I will tell you when to come home."

And Jacob's father, Isaac, said to him, "While you are at Laban's house, you should choose a wife."

Then Isaac who was old and blind prayed a special prayer for his son, Jacob. He said, "May God give you a big family, and may He give the blessing to you that He gave to your grandfather, Abraham. May God give the land He promised to

Abraham to you and your children and grandchildren."

Then Jacob left his father and mother and went to a different country. Jacob traveled a long way, and he probably traveled as fast as he could because he was afraid of his brother, Esau. That night Jacob was very tired. He took a stone and put it under his head for a pillow. Soon he was fast asleep.

While Jacob slept, he had a dream. He saw a ladder that stretched all the way from earth to Heaven. And angels of God were walking up and down the ladder.

God spoke to Jacob in the dream and said, "I am the Lord. I am the God of Abraham and the God of Isaac. The land on which you are sleeping will belong to you and your children and their children. You will have a very large family, and someone in your family will bring good news to everyone on earth."

God made another promise to Jacob. He said, "I am with you, and I will take care of you and bring you back to this land. I will keep my promise."

When Jacob awoke, he said, "This is a very special place because God was here. I will set up this stone that I used for a pillow to remind me that God spoke to me here."

So Jacob set the stone up, poured oil on the top of it, and called the place Bethel, which means "The house of God." Then he continued on his journey to his uncle's house, but he never forgot the wonderful dream.

From *A Child's First Book of Bible Stories* by Wanda Hayes. Standard Publishing, pp. 24-26.

REMEMBERING GOD'S TRUTHS: You will need four picture cards from your picture file for today's lesson.

- In our story, Jacob was running away from home because his brother, Esau, was angry at him. Do you think Jacob might have been afraid of his brother?
  Who can help you when you are afraid?
  God can help me when I am afraid. (*God's Care* section)
- Jacob was a big man. He was afraid of his brother, Esau. So Jacob went far away from his home.
  When you go far away, who will take care of you?
  God will take care of me. (*God's Care* section)
- Jacob surely had a problem with his brother, Esau, but God helped him solve his problem. When you have a problem, what should you do?
  I should pray and ask God to help me. (*I Pray* section)
- When Jacob was away from his home, he was asleep. He dreamed of a ladder with angels on it. He heard God tell him that He would take care of him.
  Who takes care of you when you sleep?
  God takes care of me when I sleep. (*God's Care* section)

EXPERIENCING GOD'S TRUTHS: Provide pieces of sheet or small blankets for each child. Have the children lie down on the floor and fold their hands. Let them repeat this prayer after you: "Dear God, I thank You, that You always take care of me when I sleep. Amen." Instruct the children to cover up and pretend to be sleeping. Turn the lights off, then make a noise (Example: make the door squeak) and say, "Let's pretend this noise frightened us. Who can help you when you are afraid? They will respond, "God can help me when I am afraid." Pray together: "Dear God, help us not to be afraid. Help us to find out what made that scary noise. Thank you. Amen."

Have the children get up and help you look around for what made the scary noise. Walk around the room looking for the source of the noise till you find it. (Example: "Oh, here it is! This is a squeaky door.")

Have the children to go to the tables and give each child an activity sheet, "God's Care at Night" (p. 7, *Through the Bible Activities for Preschoolers, Book 1*). Let the children connect the dots and color the mother and the child. Stress the fact that God takes care of us when we sleep.

REVIEWING GOD'S TRUTHS: Read the book, *When I'm Afraid* by Sylvia Tester, Standard Publishing (#4900), if it is available. Or play, "It's a New Day" as described in the **Games** section, page 10.

Then review today's Bible verse.

Pray, "Thank You, God, for Your love and care. Amen."

Unit Two: God's Special People
Bible Verse: I will trust and not be afraid. (Isaiah 12:2, NIV)

Genesis 37; 39:1-6; 41—46
Lesson 8

JOSEPH AND HIS BROTHERS

AS THE CHILDREN ARRIVE: (See p. 7, for information concerning this part of the lesson.) Greet each child warmly and direct him or her to one of the learning centers.

Attendance Check Center: Help each child put a star or a sticker on the attendance chart or card. Count the number of stars or stickers they have on the chart, and let them know how happy you are that they have been faithful in their attendance. Make every child feel welcome.

Bible Word Center: Bring to class a cardboard box large enough for a child to fit inside after the box is closed. In class read Isaiah 12:2, "I will trust and not be afraid." Show the verse to the children. Then let the children take turns getting into the box. Close the top of the box loosely, and ask the question, "What should you do when you are afraid?" The child will pop out of the box as he says, "I will trust and not be afraid, Isaiah 12:2." You may need to help the child with the verse. Each child will have a turn. Encourage the children to clap for each child after he or she says the verse and reference. (Save the cardboard box for use in later lessons.)

Brothers and Sisters Center: Bring to class several play people (little people dolls or paper dolls) that represent a family. Ask the children to show you with the dolls some problems that brothers and sisters sometimes encounter. Introduce the idea of jealousy by telling make-believe stories about the dolls. (Example, one brother got new sneakers, and the sister felt jealous, etc.)

Discuss these feelings. Encourage the children to express how they feel in these or similar situations. Tell the children, "Your parents love each of their children. They want only what is best for each one. God loves each of His children. He wants us to love one another."

At the sound of music from the cassette tape or piano, have the children leave and go to the story area of the room for singing.

SINGING AND TALKING TO GOD: Sing "I Will Trust in God" (p. 38, *Songs for Preschool Children,* changing lines 2, 3, and 5 to read "Isaiah twelve, two"); "Trust in the Lord" (p. 25, SPC); "He Careth for You" (p. 32, SPC, change to "cares"); and "In His Bible Book" (p. 41, SPC, change "love" to "trust"). Sing some of the children's favorite songs.

Pray, "Father, we thank You for always taking care of us. Please help us to trust You and not be afraid. In Jesus' name, amen."

READING ABOUT GOD'S WORD: Read Acts 7:9, 10 from the *International Children's Version.* Read or tell the Bible story.

Joseph and His Brothers

Joseph's brothers were jealous of him because their father loved Joseph more than them. Jacob loved all of his sons, but because he loved Joseph the most, he gave him a special coat of beautiful colors. And when the brothers saw Joseph coming, wearing his special coat, it made them so angry they wanted to kill him.

"No! Let's not kill him," said Reuben. "Let's just throw him into a pit." Reuben planned to come back later and get Joseph out of the pit.

So the brothers took his beautiful coat and threw Joseph into a big hole. Then they sat down to eat.

While Reuben was away from the other brothers, Judah said, "See that group of men with their camels? They are going down to Egypt. Let's sell Joseph to them. Let's not kill him since he is our brother." So they sold Joseph to the traders who took him to Egypt.

Later, Reuben came back to the pit. But Joseph was not there. *Oh, no!* Reuben thought, *Joseph is gone. What am I going to tell our father?*

His brothers said, "Let's kill a goat and put its blood on Joseph's coat and tell our father a wild animal killed him." They did, and when their father, Jacob, saw the coat, he believed that Joseph was dead.

In Egypt, Joseph was far away from home, but God was watching over him. And Joseph was very smart. He could even explain the meanings of dreams with God's help. And when the Pharaoh told two of his dreams to Joseph, Joseph said, "Your dreams mean that for seven years the farmers in Egypt will grow good crops. Everyone will have plenty of food. Then for the next seven years, the farmers will not be able to grow good crops. There will not be enough food in Egypt. And you should choose someone to be in charge of saving food, now, so the people will not starve when the bad years come."

The Pharaoh chose Joseph for this job, and Joseph saved lots of grain during the seven good years. And when the seven bad years came, all of the people of Egypt had food to eat.

And way back in the land where Joseph used to live, his father and brothers did not have enough food to eat. So Jacob said to his sons, "I have heard that there is food in Egypt. Go there and buy some for us."

So Jacob's sons went down to Egypt to buy grain. They didn't know that the man who sold it to them was their brother, Joseph. But Joseph knew them, and he was very glad to see his brothers. But he didn't tell them who he was.

When Joseph learned that his father and youngest brother, Benjamin, were still alive, he said, "I will keep Simeon in prison until you go back home and return with your youngest brother. Then I will know you are not spies."

When Joseph's brothers went home and told their father what the man in Egypt had said, he was sad. But when their food was gone, Jacob sent them to Egypt again—this time with their brother, Benjamin.

And when Joseph saw Benjamin, he told them, "I am your brother, Joseph, whom you sold into slavery. But God wanted me to be in Egypt so I could save your lives."

Joseph's brothers could hardly believe what he told them. And Joseph was so happy to see Benjamin that he hugged him and cried and cried. Then he said, "Go home and bring our father and your families back to Egypt. All of you can live here and have everything you need."

From *A Child's First Book of Bible Stories* by Wanda Hayes. Standard Publishing, pp. 28, 29.

REMEMBERING GOD'S TRUTHS: Use the pictures from the picture files suggested on p. 6. You will need three picture cards for today's lesson.

- Joseph had a problem. His brothers hated him.
  When you have a problem, what should you do?
  I should pray and ask God to help me. (*I Pray* section)
- Some children have problems today, too.
  Does Jesus love children who have problems?
  Yes, Jesus loves everyone. (*About Me* section)
- Joseph had to go far away to the land of Egypt. If you go far away, who will take care of you?
  God will take care of me. (*God's Care* section)

EXPERIENCING GOD'S TRUTHS: Help the children to understand that fear is OK. Bring to class or ask a parent to supply the following: a tricycle; a wide, long strip of paper for a pretend road; a candy bar or a $1 bill; and a coat or hat that is unfamiliar to the children.

Tell the children, "We are going to talk about being afraid." Provide an opportunity for the children to relate experiences when they have been afraid.

Tell them, "There are two kinds of fear, or times to be afraid. One kind of fear is when there is a *real* thing to be afraid of, and another kind of fear is when we are afraid of something that is not real, but pretend—something you do not need to be afraid of at all." An example might be movies or TV. Stress that these are just pictures, and we do not need to be afraid of pictures.

Ask, "What is a real thing that sometimes makes us afraid?" Some will probably retell some of their fears. This time, help them to distinguish between causes of fears that are real (sharp knives) and fears that are pretend or unreal (ghosts). Be sure to convey the idea that the fear itself is always real. Here are some suggested ways of answering the children:

Thunder and other noises: "I used to be afraid of thunder, too. But now I know that loud noises don't hurt me. So when I hear thunder, I pretend that the angels are playing their drums. When we hear thunder, we can say, *'God can help me when I am afraid.'*"

Robbers and other bad people: "Robbers are

real, and we should be afraid of them. That's why we lock the doors and windows of our houses—to keep out the robbers. So if you think a robber is coming to your house, you can say, *'God can help me when I am afraid.'* Then you can talk to your mommy or daddy about how you feel."

Ghosts, monsters and other pretend things: "Some people are afraid of ghosts. But did you know that ghosts are only pretend? We do not need to be afraid of pretend things. So if you get afraid of a pretend thing, you can say, *'God can help me when I am afraid.'* Then you can talk to your parents about how you feel." (Never tell a child that it is silly, dumb, or stupid, etc., to be afraid of something. Fear is real, even if the object of the fear is pretend. Always encourage children to talk about their fears. Talking helps them to get over them.)

Big dogs or other real dangers: "Being afraid is sometimes God's way of telling us to be careful. Being afraid of something helps us to know that we must stay away from it. Who can help you when you are afraid? God can help me when I am afraid. So if you see a big dog, you can say, 'God, I am afraid. Please help me to get away from the dog.' Then you can walk to your house."

After discussing their fears, provide time for role playing some real fears. Stress that there are times when we need to ask God to help us. (Read *Act It Out,* p. 9.)

1. Pretend that the tricycle is a real car. The long, wide strip of paper is a road. "Who would like to ride the tricycle fast on our pretend road?" Let one child ride the tricycle while the others stand back away from the road. Talk about how we *should* be afraid of cars. Stop to pray and ask God to help us stay out of the street so we won't be hurt by cars.
2. Another thing we should be afraid of is strangers. Put on the coat or hat. Pretend to be a stranger. Say, "Remember, I am not Mr./Ms. (your name). I am now a stranger." Offer one child a candy bar or dollar bill and ask him to come with you. See if the child refuses. Take off the costume and talk about bad people who try to steal children. Tell the children that they should run right home and say, "God will help me" while they are running. Put the costume on again and repeat the scene, using different words, until the children automatically run and pray without talking to the stranger.

Have the children return to the tables. Give each child an activity sheet, "When I am Afraid", (p. 8, *Through the Bible Activities for Preschoolers, Book 1*). Discuss the two pictures. Scott was afraid of something real, and this fear is God's way of telling him to be careful. What should Scott do? (Walk slowly toward his house and remember, "God can help me when I am afraid.")

The older boy is telling Scott that a monster is going to eat him up. Scott remembered that "God can help me when I am afraid." He remembered that monsters are only pretend, and he didn't have to be afraid of pretend things. What should Scott do? (Say to the big kid, "I know you are just kidding me," and go on with his playing.)

Have the children color the pictures.

REVIEWING GOD'S TRUTHS: If you did not read *When I'm Afraid* by Sylvia Tester, last week, be sure to read it today.

Play the game, "It's A New Day", page 10, and relate it to Joseph's waking up one morning in the strange land and remembering God's Word early in the morning.

Review today's Bible verse. Ask, "What should you do when you are afraid?" Encourage the children to answer, "I will trust and not be afraid, Isaiah 12:2."

For the closing prayer, the teacher will pray for each child, by name, and ask God to help that child with the specific fear he or she stated earlier.

Unit 3—God's Special Man—Moses

GETTING READY FOR UNIT THREE

The theme of this unit will be that God used Moses as a special leader. He cared for Moses as a baby and prepared him to be a great leader of His people. It was through Moses that God gave His people rules for living.

Learning Objectives: Some things you should expect your children to accomplish in this unit:

The children should know (1) God kept baby Moses safe; (2) God will give us courage; (3) God wants us to trust Him; (4) God wants us to obey Him.

The children should feel (1) Thankful to God; (2) Happy that God will help him; (3) Assured that God will help him when afraid; (4) Sorry when he disobeys.

The children should be able to (1) Tell the highlights of the Bible stories; (2) Say the Bible verses; (3) Name three of God's rules; (4) State simple answers to concept questions.

Books: Several books are suggested for reading at the end of each lesson, if time permits. These books may be placed in the quiet, reading corner of your room. *Kindness; Courage; Baby Moses in the Basket; Doing Right Makes Me Happy* are suitable for the ages of the children and for the subjects being studied.

Bible Verses: Three review verses and one new verse are in this unit. Use the teaching aids prepared in previous lessons for reviewing the familiar verses. Follow the suggestions in Lesson 12 for introducing the new Bible verse. Music and actions aid the children in learning the verse.

Bulletin Board: There will be murals made in the centers that need to be displayed on the bulletin board or wall space near the story circle. They will be "Babies," pictures involving "courage," and "Rules, Rules, Rules." You may want to display pictures of Moses using the name of this unit for the heading.

THINGS TO DO:

Lesson 9: Collect pictures of babies and toddlers. Provide a strip of shelf paper and glue. Collect baby items (see p. 34).

Lesson 10: You will need stars or stickers; small toys that have to do with transportations (see p. 36); a bag; the book, *Courage* by Jane Belk Moncure; and pictures that illustrate situations where courage is needed (see p. 37).

Lesson 11: You will need a strip of light blue paper or cloth and play people or paper dolls (see p. 38); paper cups, grape juice, crackers, two bricks, a board four inches wide and at least four feet long; (see p. 39).

Lesson 12: Familiarize yourself with the actions used for learning the Bible verse. Get a large sheet of shelf paper for making a rebus lists of rules (see p. 40); a toy gun; a popular child's toy; a kitchen knife; a chocolate candy bar; and a bag for these items.

Unit Three: God's Special Man—Moses
Bible Verse: God is good. (Psalm 73:1, NIV)

Exodus 2:1-10
Lesson 9

A BABY IN THE BULRUSHES

AS THE CHILDREN ARRIVE: (See p. 7, in the front of this book for information concerning this section of the lesson.) Have the room ready at least ten minutes early, and be ready to welcome warmly each child and direct her to the learning centers.

Attendance Check Center: Help the children to place stars and stickers on the attendance chart or cards. Make each child feel important!

Bible Word Center: Use the cards made in Lesson 1 (see p. 12). Scatter the words and have the children put them in order. Ask, "What does the Bible tell us about God?" Encourage the children to answer, "God is good. Psalm 73:1." Discuss the good things God has done for them this day.

Babies Center: Bring to class pictures of babies and toddlers that you have cut from magazines or store catalogs. Provide a long strip of shelf paper and glue. In class, let each child paste a picture of a baby on the paper and tell about a baby he or she knows.

You might want to bring pictures of baby items like strollers, toys, bottles, etc., for your students to add to the picture. Tell the children that God provides mothers, fathers, brothers and sisters to love babies and to take care of them. Let each child tell how he or she can help with a baby.

At the sound of music from the cassette tape or piano, have the children go to the story area of the room for singing.

SINGING AND TALKING TO GOD: Sing "Trust in the Lord" (p. 25, *Song for Preschool Children);* "God Loves Me" (p. 36, v. 3, SPC); "Sing, Little Children, Sing" (p. 37, SPC); "God Is Good" (p. 38, SPC, add a second verse, "Psalm 73, one. God is good."); "I Will Trust in God" (p. 38, SPC); and "Let Us Love One Another" (p. 29, SPC).

Prayer: "Thank You, God, for taking such good care of us. In Jesus' name, amen."

Sing the "Action Song" (p. 5, SPC) in preparation for listening to the Bible story for today.

READING ABOUT GOD'S WORD: Read Acts 7:20-22 from your copy of the *International Children's Version.*

Now read or tell the Bible story.

Exodus 2:1-10 CR p. 40, 41. Bible in Pictures

A Baby in the Bulrushes
CR - My Bible Friends

"Shh! Don't Cry," Jochebed said, as she looked at her beautiful baby boy. She was sad because the wicked, mean ruler of Egypt, the Pharaoh, wanted to kill her baby. He wanted to kill all the Hebrew boy babies as soon as they were born. Jochebed loved her baby and didn't want him killed. So she hid him in her house.

Jochebed thought as she watched her little boy sleep, "I cannot hide him much longer. He cries louder now, and one of the Egyptians could hear him. If the bad Pharaoh hears him, he will have him killed."

So Jochebed said, "Miriam, I know what I am going to do. I will make a little basket-boat and put your brother in it. Then I'll ask God to protect him."

Jochebed made the boat and put her little boy in it. Then she carried the basket-boat down to the river. It floated on top of the water where the tall bulrushes grew. Miriam hid where no one could see her and watched the basket.

Soon Miriam saw someone coming to the river to take a bath. It was a princess, the Pharaoh's own daughter! And when the princess saw the basket-boat, she said to her maids, "I see a basket. Bring it to me." Then the princess looked inside, and saw the beautiful little boy.

"I'll keep this little Hebrew baby," the princess said. And she named him Moses.

Then Miriam came to the princess and said, "May I get one of the Hebrew women to care for this baby for you?"

The princess said yes, and Miriam ran as fast as she could to get her mother, Jochebed!

From *A Child's First Book of Bible Stories* by Wanda Hayes. Standard Publishing, p. 31.

REMEMBERING GOD'S TRUTHS: You will need to use four picture cards from the picture files suggested on p. 6.

- Sister Miriam was alone and sad as she watched her baby brother in the basket in the water.

    When you are alone and sad, what should you do?

    I should pray and ask God to help me. (*God's Care* section)

- Moses was sleeping in the basket on the water.

    Who takes care of you when you sleep?

    God takes care of me when I sleep. (*God's Care* section)

- God took care of Moses.

    Who is God?

    God is our Heavenly Father. (*Heavenly Father* section)

- Our Heavenly Father took good care of baby Moses. The princess took him out of the water. He was not killed by the wicked Pharaoh. Miriam was so happy.

    When you are very happy, what should you do?

    I should thank God for making me happy. (*I Pray* section)

EXPERIENCING GOD'S TRUTHS: Obtain the book *My Baby Brother Needs Me* by Jane Belk Moncure, Standard Publishing (#4901), or another book about a preschooler caring for a baby brother or sister. Bring baby items (bottles, rattle, diapers, cradle, etc.) for the children to use as they pretend to care for a baby, a basket or box to hold a pretend baby Moses in the pretend water, several dolls, and a blue blanket for the pretend water.

Let the children pretend to be babies. Let them lie on the floor and kick. Let them crawl around the room.

Gather the children in the story area and read the book about caring for a baby. Give the children a few minutes to play with the dolls and baby things you brought. Tell the boys that Moses had a big brother named Aaron. The boys can pretend to be Aaron. The girls can pretend to be Miriam.

Let the children act out the story as you retell it, letting them do the talking when it is appropriate. Place the doll in the basket, and the basket in the water (blue blanket). Place chairs on one side of the water, and tell the children to pretend that the chairs are bulrushes, or high grass, growing near the water. One girl should be Miriam, and one boy should be Aaron. Let another girl be the princess who comes and finds the baby. Miriam will hide among the chairs (bulrushes), and come out to speak to the princess, "I know a good nurse who will take care of the baby for you." Miriam then goes to get the mother of Moses, another girl in your class. Let the children clap because they are happy that God has kept baby Moses safe. Ask, "When you are very happy, what should you do?" Let them answer, "I should thank God for making me happy." Then, lead the children in a prayer of thanks for keeping baby Moses safe and keeping us safe, too.

Direct the children back to the tables, and give each child an activity sheet, "Peek-A-Boo" (p. 9, *Through the Bible Activities for Preschoolers, Book 1*). Be sure that each child's name is printed on the back of his or her paper. Give each child a pink crayon and tell him to color only the face and hands of the baby and the brother. Draw a happy face on the paper of the ones who follow your directions.

REVIEWING GOD'S TRUTHS: Play "Hide the Picture Cards" as described on page 9.

Ask the children, "What does the Bible tell us about God?" Encourage the children to answer, "God is good, Psalm 73:1."

Have a closing prayer, "Father, please help us to be kind to our younger brothers and sisters. We thank you for them. In Jesus' name, amen."

Note: If time permits, read the book, *Kindness* by Jane Belk Moncure, Standard Publishing (#4929). Talk about pages 8, 11 and 12 which have pictures of a child helping a younger sibling.

Unit Three: God's Special Man—Moses
Bible Verse: I will trust and not be afraid. (Isaiah 12:2, NIV)

Exodus 3; 4; 7—12
Lesson 10

MOSES LEADS GOD'S PEOPLE

AS THE CHILDREN ARRIVE: Greet each child warmly and help him put any items he may have brought in the Safe-Keeping Box (see p. 7). Direct the child to a learning center.

Attendance Check Center: Help the children use the stars or stickers provided to place on the attendance chart or cards.

Bible Word Center: Use the large cardboard box suggested in Lesson 8 (p. 30) to review the Bible verse. Let the children be the Jack-in-the-Box, and pop up as they say the verse. Ask, "What should you do when you are afraid?" The child jumps up saying, "I will trust and not be afraid, Isaiah 12:2." Let every child have a turn, and clap for each child after he or she says the verse.

Transportation Center: Bring to class or ask some of the parents to bring to class small toys that have to do with transporting people and goods. (Examples, cars, trucks, airplanes, ships, horses, space ships, donkeys, motorcycles, etc.) Place these toys in a bag to hide them from view, and put the bag on one side of the table.

As the children arrive, talk about the word, "transportation." Let the children take a motor toy from the bag, and use the toy to get from one side of the table to the other.

Tell them that people in Bible days did not have any of these ways to get from one place to another. Put the motor toys back into the bag.

In Bible days, they had to walk or ride donkeys, horses, or camels. Let the children walk their fingers across the table and then walk an animal across the table.

Tell them, "In our lesson today, God's people had to follow Moses on a long journey. Most of them walked."

At the sound of music from the cassette tape or piano, have the children go to the story area of the room for singing.

SINGING AND TALKING TO GOD: Sing "Thank You, God" (p. 40, *Songs for Preschool Children,* change "the Bible" to "courage"); "Bible Song" (p. 41, SPC, use "Moses" instead of "Jesus"); "I Will Trust in God" (p. 38, SPC); "God So Loved" (p. 42, this book); and "Give Thanks" (p. 23, this book).

Have a special time for talking to God. Ask the children, "How did God take care of you this past week?" Let each child have a chance to talk. Start with the child whose name begins with the letter A. Go in alphabetical order, and assure the children that each one will have a chance to talk. Stress that they must listen to what their friends have to share. Pray, "Father, You have taken such good care of us this week. Thank You for taking care of people who love You. We love You. Amen."

Sing "Head and Shoulders" (p. 5, SPC) and have the children do the motions. This activity will help them to be better listeners.

READING ABOUT GOD'S WORD: Read Hebrews 11:27 from your copy of *International Children's Version.* "It was by faith that Moses left Egypt. He was not afraid of the king's anger."

Read or tell the Bible story.

Exodus 3, 4, 7-12 CR P. 42, 43 44, 45

Moses Leads God's People

The people of Israel lived in Egypt a long time. They worked very hard, but the harder they worked, the meaner the Egyptians were to them.

When Moses grew to be a man, he saw how unhappy the Israelites were. They had been made slaves to the Egyptians, and it made him angry and sad. But God had a special way for Moses to help his people.

God had heard the cries of the Israelite people as they begged Him to help them. So God chose Moses to lead the Israelites out of Egypt.

Moses went to the Pharaoh and asked him to let the Israelite people leave Egypt. Pharaoh kept saying no. So God punished the Egyptians with bad things called plagues. First, He turned their river to blood so they could not drink it or wash in it, but even then Pharaoh would not let the people go.

Then God sent millions of frogs to hop all over Egypt—even in the houses, but still Pharaoh would not let the Israelites leave.

God punished the Egyptians ten different times with bad plagues. Sometimes Pharaoh would say, "Yes, you may leave," but when the bad things were over, he would change his mind.

Finally, God sent one last terrible punishment on the Egyptians. God knew this last bad thing would be sure to make Pharaoh let the people leave. So God had Moses tell the Israelites to get ready to leave.

And that night, God sent His death angel to every Egyptian home and the oldest son died. But no one died in the homes of the Israelites, because God had told them what to do. And just as God had said, Pharaoh let the Israelites leave Egypt.

From *A Child's First Book of Bible Stories* by Wanda Hayes. Standard Publishing, p. 34.

REMEMBERING GOD'S TRUTHS: You will need four picture cards from your picture file for today's lesson. The first card is found in the *Jesus* section, and the rest are found in the *Heavenly Father* section.

- God's people were living in Egypt. But they had a problem. Pharaoh made God's people work very hard. Sometimes we have problems, too.
  Does Jesus love children who have problems?
  Yes, Jesus loves everyone.
- Pharaoh was mean, and he did not love God. He didn't even know who God is. But you know.
  Who is God?
  God is our Heavenly Father.
- You know many things about God that Pharaoh did not know. Here are two questions about God.
  Where is God?
  God is everywhere.
  Who made the world?
  God made the world.

EXPERIENCING GOD'S TRUTHS: Exercise to work out the wiggles. Have the children wiggle their fingers, toes, nose, shoulders. Make a fun game of it. Say, "Now no more wiggles are left in me, and I can now sit as quietly as can be."

Read *Courage* by Jane Belk Moncure, Standard Publishing (#4930), if it is available. Talk with the children about each incident in the book that required courage. For younger children, you may want to choose only three or four incidents.

If the book, *Courage,* is not available, find pictures to illustrate three or four of the following ideas that are taken from the book:

It takes courage to be brave when you get a shot at the doctor's office or go to the dentist's office.

It takes courage to tell someone not to hurt a small child.

It takes courage to admit that you have done something wrong.

It takes courage to say "I'm sorry" when you did something wrong, or you have hurt someone.

It takes courage to say "good-bye" to your parents when they must leave you for a while.

It takes courage to do something new—like slide down a big slide or go to a new class.

Let the children tell you what they think the picture is about.

Say, "We can pray and ask God to give us courage when we are afraid." Say this every time you talk about a new fearful situation. Let the children act out one of the incidents (see, **Act It Out,** p. 9).

Direct the children to return to the tables. Give each child an activity sheet, "Courage" (p. 10, *Through the Bible Activities for Preschoolers, Book 1).* Let each child color Mike's clothes and glue sequins to his skates. Talk about how it feels to try to do new things. Use the phrase, "We can pray and ask God to give us courage."

REVIEWING GOD'S TRUTHS: Play the "Pop-Up Game" as described on page 9. If any child is hesitant to play, stop and talk about how it takes courage to do something we do not usually do.

Review the Bible verse. Ask, "What should you do when you are afraid?" Encourage the children to answer, "I will trust and not be afraid."

Closing prayer: "Dear God, thank You for giving us courage when we ask for it. You are so good to us. In Jesus' name, amen."

Unit Three: God's Special Man—Moses

Bible Verse: I will trust and not be afraid. (Isaiah 12:2, NIV)

Exodus 13:17-22

Lesson 11

CROSSING THE RED SEA

AS THE CHILDREN ARRIVE: Greet each child as he or she enters and make each child feel special. Comment on something personal and special about each child. (Examples: Sally, I really like to see your smiling face, or Tommy, you were so kind to Jimmy when you came into our room.) Direct the children to a learning center.

Attendance Check: Help the children to put their stars or stickers on the attendance chart or cards. Check to see how many meetings they have been present. Help them count their stars or stickers.

Bible Word Center: Today's Bible verse is a review of the one taught in Lessons 8 and 10. For variety, substitute a large blanket for the box, and let the child pop out from under the blanket when they say the verse. Ask, "What should you do when you are afraid?" The child answers, "I will trust and not be afraid. Isaiah 12, verse 2." as he or she jumps out from under the blanket.

Solving a Problem Center: Bring to class a strip of light blue paper or cloth to tape to a table. You will need lots of play people or paper dolls cut from catalogs or magazines. Set up the table like this:

Let the children pretend to walk the people up as far as the water. Then talk about the problem of how to get across the water. Let the children suggest ways to get across. Do not tell the Bible story. Only describe the problems: the need to get across; too far to swim; no boat available; and no helicopter available. Leave the problem unsolved. Tell the children, "We will hear a story later that will tell us how God solved the problem. God can do anything."

At the sound of music from the cassette tape or piano, have the children go to the story area of the room for singing.

SINGING AND TALKING TO GOD: Sing these songs: "I Will Trust in God" (p. 38, *Songs for Preschool Children);* "Trust in the Lord" (p. 25, SPC); "All Things Were Made by Him" (p. 49, SPC); "Bible Song" (p. 41, SPC, using "Moses" instead of "Jesus"); and "Sing, Little Children, Sing" (p. 37, SPC).

For the special time of talking to God, ask one child to express the verbal prayer thanking God that we can trust Him.

READING ABOUT GOD'S WORD: Say, "The Bible tells us that we can trust God. Listen while I read from my Bible about trust." Read today's Bible verse: "I will trust and not be afraid" (Isaiah 12:2, NIV). Let the children take turns passing the Bible to each other as they pretend to read the verse and say the reference.

Now read or tell the Bible story to the children.

Exodus 13:17-22 CR p. 46

Crossing the Red Sea

"Get out of my land!" Pharaoh told Moses. "You and all of the children of Israel, leave now!"

Moses did not wait. He told the Israelites, "Let's go now. Pharaoh is finally letting us leave."

So they left Egypt—thousands and thousands of Israelite men, women, and children and all of their animals. They followed Moses to the Red Sea. Then God told them to camp beside the sea.

But back in Egypt, the wicked Pharaoh was changing his mind again. *"What have we done?"* he asked himself. *"Who will work for us now that the Israelites are gone? We must go after them and bring them back."*

So the Pharaoh and his army rode after the Israelites. There were soldiers riding horses and soldiers marching. They kept going until they could see the Israelites camped by the Red Sea.

When the men and women with Moses saw the Egyptians coming, they were afraid.

"Why did you lead us here, Moses?" they asked. "We should have stayed in Egypt and died there. We don't want to die here."

But Moses trusted God, and he told the people, "Don't be afraid. God will save you today."

Then God said to Moses, "Stretch your hand over the sea and divide it. The people of Israel will walk through on dry land." And they did!

When the Egyptians saw the Israelites walking through the sea, they started to follow. But God had a plan. He told Moses, "Stretch out your hand over the sea again and make the waters come back together."

Moses obeyed God, and all of the Egyptians were drowned in the Red Sea that day.

From *A Child's First Book of Bible Stories* by Wanda Hayes. Standard Publishing, p. 35.

Note: Since there is no picture in the story book, you will need to get a picture of Moses and the Israelites crossing the Red Sea. Or, use the table used earlier in the learning center.

REMEMBERING GOD'S TRUTHS: Use the pictures from the picture files suggested on page

You will need four for today's lesson. Be prepared to teach the four concepts represented in the pictures in a fun and instructive way. Remember to use rhythm and body movement to aid learning.

- The wicked Pharaoh let the Israelite people leave Egypt. Then he changed his mind and told his soldiers to go get them and bring them back. When the Israelite people saw the soldiers coming after them, they were afraid.

  Who can help you when you are afraid?

  God can help me when I am afraid. (*God's Care* section)

- The Israelites had a problem.

  When you have a problem, what should you do?

  I should pray and ask God to help me. (*I Pray* section)

- God solved the problem for His people, the Israelites.

  What can God do?

  God can do anything. (*Heavenly Father* section)

- The Israelites were so happy that God had solved their problem.

  When you are happy, what should you do?

  I should thank God for making me happy. (*I Pray* section)

EXPERIENCING GOD'S TRUTH: Discuss the question, "What is trust?" (Bring from home: a paper cup for each child, grape juice, a cracker for each child—one that the children may not be familiar with, 2 bricks or wood the size of bricks, and a board about five inches wide and at least four feet long.)

In class say, "The Israelite people had to trust God to help them cross the Red Sea. You and I need to trust, too. You trust your mother and father. When they give you something that does not taste good, like some medicine, you always trust that the medicine will help you. So, you swallow the medicine."

Show the children the board and say, "Here is a board, and we are going to put these bricks (or blocks of wood) under the ends of the board. Do you think you can trust me to hold your hand so you won't fall when you walk on it? Which one of you would like to be first to walk across this board?" (Let one child walk the length of the board.) Give each child a turn.

"You are right. You can trust me. I held your hand so you would not fall."

Direct each child to the tables. When they are all seated, say "I am going to give each of you a cracker. Have you seen one like this before? Do you think this cracker is OK to eat? Can you trust me when I say that this cracker will not hurt you? Yes, you can trust me because you know that I love you, and I would not do anything to hurt you." (All eat crackers.)

Repeat with the cup of grape juice. Emphasize the concept of trust. Say, "God loves you very much. You can trust Him." Pray, thanking God that we can trust Him.

Give each child an activity sheet, "I Can Trust" (p. 11, *Through the Bible Activities for Preschoolers, Book 1*), and instruct the children to color the child only. Cut strips of blue crepe paper to be glued on the picture for water.

REVIEWING GOD'S TRUTHS: Play "Musical Picture Cards" (see p. 10).

Closing prayer: "Dear God, there are many times when we can trust You. You have done so very much for us. Please help us to trust You more. In Jesus' name, amen."

Unit Three: God's Special Man—Moses
Bible Verse: Children, obey your parents. (Ephesians 6:1, NIV)
Exodus 19; 20:1-17
Lesson 12

RULES FOR GOD'S PEOPLE

AS THE CHILDREN ARRIVE: Let each child know you are glad that he or she is present. Direct each child to a learning center.

Attendance Check Center: Help each child place a star or sticker on the attendance chart or card. If you are using cards, this will be the last week for using them, and you may give the cards to the children to take home.

Bible Word Center: Read the verse from the Bible. "Do what is right and good" (Deuteronomy 6:18). Teach the verse and reference by using the following song and game technique. Have the children form a circle, holding hands. Walk to the right as you sing this verse and reference to the tune of "Farmer in the Dell." Repeat the verse as you walk to the left. Then have two children hold each other's hands up in the air to form a bridge while the other children walk under the bridge. The children are to repeat the song as they walk under the bridge, form a circle again after walking under the bridge, and clap the rhythm as they sing the song again.

Rules, Rules, Rules Center: You will need a large piece of paper and a magic marker. Write the heading, **Rules, Rules, Rules,** at the top of the paper.

Talk with the children about the rules they obey at home. Write the rules on the paper. Let the children draw pictures to represent the words wherever possible. Examples: "Do not run in the house."

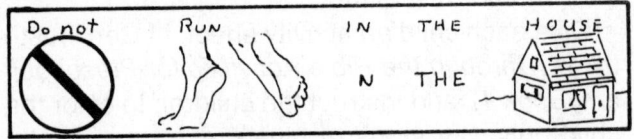

Or, "Wipe your feet at the door."

List as many rules as time permits.

At the sound of music from the cassette tape or piano, have the children go to the story area of the room for singing.

SINGING AND TALKING TO GOD: Sing these songs: "Pleasing God" (p. 26, *Songs for Preschool Children,* add verse four using the Scripture, Ephesians 6:1, and for verse five use the Scripture, Deuteronomy 6:18); "Help Me to Forgive" (p. 71, SPC); "Thank You, God" (p. 40, SPC); "In His Bible Book" (p. 41, SPC, change "love" to "obey").

Pray, saying a few words at a time and letting the whole group repeat the words: "Dear Father, thank You for our parents. They help us to know about You. Please help us to obey them each day. Amen."

READING ABOUT GOD'S WORD: Read Hebrews 8:10, from the *International Children's Version.* "I will put my laws in their minds, and I will write them on their hearts. I will be their God, and they will be my people."

Now use the NIV to read Ephesians 6:1 and Deuteronomy 6:18. Then read or tell the Bible story.

Exodus 19, 20:1-17 CR p. 51.

Rules for God's People

God's people needed two things to help them become a good nation. They needed to know how to worship and obey God, and how to treat other people.

Moses told everyone, "Wash your clothes so that you will be clean, because in three days God is going to come down to the top of this mountain. And God said that you must not touch the mountain or even come close to it."

The Israelites did everything Moses told them, and three days later God came to the top of Mount Sinai in the morning. No one could see God because the mountain was covered by a thick cloud. There was thunder and flashes of lightning. Then a trumpet sounded so loud that all of the people shook with fear.

Moses and the Israelites waited at the bottom of the mountain. When the sounds of the trumpet grew louder and louder, Moses spoke, and God answered him with a voice that boomed like thunder. Then God called Moses to come up to the top of the mountain. There God told Moses to warn the people not to come near the mountain because God would be too bright and shiny for them to look at. So Moses went back down from the mountain and warned the people not to come near the mountain while God was there.

Then the people moved farther back from the mountain. They watched Moses go up, up, up again into the thick cloud that covered the mountain where God was.

Moses was on the mountain with God a long time. When he came down, he brought stone tablets with ten special laws written on them. We call these ten special laws the Ten Commandments.

From *A Child's First Book of Bible Stories* by Wanda Hayes. Standard Publishing, p. 37.

REMEMBERING GOD'S TRUTHS: You will need four picture cards from your picture file for today's lesson.

- God is always watching over us. He is taking care of us, and He helps us obey His rules.
  Where is God?
  God is everywhere. (*Heavenly Father* section)
- God gave laws to His people because He wanted them to obey.
  Who helps you to obey?
  God helps me to obey. (*About Me* section)
- Sometimes we disobey God.
  When you do something wrong and then say, "I'm sorry, God," what does God say?
  "I forgive you." (*I Pray* section)
- Some people think that if they obey God's laws, God will let them go to Heaven, but you know the right way to go to Heaven.
  Who can go to Heaven?
  All people who love and trust Jesus can go to Heaven. (*Heavenly Father* section)
  Be sure to explain to the children what it means to love and trust Jesus.

EXPERIENCING GOD'S TRUTHS: Play the "Obeying Game." Have the children get in a line side by side against one wall. The teacher explains the game by saying, "I will tell you what to do, and I'll watch to see who obeys. Please do only what I tell you to do."

The teacher says, "You may obey by taking three giant steps." The children obey, and the teacher thanks them for obeying.

Say, "You may obey by jumping on one foot until I say stop." The children jump until the teacher says, "Stop! Thank you for obeying."

Repeat the statements, using different actions such as take two baby steps; pat your head; stretch your arms up high; take one elephant step; or take two jumping steps. Always say, "Thank you for obeying," after each exercise.

Help the children to see that it is important to obey God's laws at play time. You will need several items that you can bring from home or ask a friend with children to lend them to you. Do not use toys that belong to any child in your class. You will need: a toy gun, a large or special toy that might cause a child to covet or wish he had it, four or five other toys, a kitchen knife, a chocolate candy bar, and bag to hide these items in.

Say to the children, "God gave laws to His people. Were the laws only for grown-ups to obey?" Allow time for the children to say, "No!" Then continue your questions: "Should children obey God's laws, too? Yes! Can you remember any of the laws God told to His people?" Let the children respond. See how many of the laws they can remember. Say, "We are going to talk about some of the laws God gave us. I am going to show you an object, and I want you to think of a law about that object." Show the gun. Let the children try to remember the law that says we should not kill. Help them if they can't recall the law. Discuss with the children that pretending to kill is not good because pretending is teaching. So, if we pretend to shoot someone, we are teaching ourselves to disobey God. Expect some children to disagree, but stress that guns are not good toys.

Take out the very attractive toy. Tell them to pretend that this toy is in a store, and their parents are not planning to buy it. Ask the children to think of a law about toys in a store. Help them to recall the law about stealing. Say, "God does not want us to take anything that is not ours. If we see something that we can't have, God wants us to be happy even though we can't have it. If our parents say we can't have something, God wants us to act kind and be happy about the toys we do have at home. He does not want us to keep thinking about the toy we can't have."

Repeat using the candy bar. First tell the children to pretend they cannot eat chocolate, but they see a candy bar in a store. They want it very much. Use the same statements as before.

Now spread all the remaining toys on a table. Explain that they are to look at the toys, but they will not be able to play with them because they are not theirs. Ask the children, "What things are best to play with?" Talk about the gun and the knife as poor choices because they are dangerous. Praise the child who is willing to choose simple, safe toys.

Close this section of the lesson by asking God to help us remember His law about not taking things that are not ours.

Have the children return to the tables and give each child an activity sheet. "Timmy Obeys God's Law" (p. 12, *Through the Bible Activities for Preschoolers, Book 1*). Print each child's name on the back of her paper. Tell the children, "Timmy and Jeff are playing with Jeff's super heroes. Jeff tells his super hero to shoot Timmy and kill him. Timmy says, 'Jeff, God's law says don't kill. I think our super heroes should do kind things.' Timmy is pleasing God by obeying His rules." Let the children color the super heroes.

REVIEWING GOD'S TRUTHS: Play "Musical Picture Cards" as described on page 10 of this book.

Discuss pages 12 and 14 in the book, *Courage,* by Jane Belk Moncure. This is the book suggested for reading in last week's lesson. These pages are about telling the truth when you have done something wrong. Explain that one of God's laws tells us to never tell a lie.

Review the Bible verse. Ask, "What does the Bible say about obeying?" Encourage the children to answer, "Children, obey your parents (Ephesians 6:1, NIV)." Then ask, "What does the Bible say about doing what is right?" Encourage the children to answer "Do what is right and good. (Deuteronomy 6:18, NIV)."

Closing prayer: "Dear God, sometimes it is hard to do what is right and good. But we know you can help us. We love You. In Jesus' name, amen."

God So Loved

John 3:16 (NIV)

June George

Unit 4—God's Special People

GETTING READY FOR UNIT FOUR

The theme of this unit is that God provided special people to carry on the work Moses started. Joshua led the Israelites into the Promised Land to conquer the enemies of God's people. Hannah trusted God for a son, and Saul was chosen as king.

Learning Objectives: Some things you should expect your children to accomplish in this unit:

The children should know (1) God keeps His promise; (2) God wants us to tell the truth; (3) God is most powerful; (4) God wants us to talk to Him.

The children should feel (1) They should tell the truth; (2) Thankful that God can do anything; (3) They can talk to God anytime; (4) God will help them make right choices.

The children should be able to (1) Tell the highlights of the Bible stories; (2) Say the Bible verses and state simple answers to concept question; (3) Pray a simple prayer; (4) Make some right choices that please God.

Remember, because of the differences in age and maturity, some children will meet more of these objectives than others will.

Bible Verses: The four Bible verses in this unit are review verses.

Books: Several books are suggested for reading at the end of each lesson, if time permits. These books may be placed in the quiet, book corner of your room. *Thank You, God, for Wonderful Things; I Can Pray to God; Choosing Is Fun;* and *Happy Hannah* are suitable for the ages of the children and for the subjects being studied.

Bulletin Board: Place on the bulletin board, or wall, pictures of Joshua and Caleb, Joshua leading the Israelites around the walls of Jericho, Hannah with the child Samuel, and Samuel choosing Saul to be king. Build this bulletin board as you tell the Bible stories each week. Use the heading: *God's Special People.*

THINGS TO DO:

Lesson 13: You will need materials for making new attendance charts. Arrange for a helper to role play situations suggested in the chart on page 45. Be sure to have the appropriate props available for this.

Lesson 14: Gather the materials needed for the learning centers (see p. 46). Collect pictures of super heroes or objects that remind the children of super heroes. Practice the motions used for the "Super Game." Scatter six pictures round the room, as suggested on pages 47 and 48.

Lesson 15: Be sure you have stars or stickers for the attendance chart; drawing paper and crayons; and the objects for role playing the stories on page 50.

Lesson 16: You will need to gather the objects needed for the **Choosing Center** (p. 51). Be prepared to use the expressions suggested. You will need glue and crayons for the activity sheet.

Unit Four: God's Special People
Bible Verse: God is good. (Psalm 73:1, NIV)

Numbers 13; 14
Lesson 13

THE PROMISED LAND

AS THE CHILDREN ARRIVE: Be sure to greet each child warmly, and direct him or her to a learning center.

Attendance Check Center: Give each child a sheet of light-colored construction paper. Ask each child to use crayons to draw a picture of himself or herself on the paper. Attach the pictures on the wall at the children's eye level. Stickers are to be added each week the child is present.

Bible Words Center: Review two Bible verses. Use the teaching materials made in previous lessons.

"God is good." (Psalm 73:1, NIV)—Word cards, Lesson 1.

"For God so loved the world that he gave his one and only son." (John 3:16, NIV)—Actions, Lesson 7.

Believing God Center: Play the "Believing God" game. Cut nine strips of paper 1" x 3". On five strips write a memory verse beginning with this week's Bible verse and using four other verses from previous lessons. On the four remaining strips, write one of the following **false** statements on each:

It is OK not to believe in God.

It is OK to tell lies.

You should watch TV a lot because everything on TV is good.

It is OK to be nasty to people if they are nasty to you.

Place these strips of paper in a box. During class, place the box of statements at one end of the room and the children at the other end. (Have the children standing side by side against the wall.) Tell the children that this is a game of deciding whether or not to believe what we hear. Let one child run down to the box, get a strip of paper and run back. The teacher reads the statement and then says, "Can we believe this?"

In the case of a Bible verse, the teacher helps the children to respond, *"Yes, we can always believe the Bible because the Bible is the Word of God, and God always tells the truth."*

In the case of the false statements, the teacher should listen to the children's ideas and lead them to see why the words are a lie. Emphasize the truth, "We can always believe God and He will reward us for believing Him."

At the sound of music from the cassette tape or piano, have the children go to the story area of the room for singing.

SINGING AND TALKING TO GOD: Sing, "God Is Good" (p. 38, *Songs for Preschool Children*); "Please Him, Please Him" (p. 39, SPC); "God's Friends" (p. 86, SPC, using "Joshua" when singing the first verse and "Caleb" when singing the second verse); "Give Thanks" (p. 23 this book); "Clap, Clap Your Hands for Joy" (p. 54, SPC); and "I Will Trust in God" (p. 38, SPC).

When talking to God in prayer, be sure to thank God that we know about Him and can believe in Him.

Lead the children in a walk around the room as they pretend to be God's people walking to the promised land.

READING ABOUT GOD'S WORK: Read or tell the Bible story.

Numbers 13, 14   CR p. 56

The Promised Land

"Here they come!" said the excited men and women. "Joshua and Caleb and the other spies are back from Canaan."

Twelve men had gone into the Promised Land to do a very important job. Moses had told them, "See if the land is good or bad. See what the people are like. Come back and tell me if the cities are open or have walls around them. And tell me if the land is good for growing crops."

Everyone wanted to hear what the men had to say. First, they had some good news.

"It is a good land for growing crops. Just look at this fruit," they said. The grapes were so big that it took two men to carry one bunch between them on a pole.

But what about the people in Canaan, everyone wanted to know. And the spies told them, "The people who live in Canaan are big and strong. They live in big cities with walls around them."

When the people heard this, they were afraid. They began to worry and complain. But Joshua and Caleb, two of the spies, said, "We can take this land and live in it. If God is pleased with us, He will help us take this land."

God was sorry that the people were afraid to go into the land He had promised to give them. So God said that the people who were afraid would wander in the wilderness for forty years—until they all grew old and died. They would not get to live in Canaan.

God also said, "Joshua and Caleb will get to go into the Promised Land of Canaan, because they gave a good report and because they believed in me."

From *A Child's First Book of Bible Stories* by Wanda Hayes. Standard Publishing, p. 39.

REMEMBERING GOD'S TRUTHS: You will need four picture cards from your picture file for today's lesson.

- Joshua and Caleb went into the Promised Land. They saw the huge grapes and the other food growing.
    Who gives you food?
    God makes food grow for me. (*God's Care* section)

- Joshua and Caleb said that the land was good and that the people should go into the land. Joshua and Caleb believed that God would take care of them.
    Who is God?
    God is our Heavenly Father.
    Where is God?
    God is everywhere. (*Heavenly Father* section)

- The people did not want to go into the Promised Land because they were afraid.
    Who can help you when you are afraid?
    God can help me when I am afraid. (*God's Care* section)

EXPERIENCING GOD'S TRUTHS: Help the children to understand what a reward is. Bring a simple cookie treat for each child. Place the treat in a small bag with the child's name on it. Tell the children that you have a reward waiting for each of them if they can answer one of the questions from the picture cards. Ask the questions and give the cookie reward to each child after he or she answers the questions. Help the children with the words if necessary.

Before class, ask a teen or an adult to help you with this part of the lesson. Be sure the helper has a copy of the chart that explains the stories and that he is well prepared. This helper will act out each story on the chart. He will pretend to be the person listed in the "Visitor"

ROLE PLAY CHART							
Prop	Visitor Says	Proclaims	Children Respond	Teacher Responds	Children Respond	Teacher Responds	
Covering for back of head	I am Caleb, and I have seen the Promised Land.	We should believe that God will help us, and we should go into the Promised Land. Isn't that right?	Yes	Should Caleb believe God? Does God always tell the truth? Does God reward people who believe Him?	Yes Yes Yes	God rewarded Caleb and Joshua by letting them go into the Promised Land later on. The other spies who did not believe God were not allowed to go in.	
Bathrobe and children's book that advocates belief in witches, space people or super heroes	I am a father/mother reading a book to you.	(Alter these words according to what book you bring.) The super hero can save you. He is the one you should follow.	No	Should we believe this book is really true? Is this just a fairy tale?	No Yes	Fairy tale books are not stories that we believe. They are just fun stories. God is the one we obey and believe.	
Back of head covered with sheet	I am pretend Noah.	God told me to build an ark to be safe from a storm. Should I believe God?	Yes	Opens Bible and pretends to read and says, "Yes, God told you to do it, Noah, and you can always believe God."		Does God reward people who believe Him? How did God reward Noah?	Yes He saved him so he would not drown.
Box of sugar or chocolate cereal with extra stars or glitter added to it	I am the kid on TV.	This is the world's most wonderful cereal. It has chocolate, sugar, marshmallows, candy pieces, and toys in it. Will it make you strong?	No	Should we believe this TV person? Will that sugar cereal be good for your body?	Let children answer.	People on TV do not always tell the truth. We should always be thinking, "Is that true?" If God tells us something different, then we should believe God, not the TV person.	

column, and he will wear or carry the prop listed in the "Prop" column. He will say the words listed in both the "Visitor Says" column and the "Proclaims" column. Be sure you have all the props needed for your actor-helper and that he or she knows how to use them.

Explain to the children that there are many people in the world who do not tell us the truth. We should not believe them. We should always believe God, because God always tells the truth. When we believe God, He rewards us. His reward is that we are happy, or He gives us something, or He keeps us safe, or in another way He shows us that He is pleased with us because we believed Him.

Say, "We are going to pretend some stories in which people must decide to believe God, or not to believe the person who is talking because that person is telling lies."

Introduce the actor-helper, and explain that he or she is going outside the door. When the helper comes back, pretend that he is another person.

Now follow the chart. Encourage the children to talk and interact as much as possible. Lead them as they clap after each skit.

Following the skits, have the children go to the tables. Give each child an activity sheet, "Believing God" (p. 13, *Through the Bible Activities for Preschoolers, Book 1*). Write the children's names on the papers. Discuss what the little boy is doing in the picture. Tell the children to look for the six hidden objects and circle them. Discuss how these hidden pictures are related to their Bible lesson. Then say, "Sometimes people tell lies, and we cannot believe them. God rewarded Joshua and Caleb for telling the truth. They got to go into the promised land. You can always believe God."

REVIEWING GOD'S TRUTHS: Continue playing the "Believing God" game (see learning center) with the whole class as long as interest lasts. Or, read the book, *Thank You, God, for Wonderful Things* by Ruth Odor, Standard Publishing (#4921).

Closing Prayer: "Thank You, God, for always telling us the truth. We know we can trust You. You know what is best for us. We love You. Amen."

Unit Four: God's Special People

Bible Verse: I will trust and not be afraid. (Isaiah 12:2, NIV)

Joshua 1:1-9; 2; 5:13—6:21

Lesson 14

THE WALLS OF JERICHO

AS THE CHILDREN ARRIVE: (See p. 7 for information concerning this section of the lesson.) Greet each child warmly and direct him to one of the learning centers.

Attendance Check Center: The children will place a star or sticker on the new cards that were made last week. Make each child feel special.

Bible Words Center: Today's Bible verse was first introduced in Lesson 8. Using a large cardboard box, let the children be Jacks-in-the-Box and pop-up when they say the verse. Ask, "What should you do when you are afraid?" The child answers, "I will trust and not be afraid, Isaiah 12:2." Everyone claps to show approval.

Strong Walls Center: Let the children build walls with blocks. Talk to them about the fact that long ago cities often had strong walls around them to keep enemies out.

At the sound of music from the cassette tape or piano, have the children go to the story area of the room for singing.

SINGING AND TALKING TO GOD: For song time, sing, "God Is Good" (p. 38, *Songs for Preschool Children*, add another verse, "Psalm 73:1, God is good."); "I Will Trust in God" (p. 38, SPC); "In His Bible Book" (p. 41, SPC, use the word "trust"); "In Our Church Building" (p. 35, SPC, change the words "We're Here in Our Church" to "In Our Church Building" in the title and lines 4 and 8); and "God's Friends" (p. 86, SPC, using "Joshua" instead of "Noah").

In this special time of talking to God, thank Him that He is so powerful. There is no one as powerful as He.

Lead the children in a march around the room. Tell them, "We are going to march like soldiers. In our story we will hear about some marching men."

READING ABOUT GOD'S WORD: Read Luke 1:37 from your copy of the *International Children's Version.* "God can do anything!" Show the children the words in the Bible. Have them say the words together.

Now read the Bible story.

Joshua 1:1-9, 2, 5:13—6:21 CRp. 65, 67

The Walls of Jericho

After Moses died, God said to Joshua, "It is now time for the people of Israel to go into the land I have promised them. Be strong and don't be afraid."

Now Joshua knew that his armies would have to take the land away from the people who live there. So Joshua sent two spies to visit the city of Jericho. He told them to see what the land was like, and then come back and tell him.

When the spies returned to Joshua after three days, they said, "God has given us this land. The people who live there are afraid of us."

Later, God told Joshua exactly how to take over the city of Jericho. God said that some of Joshua's soldiers should line up and march around the city. They were to be followed by seven priests carrying trumpets and other priests carrying the ark of the covenant.

Then Joshua told everyone, "Do not say a word until I tell you. We will march quietly around the city of Jericho for seven days. Then on the seventh day when I tell you to shout, shout as loud as you can."

For six days the soldiers and priests marched all the way around the city of Jericho, one time each day. The priests blew their trumpets the whole time. The people inside Jericho were afraid. They did not dare to go outside. They wondered what would happen next.

On the seventh day, the soldiers and the priests carrying the ark of God's covenant marched around the city seven times. And then when the other priests blew their trumpets, Joshua told the people, "Shout!" The people shouted as loud as they could, and the walls of Jericho fell down flat.

From *A Child's First Book of Bible Stories* by Wanda Hayes. Standard Publishing, p. 41.

REMEMBERING GOD'S TRUTHS: Use the picture cards from the picture files suggested on page 6. You will need four for today's lesson.

- God is more powerful than any person.
  Who made the world?
  God made the world. (*Heavenly Father* section)
- One of the powerful things that God did was to change His Son in Heaven into a little baby to live on earth. We usually talk about that at Christmas.
  What is Christmas?
  Christmas is the time we celebrate Jesus' birthday. (*Jesus* section)
- One of the ways God shows His power is by making people.
  Who made you?
  God made me. (*About Me* section)
- Another way God showed His power was by making Jesus alive again after He died.
  Will Jesus ever die again?
  No, Jesus will live forever. (*Jesus* section)

EXPERIENCING GOD'S TRUTHS: Children spend a great amount of time viewing, playing, and talking about super heroes. Your goal in this lesson is to teach that super heroes are pretend, and they have only pretend power. In contrast, God is the most powerful, and God's power is real. Begin your preparation by listing the names of super heroes your students talk about. You may want to use different super heroes than those suggested here. You will need to have pictures or an object to remind the children of each super hero, as well as several pictures of Jesus placed in a bag.

Play the "Super Game." Teach the children two hand motions. A loud definite clap of the hands means "real." A loose waving motion of the arms means "pretend." Practice these motions while saying the words. Place the objects or pictures of the super heroes and pictures of Jesus in a bag. Remove the items from the bag one at a time, and talk about which is real and

WHO IS MOST POWERFUL?			
PICTURE OF	SCRIPTURE	CONTRAST WITH	GO TO THE NEXT PICTURE
Jesus feeding the 5,000	Matthew 14:19-21 "(Jesus) took the five loaves of bread and the two fish.... He ... thanked God for the food.... He gave them ... to the people. All the people ate and were satisfied.... There were about 5,000 men there who ate, as well as women and children."	Can Wonder Woman feed 5,000 people with five loaves of bread and two fish? No, she can't because she has no power. She is only pretend.	Pretend to be Jesus' disciples giving out the food.
Jesus walking on the water	Matthew 14:25, "Jesus' followers were still in the boat. Jesus came to them. He was walking on the water."	Can Superman walk on water? No, we pretend that he can fly, but that is only pretend. Jesus is really powerful. He can walk on water.	Pretend to swim because we are not powerful enough to walk on water.
Parting of the Red Sea	Acts 7:36, "(God) worked wonders and miracles ... at the Red Sea."	Mr. T. is very strong and sometimes we pretend he can do super things. But can Mr. T hold back the water so that God's people can walk on dry land? No, only God is that powerful.	Skip and sing for joy because we are so happy that God is powerful and could save His people at the Red Sea. Sing "Please Him" (SPC 39. substitute "God is powerful" for "God is love").
Jesus changing water to wine	John 2:7, 9, "Jesus said to the servant, 'Fill the jars with water.' ... the servant took the water to the master. When he tasted it, the water had become wine."	Can Batman and Robin change water to wine? No, Batman and Robin can't do impossible things—for they are only pretend. (He Man or Spiderman could be used instead of Batman.)	Walk, clap, and say, "God is the most powerful."
Jesus calming the storm	Luke 8:23-24, "A big storm blew up on the lake.... They were in danger.... They said, 'Master! We will drown!' Jesus ... gave a command to the wind and the waves. The wind stopped and the lake became calm."	Can Luke Skywalker make a storm stop? No, he is only pretending to do powerful things. Only God can stop a storm.	Pretend to row our boats.
Jesus	Matthew 9:6, "... (Jesus) has power on earth to forgive sins."	Popeye always tries to save Olive Oyl. But, can Popeye save people from sin? No, only God can forgive sin.	

powerful (Jesus) and which are pretend (super heroes). Do not be surprised if some children resist the idea that super heroes are only pretend. They have had many hours of TV indoctrination to teach them otherwise. Put the items back in the bag. Now remove the items one at a time, and have the children say the word and do the motion to indicate whether the person is real or pretend. Do again, this time having the children do only the motion to indicate real or pretend.

Discuss who is most powerful. You will need to use the chart to guide you in the discussion and activity for each Scripture reference. Scatter the six pictures or objects around the room. Have the children sit in the area near the first picture/object. Read Matthew 14:19. Let the children talk, but do not let the conversation center on the super hero side of each contrast. *God's power is the emphasis of the lesson.* Then let the children walk around the room as they pretend to be Jesus' disciples giving out the bread and fish. Stop walking and sit in front of the next picture/item (Jesus walking on water). Follow the same procedure for each picture or object.

At the tables, give each child an activity sheet, "God Is the Most Powerful" (p. 1, *Through the Bible Activities for Preschoolers, Book 2)*, and be sure to write the child's name on the paper. Encourage the ones who can write their own names to do so. Discuss the paper. Have the children circle the picture of the most powerful person on the page, and put an X on the cartoon person who is only pretend powerful.

REVIEWING GOD'S TRUTHS: Let the children retell the Bible story, acting out the marching and trumpet blowing. Or ask the children to think of an animal (Example, lion, tiger, elephant, leopard). Ask them how they feel when they are acting like a powerful tiger, for example. Then ask, "Is a tiger more powerful than God? No, God is the most powerful!" Repeat the emphasis on God's power after pretending each animal action.

Review the Bible verse. Ask, "What should you do when you are afraid?" Encourage the children to answer, "I will trust and not be afraid (Isaiah 12:2)."

Have a closing prayer. "Thank You, God, for Your love and Your power to do things that no one else can do. Please help us to trust You and not be afraid. In Jesus' name, amen."

Unit Four: God's Special People

Bible Verse: Give thanks to him and praise his name. (Psalm 100:4, NIV)

1 Samuel 1

Lesson 15

HANNAH TRUSTED GOD

AS THE CHILDREN ARRIVE: Greet each child warmly and direct him to one of the learning centers.

Attendance Check: Help each child place a star or a sticker on his attendance chart. When the child is finished, he is to go to another learning center.

Bible Word Center: Today's verse was first introduced in Lesson 4. Review the verse by acting it out. The children are to fold their hands and bow their heads when they say, "Give thanks to him." They are to clap their hands as they say, "and praise his name." They are to jump in place when they say, "Psalm 100:4." Ask the question: "What does the Bible say about giving thanks?" Encourage the children to answer as they act out the Bible verse.

Asking God Center: You will need drawing paper and crayons. Ask each child to think about a time when he or she asked God for something special. After each child has told about his request, give each child a piece of drawing paper and ask him or her to draw a picture of the time he asked God for something. Print a sentence on his paper which expresses what the child said. Print the child's name on the drawing, and let her take it home after class.

At the sound of music from the cassette tape or piano, have the children go to the story area of the room for singing.

SINGING AND TALKING TO GOD: Sing, "Bible Song" (p. 41, *Songs for Preschool Children,* substitute "Hannah" for "Jesus"); "Trust in the Lord" (p. 25, SPC); "I Will Trust in God" (p. 38, SPC, change lines 2, 3 and 5 to "Isaiah 12:2."); "God Loves Me" (p. 36, v. 2, SPC); and "I Can Talk to God" (p. 80, SPC).

For this lesson, it would be appropriate to thank God that He always hears us when we talk to Him.

Let the children clap and march around the room as they sing the "Bible Song" listed above.

READING ABOUT GOD'S WORD: Read James 5:13 from the *International Children's Version.* "If one of you is having troubles, he should pray."

Now read the Bible verse, Psalm 100:4 (NIV). "Give thanks to him and praise his name."

Read or tell the Bible story.

1 Samuel 1   CR p. 74

Hannah Trusted God

Every year Hannah and her husband, Elkanah, went to God's house, the tabernacle, to worship God at a special service. But every year when it was time to eat the special meal, Hannah would be so sad she couldn't eat.

Elkanah knew that his wife, Hannah, wanted a son more than anything else in the world. She wanted to be a mother, but she had no children.

"I know what I am going to do," Hannah said to herself. *"I will make a special promise to God when I pray."*

When the meal was over, Hannah went to the big tent to pray. She was so sad when she prayed that she was crying very hard. Her lips moved as she talked to God in Heaven, but she didn't say any words out loud.

And this is what Hannah prayed, "O God of hosts, if you will give me a son, I will give him back to You for all of his life. To show that he is a special gift for You, I will never cut his hair." Hannah prayed a long time.

Eli, the priest, said to Hannah, "Go in peace, and may God give you what you have asked for."

Hannah and Elkanah got up early the next morning and worshiped God again. Then they went back home.

After awhile, Hannah's prayer was answered. A baby boy was born to her and her husband, and they named him Samuel. Hannah was very happy. She stayed home and took care of Samuel.

And when Samuel was a young boy, Hannah

did what she had promised. She took Samuel to Eli the priest and said, "I am the woman who prayed for a son. God answered my prayer. Here is the boy God gave me. I have brought him to live with you here and to serve God the rest of his life."

From *A Child's First Book of Bible Stories* by Wanda Hayes. Standard Publishing, p. 43.

REMEMBERING GOD'S TRUTHS: You will need four picture cards from the *I Pray* section of your picture file for today's lesson.
- Hannah prayed to God. We pray, too.
    Does God hear you when you talk to him?
    Yes, God always hears me when I talk to Him
    Where can you pray?
    I can pray anywhere.
    When can you talk to God?
    I can talk to God anytime.
    When you pray, what are you doing?
    When I pray, I am talking to God.

EXPERIENCING GOD'S TRUTHS: Bring from home an object or objects that pertain to each of the following stories. Tell the stories, one at a time, and allow the children to role play them, using the props you brought from home. (Read **Act It Out,** p. 9.) Help the children actually pray for the thing the child in the story prayed for. After each story, talk about what the child prayed for. Explain that God will answer the child's prayer. He will give the child what he or she asked for if it is best for the child. But, God will say, "No," and not give the child his request if it is best for the child not to have his wish.

Story One
Shawn had a tricycle that he loved to ride back and forth on the pavement in front of his house. His friend Kevin, who was older, got a bicycle, with only two wheels. Shawn would watch Kevin ride his two-wheeler, and Shawn would wish he could have a two-wheeler. Before he went to bed one night, Shawn prayed for a two-wheeler. The next night he prayed again for a bicycle. And the next . . . and the next! He asked God every night for a whole week. Do you know what happened? Shawn did *not* get a two-wheeler.

Shawn was upset, so he asked his parents why God had not given him a bicycle. His dad said, "Son, God does not give you things that are not best for you. God loves you and wants what is the very best for you, because you are His child." His mother said, "When you are older and bigger, maybe God will think you are ready for a bicycle."

At first Shawn was upset. But after talking it over with his parents several times, he felt better. Then he went outside and rode his tricycle.

Story Two
Joy was invited to go swimming in an indoor pool with her friend Terry on Saturday. Joy was very disappointed when her mother said, "Joy, you have a cold and I don't think you will be able to swim by Saturday." That made Joy angry, and she started to cry. Then she decided to stop crying and pray about the problem. "Dear God," Joy prayed, "please make my cold go away so I can swim Saturday with Terry." Joy waited. She got lots of sleep and reminded her mother to give her vitamins each day. By Friday her nose had stopped running, and she did not have a cough. When she woke up on Saturday morning, she ran to her parents' bedroom and asked, "Can I go, can I go?" "Yes," said her dad, "you can go, because your cold is better." "I knew God would hear me when I prayed," said Joy. "And he answered my prayer with a YES."

Following the discussion of the two stories, have the children return to the tables. Give each child an activity sheet, "Shawn's Answer", (p. 2, *Through the Bible Activities for Preschoolers, Book 2).* Have the children connect the dots to see what answer Shawn got to his prayer. Ask, "What is Shawn riding?" Stress the fact that God answers "Yes" if what we ask for is best for us at that time. God's timing is best!

REVIEWING GOD'S TRUTHS: Play the "Pop-Up Game" as described on page 9.

Read the book *I Can Pray to God* by Sandra Brooks.

Review the Bible verse. Ask, "What does the Bible say about giving thanks?" Encourage the children to answer, "Give thanks to him and praise his name, Psalm 100:4."

Closing prayer: "Thank You, God, for answering our prayers with only what is best for us. We know You hear and answer our prayers. We love You and praise You. Amen."

Unit Four: **God's Special People**

Bible Verse: Do what is right and good.
(Deuteronomy 6:18, NIV)

1 Samuel 8—10

Lesson 16

CHOOSING A KING

AS THE CHILDREN ARRIVE: Have the following centers ready ten minutes ahead of class time so children may get involved with a learning activity as soon as they arrive. Continue the learning centers for five minutes into the class time and then have the children assemble for the singing and talking to God time.

Attendance Check Center: Greet each child warmly and help him place a star or sticker on his attendance picture.

Bible Words Center: Today's Bible verse was first introduced in Lesson 12. Review the verse by singing it to the tune of "Farmer in the Dell." See page 40, for directions for putting actions with the song.

Choosing Center: Preschoolers often have difficulty making choices. Here is a fun way to help them.

Bring to class five to ten items from three or four different categories of items. (Examples, ten different colored crayons, five different children's shirts, six or eight different small toys like matchbox trucks or little people, or five different fruits.)

Tell the children, "Each of us has times when we can choose what we want. We are going to play a choosing game. You will choose the thing you want to hold. You will not take the item home because it does not belong to you. We will watch to see which child chooses which item."

Then spread out the items from one category (Example, the crayons) and ask, "Which color do you want to choose?" Give each child a chance to choose, and talk about why he chose that item.

Put those items away and repeat with another set of items.

Use expressions like these:

"Your eyes will help you choose."

"Your brain is working hard trying to choose."

"Different people choose different things."

"Sometimes it's hard to choose."

"All of these things are good, but you must choose what you think is best."

"Thanks for choosing."

At the sound of music from the cassette tape or piano, have the children go to the story area of the room for singing.

SINGING AND TALKING TO GOD: Sing, "Pleasing God" (p. 26, *Songs for Preschool Children* using these words, "Deuteronomy 6, verse 1, is a very good verse for me; It's message tells me what to do; it's a very good verse for you. 'Do what is right and good, Do what is right and good, This is what you ought to do, Do what is right and good.'"); "In His Bible Book" (p. 41, SPC, change "love Him" to "choose Him"); "Clap, Clap Your Hands for Joy" (p. 54, SPC); and "God's Friends" (p. 86, SPC, change "Noah" to "Samuel").

Have a special time for talking to God. For this lesson it would be appropriate to ask God to help us choose to do what is right.

Say, "We are going to go around the room. You may choose whether you want to hop, skip, or walk." Let each child make his choice and then go around the room.

READING ABOUT GOD'S WORD: Read Acts 13:21 from the *International Children's Version*. "Then the people asked for a king. God gave them Saul."

Read or tell the Bible story.

1 Samuel 8-10   CR p. 78

Choosing a King

Samuel was now an old man. He had been telling the people to obey God's laws and helping them when they had problems for many years. He had served God from the time his mother, Hannah, had brought him to God's house when he was a little boy.

One day the leaders of the Israelites came to Samuel with an idea. "We want a king to rule us," they said.

"Why do you want a king?" Samuel asked.

"We want to be like the other nations around us," the men said. "If we have a king to lead us, we will win all of the battles we fight."

Samuel listened to everything the men had to say, and he did not like their idea. But he prayed to God about it, and God told him, "Don't be angry with them, Samuel. But be sure they know what it will be like to have a king."

Samuel told the people, "A king will want you to work for him and give him presents."

"We still want a king," the people answered Samuel.

Then God said, "Give them a king."

So Samuel called all of the tribes of Israel together, and then he chose the tribe of Benjamin. He knew that the king God had chosen was in that family. Samuel asked for Saul, the son of Kish, to step forward.

"Where is Saul?" the people asked. But the new king was shy. He was hiding. So the people ran and got Saul and stood him in front of everyone.

Samuel said, "Look at the man God has chosen to be your king. There is no one like him."

To show that God had chosen Saul to be the king of Israel, Samuel poured drops of oil on his head.

From *A Child's First Book of Bible Stories* by Wanda Hayes. Standard Publishing, p. 46.

REMEMBERING GOD'S TRUTHS: Use the picture cards from the picture file suggested on page 6. You will need four for today's lesson.

- Samuel had been telling the people to obey God's laws.
    Who helps you obey?
    God helps me to obey. (*About Me* section)
- The people told Samuel, "We want a king to rule us." Samuel did not know what to do. So he prayed.
    When you pray, what are you doing?
    When I pray, I am talking to God.
    Does God hear you when you talk to Him?
    Yes, God always hears me when I talk to Him.
    When you have a problem, what should you do?
    I should pray and ask God to help me. (*I Pray* section)

EXPERIENCING GOD'S TRUTHS: God did not tell His people to have a king; He let them choose. The people chose to have a king, and God said that Saul should be the one. God expects us to choose sometimes, too. Sometimes we must choose between something that is *good* and another thing that is *best*.

Bring to class a Bible, a storybook, a child's swimsuit, a girl's dress, a picture of Jesus, a super hero item, a table cloth, an apple, and a package of mints.

Tell the children to hide somewhere in the room and to hide their eyes while you count to ten. While the children are hiding, place the apple and mints on the table. Cover these items with the table cloth to add a little mystery to the game. Find each child and send him back to the table, but tell him not to touch the things on the table.

When all the children are found and seated, tell them, "Sometimes we must choose between one thing that is good and another thing that is the best." Remove the table cloth and ask, "Which of these is best for your body?" Help them to understand that the mints are good, but the apple is best for their bodies.

Repeat the game using the storybook as good, and the Bible as best. Play it again with swimming (the swim suit) as a good place to go, but the church building (represented by the dress) for your meeting is the best place to go. Play it again with the super hero as a fun person and Jesus as the best person.

After explaining this to the children, pass out the activity sheet, "Jesus Is Best" (p. 3, *Through the Bible Activities for Preschoolers, Book 2*). Help the children fold the paper on the dotted lines. Some may be coloring the picture of Jesus as they wait for your assistance. Help each child write his or her name on the line which completes the statement, "Jesus is most important to _____!" Help the children glue the tri-folded picture so it will stand up and remind them to do what is right and good. Tell the children to take their folded picture home and place it on their dresser or table.

REVIEWING GOD'S TRUTHS: Play "Pop-Up Game" as described on page 9.

Read *Choosing Is Fun* by Mary Bachman, if it is available.

Closing prayer: "Thank You, God, for helping us to make the right choices. We want to do what is right and good. Amen."

Unit 5—God's Special Man—David

GETTING READY FOR UNIT FIVE

The theme of this unit will be that God used His servant, David, throughout his life. David had special talents and abilities that God had given him. God gave David courage to do difficult tasks, and God loved him. God loves each child.

Learning Objectives: Some things you should expect your children to accomplish in this unit:

The children should know (1) God can help them when they are afraid; (2) Friendships are important; (3) God is real.

The children should feel (1) It's OK to be afraid; (2) Happy that Jesus is their best friend; (3) Happy that God takes care of them; (4) Happy that Jesus will forgive them when they ask for forgiveness.

The children should be able to (1)Tell the highlights of the Bible stories; (2) Say the Bible verses and state simple answers to concept questions; (3) Choose kind responses in given situations; (4) Pray a simple prayer.

Remember, because of the differences in age and maturity, some children will meet more of these objectives than others will.

Bible Verses: There is only one new verse in this unit. The others are review verses. Learn the suggested actions to the new verse and use them when teaching it. Use the Bible words, help the children "read" them in the Bible, and sing them at every opportunity. Be sure to keep the teaching aids used at the Bible Words Center for use in later lessons.

Books: Several books are suggested for reading at the end of each lesson, if time permits. These books may be placed in the quiet, book corner of your room. *When I'm Afraid; Kindness; Jesus Is My Special Friend;* and *David the Shepherd* are suitable for the ages of the children and for the subjects being studied. Check your church library, your Bible bookstore, or order from Standard Publishing.

Bulletin Board: Place pictures of David on the bulletin board, or wall space, near your story circle. Use the heading of the unit: *God's Special Man—David.*

THINGS TO DO:

Lesson 17: You will need a piece of shelf paper ten feet long, masking tape, pieces of brick, wood, and sand to glue on the activity sheets.

Lesson 18: Make four cardboard signs as suggested on page 56. Have the housekeeping corner of the room ready for role playing. Secure the props needed for role playing (see p. 58).

Lesson 19: Bring a real and a toy bird, a real and an artificial flower; a real baby and a doll; real and plastic foods; a Halloween mask of an animal or person; and adult clothes (see p. 59). You will need pictures of Santa Claus, the Easter Bunny, the Sandman or a Care Bear, and a Tooth Fairy pillow. Arrange these pictures around the room as suggested on page 60.

Unit Five: God's Special Man—David
1 Samuel 17:1-54
Bible Verse: I will trust and not be afraid. (Isaiah 12:2, NIV)
Lesson 17

A BOY MEETS A GIANT

AS THE CHILDREN ARRIVE: Greet each child warmly and direct him or her to a learning center.

Attendance Check Center: Help each child place a star or a sticker on his or her attendance chart. Tell each child you are glad he or she is in your class today.

Bible Words Center: Today's verse, "I will trust and not be afraid" (Isaiah 12:2, NIV), was introduced in Lesson 8. Here is a fun way to review the verse.

Bring rhythm band instruments for the children to use while they sing this verse. Page 38 of *Songs for Preschool Children* suggests you use the tune, "Fishers of Men." For this curriculum, change the second, third and last lines to read, "Isaiah 12:2," so that the children will learn the reference. If you do not have a set of rhythm band instruments, make your own. Two wood blocks, two jar tops, bells, or sticks to bang together are good instruments. An empty oatmeal box is a good drum. Empty plastic food containers, with a little rice inside and the top taped on, make shakers.

In class, read the verse from your Bible. Then teach the verse by letting the children sing it as they play their instruments.

How Big Was Goliath? Center: Bring from home a tape measure, a piece of shelf paper ten feet long, and masking tape. Tape the shelf paper on the floor. Show the children how you measure it with the tape measure and mark off each one foot segment.

Tell the children, "If Goliath lay down on our floor, he would be this long." Let the children lie on the paper (with shoes off) as if they were standing on one anothers' shoulders. Point out that it would take three children, standing on each others' shoulders, to be as tall as Goliath.

At the sound of music from the cassette tape or piano, have the children go to the story area of the room for singing.

SINGING AND TALKING TO GOD: Sing, "Trust in the Lord" (p. 25, *Songs for Preschool Children*); "I Will Trust God" (p. 38, SPC); "God Loves Me" (p. 36, v. 3, SPC); "In His Bible Book" (p. 41, SPC, change "love" to "trust"); and "All Things Were Made by Him" (p. 49, SPC).

In a special time of talking to God, it would be appropriate, for this lesson, to thank God that He helps us when we are afraid.

Following the prayer, lead the children in singing "Heads and Shoulders" (p. 5, SPC). Doing this activity will enable the children to be better listeners.

READING ABOUT GOD'S WORD: Read Hebrews 13:5b, 6, from the *International Children's Version*. "God has said, 'I will never leave you; I will never run away from you.' So we can feel sure and say, 'The Lord is my helper; I will not be afraid. What can man do to me?'"

Read or tell the Bible story.

1 Samuel 17:1-54   CR p. 79, 80

A Boy Meets a Giant

David was excited. He was going to the battlefield where the army of Israel was facing the army of the Philistines. The young shepherd boy was going to take food to his three older brothers who were in the army of Israel.

"Come back and tell me how your brothers are," Jesse told his son.

"I will," David said, and hurried away.

As David got close to the valley where the army of Israel was, he heard a loud voice coming from one of the mountains.

"Why do you come to fight us in a battle?" the voice shouted to the army of Israel. "Just send someone to fight me. If he kills me, then the Philistines will serve you. But if I kill him, then you will serve us."

As David got closer, he could see the man standing on a mountain across the valley. It was Goliath, a man almost ten feet tall. David had never seen anyone so big! He was a giant!

Again Goliath yelled to the Israelite army, "I dare you, army of Israel. Send one of your soldiers to fight me today." But no one wanted to fight Goliath. They were all too afraid. When King Saul and the whole army of Israel heard Goliath, they shook with fear.

For forty days, Goliath had been shouting across the valley to the army of Israel, "Send someone to fight me." And for forty days no one had gone to fight him.

When David got to the Israelite army's camp, he went to King Saul and said, "No one should be afraid because of Goliath. I will go and fight him."

"But you are too young," the king told David. "Goliath has been a soldier for a long time. He knows how to fight better than you do."

Then David answered, "When I was taking care of my father's sheep, I killed both a lion and a bear to protect them. And I will kill this Philistine, too."

Saul knew how much David trusted God, so he said, "Go and fight the giant, and may God be with you and help you."

King Saul gave David a helmet to protect his head and armor to protect his body. But David wasn't used to wearing them, and he took them off. David did not even take a sword to fight Goliath. Instead, he chose special weapons—a big stick, his sling, and five smooth stones from a creek. David put the stones into his shepherd's pouch and walked toward the battle line.

Goliath was wearing heavy armor and a man was carrying a shield in front of him. Goliath looked down at David. He laughed and made fun of him, but David wasn't afraid.

David said, "You come to me with a sword and a spear, but I come to you in the name of the Lord, the God of the armies of Israel. You made fun of God, but today He will help me kill you, and I will cut your head off. Then everyone will know that God leads Israel."

Goliath did not like David's brave words, and he moved forward toward him. Quickly, David ran forward toward Goliath. He put a stone into his sling and sent it flying through the air. The stone struck Goliath in the forehead. It sank deep into Goliath's head and killed him, and he fell on the ground.

Then David ran and took the giant's own sword and cut his head off with it. Now the Philistines were afraid. They ran away, and the army of Israel ran after them and won the battle.

From *A Child's First Book of Bible Stories* by Wanda Hayes. Standard Publishing, pp. 47, 48.

REMEMBERING GOD'S TRUTHS: You will need four picture cards from your picture file for today's lesson.

- David was going to the battlefield to take food to his brothers who were in the army. God had provided the food for them.
  Who gives you food?
  God makes food grow for me. (*God's Care* section)
- The armies of Israel were afraid of Goliath because he was almost ten feet tall.
  Who can help you when you are afraid?
  God can help me when I am afraid. (*God's Care* section)
- David was not afraid of Goliath. He knew that God had made his body strong, and that God would help him.
  Who made you?
  God made me. (*About Me* section)
- David knew that he could ask God to help him, and God would help. God could help because He is so powerful.
  What can God do?
  God can do anything. (*Heavenly Father* section)

EXPERIENCING GOD'S TRUTHS: Use the paper from the **How Big Was Goliath? Center**, and point out how big Goliath was.

Say, "No wonder the soldiers were afraid. Goliath was a huge man!" Ask the children if they have ever been afraid of a very big thing. Let them describe their fears.

Tell them, "It's OK to be afraid of something. Being afraid is God's way of telling us to be careful. All people are afraid sometimes. When we read in the Bible about David and Goliath, we read that all the big soldiers in the army were afraid of Goliath."

Tell the children that someone else in the Bible was afraid, and he shows us what we should do when we are afraid. Read Matthew 14:29-31, "Jesus said, 'Come, Peter.' And Peter left the boat and walked on the water to Jesus. But when Peter saw the wind and the waves, he became afraid and began to sink. He shouted, 'Lord, save me!' Then Jesus reached out his hand and caught Peter."

Ask the children, "Who can help you when you are afraid?" Help them answer, "God can help me when I am afraid."

Now, talk about a time when they might be afraid. Give the children an opportunity to pretend that they see a big dog, and they are afraid. Say, "When we see a big dog, what should we do?" Encourage them to remember what Peter did when he was afraid. Say, "When you are afraid, ask God to help you."

Let a child pretend to be the big dog. The "dog" is to go out of the room. The other children will pretend to go on a walk. Suddenly the "dog" appears and frightens the children. Ask, "What will we say when we see the big dog?" Help the children to say, "I am afraid. God, please help me." Then the children will turn around and walk back to their pretend house. Stress that they are to walk, not run. Running might make the dog excited, and then he would chase them.

Guide the children back to the tables. Give each child an Activity Sheet, "Fear of Big Things" (p. 4, *Through the Bible Activities for Preschoolers, Book 2*). Talk about the picture.

Melissa was afraid of the big machines, and she did not want to leave her apartment or go near them. Melissa's mother told her it was OK to be afraid of big things. Being afraid is sometimes God's way of telling us to be careful. Her mother went outside with her. Ask, "Who can help you when you are afraid?" Encourage the children to answer, "God can help me when I am afraid." Help the children glue on pieces of brick, sand, and wood on their pictures.

REVIEWING GOD'S TRUTHS: Read the book, *When I'm Afraid,* by Sylvia Tester.

Or play the game, "Going on a Trip" (p. 9 this book). Remind them that David was going on a trip to see his brothers on the battlefield.

Review the Bible verse. Ask, "What should you do when you are afraid?" Encourage the children to answer, "I will trust and not be afraid, Isaiah 12:2."

Closing prayer: "Dear God, please help us to remember to ask You to help us when we are afraid. We know You will help us to know what to do when we are afraid. Thank You for taking care of us. In Jesus' name, amen."

Unit Five: God's Special Man—David　　　　　　**1 Samuel 20**

Bible Verse: Love one another. (1 John 4:7, NIV)　　　　**Lesson 18**

GOOD FRIENDS

AS THE CHILDREN ARRIVE: Have the three learning centers ready for the children to go to as they arrive. Remember some children come early, and some come late. Help the early ones to get involved at a center as soon as they come into the room. They may get to enjoy all centers. Extend the centers to five minutes after the class is to begin so that late-comers will at least get to go to one center.

Attendance Check Center: Talk to each child and help him place stars or stickers on his attendance chart. Make each child feel special.

Bible Words Center: Today's verse, "Love one another," 1 John 4:7 (NIV), is new to the children.

Prepare four cardboard signs (5" x 7") to resemble these:

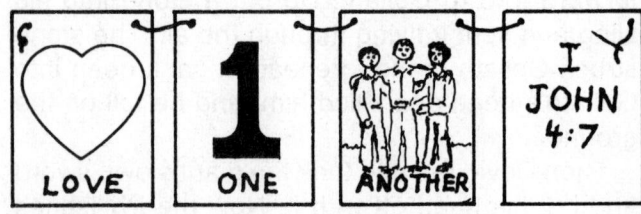

Cover them with clear contact paper to make them reusable for other lessons.

Bring a big, blunt needle and yarn to class, and allow the children to string the words onto the yarn as you help them learn the verse and reference.

Supply several sets of cards, yarn, and needles if your class is large.

Friends Center: If you have a homemaking corner or a toy area in your classroom, this activity should be done there. If not, bring some toys to class with you and set up a toy corner for this activity. As the children arrive in this area, tell them that we are going to be very good friends to each other. Talk about how good friends treat each other. As they play, talk with them about sharing, taking turns, using kind words, and being good friends.

At the sound of music from the cassette tape or piano, have the children go to the story area of the room for singing.

SINGING AND TALKING TO GOD: Sing, "Let Us Love One Another" (p. 29, *Songs for Preschool Children*); "Thank You, God" (p. 40, SPC, change "the Bible" to "friends"); "Bible Song" (p. 41, SPC, use "David" instead of "Jesus"); "My Best Friend Is Jesus" (p. 58, SPC); and "Help me to Forgive" (p. 71, SPC).

For this lesson, it would be appropriate to thank God for giving us friends. Let each child thank God for a specific friend.

Tell the children to look at each child in the room and choose a child they do *not* know. Encourage each to go to that child and say, "I want to start being your friend." Tell the children to hold the hand of this new friend and walk around the room following the teacher.

READING ABOUT GOD'S WORD: Read 1 John 4:7, 8, *International Childrens Version.* "Dear friends, we should love each other, because love comes from God. The person who loves has become God's child and knows God. Whoever does not love does not know God, because God is love."

Read or tell the Bible story.

1 Samuel 20   CR p. 81

Good Friends

David and Jonathan became good friends the first time they met. Jonathan was a prince, the son of King Saul. And David was a shepherd, tending his father's sheep.

Jonathan said to David, "I will be your friend always. To prove that I am your friend, I will give you my very own robe, my armor, my bow and arrows, and my belt."

David liked Jonathan, too, and they promised each other to be good friends always. But King Saul was not a good friend of David's. He was jealous of David, because David was such a good soldier.

David was afraid of King Saul, and so he ran away. But first he talked to Jonathan and said, "Let me know if your father, the king, plans to kill me."

"I will," Jonathan said. "But you must go away and hide for three days in our secret place. And I will find out if my father is still angry with you. Then I will come to the place where you are hiding and shoot arrows. I will bring a young boy with me to get the arrows I shoot. If I say to him, 'The arrows are beyond you,' then you will know that my father wants to kill you."

In three days, Jonathan and a little boy came to the field where David was hiding. Jonathan shot an arrow, and David heard him say to the boy, "Isn't the arrow beyond you?"

David was sorry to hear Jonathan say that. It meant that King Saul wanted to kill him.

Then David came out from his hiding place. And the two good friends kissed each other and cried, because David would have to keep running away from King Saul. They didn't know if they would ever see each other again.

From *A Child's First Book of Bible Stories* by Wanda Hayes. Standard Publishing, p. 51.

REMEMBERING GOD'S TRUTHS: Use the pictures from the picture files suggested on page 6. You will need four picture cards for today's lesson. The first three cards are found in the *Jesus* section of the file, and the fourth is found in the *God's Care* section.

- David and Jonathan were good friends. I know you have *good* friends, too, but,
    Who is your *best* friend?
    Jesus is my best friend.
- Jesus is your best friend because He is the best gift God has given you.
    What is the best gift God has given you?
    Jesus is the best gift God has given me.
- Here is another question about Jesus.
    What is Christmas?

Christmas is the time we celebrate Jesus' birthday.

- Jonathan's father, King Saul, was jealous of David so David had to hide in a secret place for three days. David was hiding all alone, and he was probably sad.

  When you are alone and sad, what should you do?

  I should ask God to help me.

EXPERIENCING GOD'S TRUTHS: Discuss kind and unkind actions to our friends. Study this list of situations where children sometimes are kind and sometimes unkind. Bring any props you might need for role playing these situations (eye patch, crackers, stuffed animals, etc.).

In class, let the children act out the situations. Describe a situation. For example, "I will pretend that I have a patch over my eye. I would like Karen to pretend she meets me and says something that is very kind to me." Then act out the kind response.

Direct the children to go to the tables. Give each child an activity sheet, "Kindness to Friends" (p. 5, *Through the Bible Activities for Preschoolers, Book 2*). You will need glue and some Play Doh or modeling clay. Let each child glue a very small piece of Play Doh or clay on the picture. Talk to the children about showing kindness toward their friends while they are working at the table and coloring the picture. Be sure to print each child's name on his paper.

REVIEWING GOD'S TRUTHS: Read the book, *Kindness,* by Jane Belk Moncure. Or, play the "Pop-Up Game" on page 9.

Closing prayer: Pray for each child by name, asking God to help him to show love to others. Close with, "Please help us to love one another. Amen."

Situation	Unkind Response	Kind Response
1. Child A sees child B with patch on B's eye.	"What's that ugly thing on your eye?"	"Hi, my name is.... Do you want to play?"
2. Child sees a child who was mean to him yesterday.	"You were mean yesterday."	"Let's play together and be real kind today."
3. Child eating crackers when friend walks up.	"You can't have any."	"Would you like a cracker to eat?"
4. Child A has pet cat. Child B asks to hold it.	Child A says, "No, it's my cat."	Child A says, "OK, you can have a turn."

Unit Five: God's Special Man—David

Bible Verse: We love (Him) because he first loved us. (1 John 4:19, NIV)

Psalm 8

Lesson 19

A SONG OF DAVID

AS THE CHILDREN ARRIVE: Greet each child warmly and direct him to one of the learning centers.

Attendance Check Center: Help each child place a star or seal on his or her attendance chart.

Bible Words Center: Today's verse is, *"We love (Him) because He first loved us"* (1 John 4:19, NIV).

Since movement aids learning, tell the children to do the following actions as they say the words:

"We"—touch shoulders of people beside you.
"love"—give yourself a hug.
"Him"—point upward with left hand.
"He"—point upward with left hand.
"first"—hold up right index finger.
"loved"—hug yourself.
"us"—touch shoulders of persons next to you.
"1 John 4:19"—march in place five times to the rhythm of the words.

First read the verse from your Bible. Then, have fun playing out the verse and reference with your class.

What Is Pretend? Center: Help your students distinguish between real and pretend by bringing objects to class and talking about them. Here are some suggestions:

1. Real bird and a toy stuffed bird
2. Real flower and a plastic flower
3. Real baby and baby doll
4. Real food and plastic food from toy tea set or an artificial fruit arrangement.
5. Halloween mask of an animal or person
6. Adult clothes for children to wear

Keep these items hidden. Show them one at a time and talk about them. Here are some conversation suggestions:

1. Kristen is sharing her bird with us so that we can look at him. Is your bird real or pretend, Kristen? Yes, he is real. He eats and sings and moves. How about this stuffed bird? Is he a real bird? No, he is a pretend bird that children play with. We just pretend he is real, when we play with him.
2. Here is some plastic food. Is it real food? Can you eat it? Now, here are some grapes. Are they real? Yes, would you like to eat one? The grapes you can eat are real. These plastic grapes are pretend grapes.
3. I'm going to put on this mask. When I put it on will I be a real tiger? No, I will be a pretend tiger. A real tiger is a big animal that roars and runs through the jungle. (Put on false face.) I am a pretend tiger.

Stress the fact that the stories we read in the Bible are about real people. These are true stories, not pretend ones.

At the sound of music from the cassette tape or piano, have the children go to the story area of the room for singing.

SINGING AND TALKING TO GOD: Sing, "Go to Heaven" (p. 90, this book); "We Love Jesus" (p. 69, this book); "All Things Were Made by Him" (p. 49, *Songs for Preschool Children*); "He Careth for You" (p. 32, SPC, change to "cares"); "God Loves Me" (p. 36, v. 1, SPC); "Sing, Little Children, Sing" (p. 37, SPC); and "God Is Good" (p. 38 SPC).

Have a special time for talking to God. Pray, "Thank You, God, for being real. We know You love us. We love You and thank You for making us. Amen."

Lead the children in a march around the room for exercise and then lead them to the story circle.

READING ABOUT GOD'S WORD: Read or tell the Bible story.

Psalm 8 CR p. 85

A Song of David

David was a shepherd, a soldier, and a king. And David played a harp and sang songs. All of his life, David sang songs to tell God how he felt. Some of his songs are written in the Bible in the book of Psalms. Here is one of the songs David wrote.

O God, our God,
   How wonderful is your name everywhere on the earth.
We can see your greatness in the skies.
   Even young children know how great you are.
When I think about the heavens you made with your hands,
And the moon and the stars that you put in their places.
I wonder why you made men and women and why you care for us.
But you have made men and women very special.
   You have made them beautiful and important.
You created men and women to take care of the earth.
You have made them greater than your other creations.
Greater than the sheep, the cows, all of the animals.
Greater than the birds in the sky, the fish in the seas,
Whatever creature lives in the water.
   O God, our God,

How wonderful is your name all over the earth.
—Adapted from Psalm 8

From *A Child's First Book of Bible Stories* by Wanda Hayes. Standard Publishing, p. 53.

REMEMBERING GOD'S TRUTHS: You will need four picture cards for today's lesson. The first three cards are found in the *Heavenly Father* section of your file, and the fourth card is found in the *God's Care* section.

- In the Psalms written by David, we read about how powerful God is.
  Who is God?
  God is our Heavenly Father.
- God is so powerful that He can be at all places all the time.
  Where is God?
  God is everywhere.
- God is certainly powerful. The Bible tells us that God made everything.
  Who made the world?
  God made the world.
- God is so powerful. God can do anything.
  Who takes care of you when you sleep?
  God takes care of me when I sleep.

EXPERIENCING GOD'S TRUTHS: You will be helping the children learn an important concept—God is real! He is really powerful; He really loves us—in contrast with pretend people who are incapable of being real, powerful, and loving. You want to be 100% truthful. When you are talking about God, read *from* the Bible and always say, "The Bible is true because the Bible is the Word of God."

God Is Real, Powerful, and Loving: You will need to bring a picture or article to represent each of the following pretend people:
  a. Santa Claus
  b. Easter Bunny
  c. Sandman, or a Care Bear
  d. Tooth Fairy (article could be a Tooth Fairy pillow or a picture of a tooth)

Place each of these pictures or articles in a separate grocery bag, and place each bag in four different corners of the room.

Mark the following Scriptures in your copy of the *International Children's Version,* or copy the references from the following explanation and put the paper in your Bible. It is important to open your Bible so that the children will learn the importance of God's Word. Add these references:

Luke 1:37   Matthew 19:26b
Matthew 9:6b   1 John 4:19

Take the class to the corner of the room containing the Santa bag and have them sit on the floor in that area. Remove the Santa Claus article from the bag and say, "What is this? (Picture of Santa). What does the Santa storybook tell us about Santa? (Children will have lots of ideas). Did Santa make the world? (No, God made everything.) Who is the most powerful? (God; yes, God is.) Let's see what a true book, the Bible, says about God's power, 'God can do anything' (Luke 1:37). God is real and God is the most powerful of all." (Put Santa item back in bag.)

The teacher and children should then move to the corner of the room containing the Easter Bunny bag. Remove the Easter Bunny article and say, "What is this? What do storybooks tell us about the Easter Bunny? If you do something wrong, can the Easter Bunny forgive you? No, he is only a fun friend. He is not a real friend like Jesus. Jesus died so that your sins could be forgiven. Let's read in our Bible, '(Jesus) has power on earth to forgive sins' Matthew 9:6. Yes, only Jesus can forgive our sins. Jesus is real. Jesus is the most powerful." (Put the Bunny article in the bag and move the class to the next corner.)

Remove the Care Bear or picture of the Sandman from the bag and say, "I once read a storybook that said that a Care Bear (or Sandman) comes into children's rooms at night. Can a Care Bear (or Sandman) take care of you while you sleep? (No). Who takes care of you when you sleep? (God takes care of me when I sleep.) That's right; God is real. God is the most powerful. And He loves you very much. Let's look into the Bible to find out about God's power. Matthew 19:26 tells us that, 'God can do all things.' He can even care for you while you sleep." (Put the article back in the bag and take your Bible and the children to the fourth bag.)

Here is something that will remind us of a fun friend, the Tooth Fairy. Do you play that the Tooth Fairy gives you money when a tooth comes out? Can the Tooth Fairy love you? No, fun friends can give us fun but not love. Who is a *real* friend who really loves us? (Jesus). What does our Bible say about Jesus' love for us? 1 John 4:19 (NIV) says,

'We love (Jesus) because He first loved us.' Jesus loves you more than anyone else. Jesus is real. He is the most powerful and the most loving."

Give each child an activity sheet, "Which One?" (p. 6, *Through the Bible Activities for Preschoolers, Book 2*). Print each child's name on his paper.

Give each child a red crayon. Ask, "Who is the most powerful person on this page? (Jesus). Put a **red** circle around Jesus because He is the most powerful." (Collect the red crayons and give each child a green crayon.)

"Who made the world? Yes, *God made the world.* And God's Son helped God make the world. So, draw a **green** circle around God's Son because He is the powerful one who made everything." (Give out blue crayons as you collect green ones.)

"Who in our picture can take care of you when you sleep? (God takes care of me when I sleep.) That's right; so let's draw a **blue** circle around God's Son, Jesus." (Collect blue crayons, and give out orange ones.)

"Now, when you do something wrong, and then say, 'I'm sorry,' which person on this page says, 'I forgive you?' (Jesus). Yes, Jesus is the most important person on this page because He is the only one who can forgive you. Let's put an **orange** circle around Jesus." (Collect the orange crayons.)

REVIEWING GOD'S TRUTHS: Play the "Pop Up Game" (see p. 9).

Ask the children, "Why do we love Jesus?" Encourage them to answer, "We love (Him) because He first loved us! 1 John 4:19." Act out the verse as done earlier in the learning center.

Closing prayer: "Dear God, we know You are so powerful. You made everything. Thank You, for taking care of us. Thank You for forgiving us when we say, 'I'm sorry.' Amen."

Children of God

Carole Matthews
John 1:12 (NIV)

June George

Unit 6—God's People Obey Him

GETTING READY FOR UNIT SIX

The theme of this unit will be that God wants His followers to obey Him. Solomon built a beautiful temple for God. A young servant girl told Naaman about her God who could heal him. Daniel worshiped God even when he was facing danger. God wants us to always honor Him in all we do.

Learning Objectives: Some things you should expect your children to accomplish in this unit:

The children should know (1) God is everywhere; (2) God can do anything; (3) God always hears us when we talk to Him.

The children should feel (1) Confident they can talk to God anytime; (2) Eager to tell others about God and His Son; (3) Happy they can pray anywhere.

The children should be able to (1) Tell the highlights of the Bible stories; (2) Say the Bible verses and state simple answers to concept questions; (3) List two ways they can help a sick person.

Remember, because of the differences in age and maturity, some children will meet more of these objectives than others will.

Bible Verses: All the Bible verses in this unit are review verses. Use the teaching aids to reinforce each verse.

Books: Several books are suggested for reading at the end of each lesson, if time permits. These books may be placed in the quiet, book corner of your room. *Sharing Makes Me Happy; Obedience;* and *Good News* are suitable for the ages of the children and for the subjects being studies.

Bulletin Board: Take pictures of each child and place on the bulletin board or wall. Use the heading, *God's Children Obey Him.* (For a more attractive display, back each picture with a cut-out shape, such as a heart, pumpkin, leaf, etc., that is appropriate for the season.)

THINGS TO DO:

Lesson 20: Provide building blocks for the learning center. You will need a man's hat or tie, lots of play money, an offering basket, and old clothes for one child to wear to look like a carpenter (see p. 64). Cut construction-paper blocks (1½" square) for the children to glue on their activity sheets.

Lesson 21: Bring paper lunch bags for each child. Write "Bag of Questions for (child's name)," on each bag. Bring an empty medicine bottle and a spoon, a box of tissues, a toy telephone, a blanket and pillow, and a plastic kitchen storage dish with a cover for role playing. Provide little treats for the children to enjoy.

Lesson 22: Practice cutting the number 3 (see p. 67). Bring four children's items from home: baseball hat, teddy bear, ball, game.

Unit Six: God's People Obey Him

Bible Verse: God is good. (Psalm 73:1, NIV)

1 Kings 5; 6

Lesson 20

BUILDING GOD'S TEMPLE

AS THE CHILDREN ARRIVE: Greet each child warmly and direct him to one of the learning centers.

Attendance Check Center: Help the children place a star or a seal on their attendance charts. Give each child your loving attention.

Bible Words Center: Today's verse was introduced in Lesson 1 (see p. 12). Use the word cards made then. Ask the children, "What does the Bible tell us about God?" Encourage them to answer, *"God is good. Psalm 73:1."* Scramble the cards, and let the children put them in order.

Building the Temple Center: If you do not have blocks in your classroom, you will need to bring a set of wooden building blocks with you for this activity. If possible, bring a picture of the Jerusalem temple.

Talk to the children about the word, "temple"—the place where God's People gathered to worship God in long ago days before Jesus came to the earth. Let them build a pretend temple out of the blocks. Explain that we do not go to a temple to worship God; we come to our church *building*. We can also worship God at home, in a park, or any place because God is everywhere, not just in one building.

At the sound of music from the cassette tape or piano, have the children go to the story area of the room for singing.

SINGING AND TALKING TO GOD: Sing these songs: "The Church" (p. 90, this book); "God Is Good" (p. 38, *Songs for Preschool Children,* adding this verse, "Psalm seventy-three, one, God is good."); "We're Here in Our Church" (p. 35, SPC, change the words to "In Our Church Building" in the title and lines 4 and 8); and "I'm Giving" (p. 67, SPC).

Have a special time of talking to God. For this lesson it would be appropriate to thank God that we have a church building where we can meet together. Ask the children to express their own prayers. Allow a quiet time for them to pray. Close with a sentence prayer.

Lead the children in a march around the room for exercise as you sing "The Marching Song" (p. 11, SPC).

READING ABOUT GOD'S WORD: Read or tell the Bible story.

1 Kings 5-6 CR p.89

Building God's Temple

King Solomon was a good and wise king. One day he said, "I am going to build a house of worship for God. When my father, King David, wanted to build a temple for God, God told him, 'Your son will build it. You, David, cannot build it because of all of the wars going on.'"

Solomon said, "Now there is no fighting. The land is peaceful, so I am going to build God's house."

And Solomon wanted the best of everything for God's house. So he asked for the very best workers and the very best materials—special stones, cedar and fir and olive wood, gold and brass. Smart men from other countries helped make the special carvings and furniture and dishes for God's house. Everyone worked very hard.

Because the temple was to be God's special house, everyone worked quietly around it. They did their noisy work, like sawing wood and cutting stones, away from the temple. Then they brought the wood and the big stones to Jerusalem and put them in place.

Solomon had special gold and silver bowls that his father, David, had saved for God's house. And the priests carried the most special piece of furniture for God's house—the ark of the covenant. Inside it were the stone tablets with the Ten Commandments that God had given to Moses hundreds of years before.

It took seven years to build the temple. When it was finished, Solomon called all of the men and women and children together to dedicate it to God. The people were very quiet.

King Solomon prayed a long prayer, asking God to bless the people in every way.

From, *A Child's First Book of Bible Stories* by Wanda Hayes. Standard Publishing, p. 55.

Explain to the children that the temple was a special building used by God's People for worship before Jesus came to earth [our hearts]. After Jesus came to the earth, His People knew that a temple was not important for worship. Because God is everywhere, we can worship Him anywhere. Today we meet together in a church building. We are thankful for our church building, but we realize that people are more important than buildings. Read from your copy of the *International Children's Version*, Acts 17:24 and 25a, "God ... made the whole world and everything in it. He is the Lord of the land and sky. He does not live in temples that men build! This God is the One who gives life, breath, and everything else to people." Let the children stand and pretend to be builders who are hammering and sawing.

REMEMBERING GOD'S TRUTHS: Use the pictures from your picture files suggested on page 6. You will need four picture cards for today's lesson.

- When God's people built the temple they called it God's house. But since Jesus came to earth and taught about God, we know that God does not live in a house.
  Where is God?
  God is everywhere. (*Heavenly Father* section)
- Yes, God is everywhere.
  What can God do?
  God can do anything. (*Heavenly Father* section)
- The people in our story went to the temple to pray at certain times.
  When can you talk to God?
  I can talk to God anytime. (*I Pray* section)
- We come to our church building. A church building is a place where we come to learn the Bible. But,
  What is the church?
  All people who love and trust Jesus are the church. (The Church section) Be sure to explain to the children what it means to love and trust Jesus.

EXPERIENCING GOD'S TRUTHS: Read **Act It Out** on page 9. To help the children understand giving, bring from home:
1. A man's hat or tie (for storekeeper).
2. Lots of dollar bills (real money or play money can be used, but do not use coins).
3. Two sets of wooden blocks for building a pretend church building.
4. Something to use as an offering basket.
5. Old clothes for one of the children to wear in order to look like a carpenter.

Set up your room so that one area is a pretend empty lot where a church building will be built. One area is a pretend store and one area is a large house where a church meets. Be sure the children understand each area before beginning the story.

Dress one child as a storekeeper and put him or her in the pretend store with the blocks that will be used for making the church building.

Dress one child as a carpenter and put him/her in the area designated as the place where the church building will be built.

Explain that the teacher and other students will be the church—the people who love and trust Jesus. Put the offering container in that area. Give each child several dollar bills.

As the church is seated in the pretend house, the teacher can act as the person who explains that "we will now give our money for God's work. We are happy to give our money. We give because we love Jesus."

Then explain that we will all follow the money to see how it is used. Carry the money to the pretend store to buy wood for building the church building. (Let the class go with you.) Then you and the class go to the empty lot to deliver the wood to the carpenter who then builds the church building.

Lead the children back to the tables and give each child the activity sheet, "Church Building" (p. 7, *Through the Bible Activities for Preschoolers, Book 2*). Print each child's name on the back of his paper. Provide some construction-paper blocks for the children to glue on their papers.

REVIEWING GOD'S TRUTHS: Play, *It's a New Day*, using this week's picture cards. Instructions for this game are in the front of this book in the *Games* section on page 10.

Ask the children, "What does the Bible tell us about God?" Help them to answer, "God is good, Psalm 73, verse 1."

Have a closing prayer, "We thank You, God, that we can worship You wherever we are. In Jesus' name, amen."

Unit Six: God's People Obey Him

Bible Verse: Do what is right and good.
(Deuteronomy 6:18, NIV)

2 Kings 5:1-16

Lesson 21

A YOUNG GIRL HELPS NAAMAN

AS THE CHILDREN ARRIVE: Greet each child warmly and direct him or her to one of the learning centers.

Attendance Check Center: Have stars and seals available for each child to put on his attendance chart as you talk to him in a loving manner.

Bible Word Center: See Lesson 12 for a suggested way of teaching today's verse, page 40. Ask the children, "What does the Bible say about doing what is right?" Help them answer, "Do what is right and good. Deuteronomy 6:18." Now sing the verse to the tune of "Farmer in the Dell" and do the actions.

Sickness Center: This activity should be done in the housekeeping corner of your classroom. Tell the children that we are going to pretend that the baby doll is sick, and we are the doll's family. We need to take care of the sick baby. Let the children role play this situation. Stress that God takes care of us when we are sick. He provides parents, doctors, and nurses to help us feel better. Suggest ways the children can help take care of mother, daddy, brother or sister when they are sick. (Examples: play quietly; take tissues to them; get a drink for them; say, "I love you.")

At the sound of music from the cassette tape or piano, have the children go to the story area of the room for singing.

SINGING AND TALKING TO GOD: Sing "Pleasing God" (p. 26, *Songs for Preschool Children*, putting today's verse to the music); "Praise Ye the Lord" (p. 28, SPC); "He Careth for You" (p. 32, SPC, change "careth" to "cares"); and "Thank You, God" (p. 40, SPC).

Have a special time of talking to God. Pray for a sick person whom the children know.

Lead the children in a march around the room for exercise as you sing "The Marching Song" (p. 11, SPC).

READING ABOUT GOD'S WORD: Read "A Young Girl Helps Naaman." Then read Ephesians 4:31, 32 from the *International Children's Version*. "Do not be bitter or angry or mad. Never shout angrily or say things to hurt others. Never do anything evil. Be kind and loving to each other. Forgive each other just as God forgave you in Christ."

2 Kings 5:1-16 CR p. 97, 98

A Young Girl Helps Naaman

Naaman was an important man. He was the captain of the army of the king of Syria. But Naaman had a problem. He had a sickness called leprosy that caused bad sores on his skin. And no one had been able to help him get well.

But there was someone who knew how Naaman could be healed of his leprosy—a young Israelite girl who worked for Naaman's wife. She said, "If Naaman would go see God's prophet in Samaria, he would make him well."

Naaman wanted to be made well more than anything. So he hurried in his chariot to Elisha's house.

But Elisha didn't even come out of his house and talk to Naaman. Instead, he sent a message to Naaman telling him to do something strange. Elisha said, "Go to the Jordan River and wash yourself seven times. Then your skin will be healed, and your leprosy will be gone."

Naaman was angry. He was so angry that he left Elisha's house.

Naaman started to go home, but his servants said to him, "The prophet asked you to do something easy, just wash in the Jordan River seven times. Why don't you do it?" Naaman thought about it. Then he said to himself, *Yes, I will do it.*

He went to the Jordan River and dipped himself in it seven times. The first six times, nothing happened. But when he came out of the water the seventh time, his skin was perfect. All of the sores were gone. He was well!

Naaman was so happy that he and his friends

rode their chariots back to Elisha's house and thanked him.

From *A Child's First Book of Bible Stories* by Wanda Hayes. Standard Publishing, p. 56.

Let the children stand and bend down and up seven times just like Naaman went into the water seven times.

REMEMBERING GOD'S TRUTHS: Here are the four concepts you will be teaching this session. Remove the picture cards from your file before class. Be prepared to teach them so that your time with the children is fun as well as instructive.

- Naaman had a problem.
   Does Jesus love children who have problems?
   Yes, Jesus loves everyone. (*About Me* section)
- You and I have problems sometimes, too.
   When you have a problem, what should you do?
   I should pray and ask God to help me. (*I Pray* section)
- God made Naaman well. He can do anything He wants to do.
   What can God do?
   God can do anything. (*Heavenly Father* section)
- God made Naaman well. God is the most powerful person of all. He is so powerful, He can even create things.
   Who made the world?
   God made the world. (*Heavenly Father* section)

EXPERIENCING GOD'S TRUTHS: Make a Tote Bag of Questions, using the activity on page 8, *Through the Bible Activities for Preschoolers, Book 2*. Cut, or let the children cut, the activity sheet on the black lines so that you end up with eight pieces (each containing a question and answer). Clip each set together. (For longer lasting papers, you may want to cover them with clear contact paper before cutting.)

Prepare a paper lunch bag. Write *Bag of Questions for (child's name)* on each bag.

Give each child his bag and have him put his set of questions in the bag. Let the children enjoy removing one question from the bag and answering that question. Give each child a turn, and play the game as long as interest is high. Let them take their bags home with them to play with their parents.

After playing with the bag of cards, tell the children that there are lots of ways they can help. Bring the following to class: an empty medicine bottle and a spoon; a Christian book; a box of facial tissues; a toy telephone; a blanket and pillow; and a plastic kitchen storage dish with a cover.

Ask the children, "Who would like to pretend he is sick?" The sick child uses the blanket and pillow to lie on the floor.

Ask the class, "What can we do to help a sick person?" As the children give ideas, let them act out doing that thing.

Here are some possible ideas the children might make and some suggestions about how to handle them:

Pray for the sick person—Let one or all of the children pray.

Give medicine—Let the teacher pretend to give medicine and emphasize that children never take medicine or give it to the others—only grown-ups do this.

Call the doctor—Let one of the children use the toy phone.

Go to the doctor—Let all of the children pretend to help the sick child go to the doctor's office.

Take food to a sick person's house—Use the plastic food container to take pretend food—let all of the children participate.

Visit a sick person—Take the book as you all pretend to go visit the sick person's house.

Give the sick person tissues for sneezes—Let one of the children share the tissues.

Be very quiet so the sick person can sleep—Practice whispering.

REVIEWING GOD'S TRUTHS: God made Naaman well. He was so happy to be well. Do you think that he was so happy that he might have had a party? Let's have a party to celebrate because God is so wonderful and powerful.

Provide little party treats for the children. Have fun eating together.

Closing Prayer: "Dear God, we want to help others. Thank You, for showing us ways we can help. We want to do what is right and good. Amen."

Unit Six: God's People Obey Him

Bible Verse: Do what is right and good.
(Deuteronomy 6:18, NIV)

Daniel 6
Lesson 22

DANIEL IN THE LION'S DEN

AS THE CHILDREN ARRIVE: See *As Children Arrive* on page 7. Greet each child warmly and direct him to one of the learning centers.

Attendance Check Center: Help each child place a star or sticker on his or her attendance chart. Make each child feel glad he or she came.

Bible Words Center: See Lesson 12, for a suggested way of teaching this verse. Ask the children, "What does the Bible say about doing what is right?" Encourage them to answer, "Do what is right and good. Deuteronomy 6:18."

Sing the words and do the actions that are suggested on page 40.

Be A Daniel Center: Practice cutting a paper 3 before class, and remember to fold and cut as you tell about Daniel. Follow these folding and cutting instructions:

Take a sheet of construction paper, and fold it in half then in half again. (See steps 1 and 2.) Hold the folded corner with one hand and cut a C-shape as shown in step 3. Open the paper half way and make another cut as shown in step 4. When you open the paper all the way, you will have a 3. Tell the children to listen carefully to the story to find out why the number 3 is important. Have extra paper for older children who might want to make a paper 3.

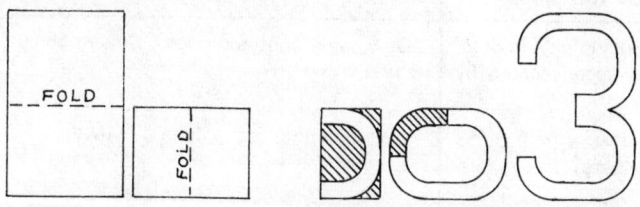

At the sound of music from the cassette tape or piano, have the children go to the story area of the room for singing.

SINGING AND TALKING TO GOD: Sing, "Trust in the Lord" (p. 25, *Songs for Preschool Children*); "Pleasing God" (p. 26, vs. 2, SPC, adding the verses Ephesians 6:1 and Deuteronomy 6:18 to the tune); "Let Us Love One Another" (p. 29, SPC); and "I Can Talk to God" (p. 80, SPC).

Have a special time of talking to God. For this lesson it would be appropriate to ask God to help us always to do what He wants us to do.

Lead the children in sing "Head and Shoulders" (p. 5, SPC).

READING ABOUT GOD'S WORD: Read Romans 12:12 from your *International Children's Version*. "Pray at all times." Also read Colossians 4:2, "Continue praying. And when you pray, always thank God."

Now read or tell the Bible story.

Daniel 6 CR p. 117, 118

Daniel in the Lion's Den

Daniel had been taken to a faraway country when he was a young man. But Daniel obeyed the laws of God even though he was away from home. He prayed to God three times a day.

King Darius, the ruler of the country where he now lived, gave Daniel a very important job. But the men who worked for Daniel were jealous of him.

"Let's get rid of Daniel," they said.

Then the men went to King Darius and had him pass a law. The law said that anyone who prayed to any god or man, other than the king himself, for thirty days, would be thrown into the lions' den.

Daniel refused to obey the king's new law. He loved God more than anyone else. So he went into his house and got down on his knees to pray as he always had.

The men hurried to tell the king, "Daniel is still praying to his God three times a day."

Now, King Darius was sorry he had made the law. He wanted to change it, but the bad men reminded him that no law could be changed. So Daniel was put in the den with the hungry lions.

That night the king was so worried about Daniel, he couldn't eat or sleep. And as soon as the sun came up the next morning, King Darius hurried to the lions' den and called out, "Daniel! Has your God saved you?"

"Oh, yes, King Darius," Daniel answered. "God sent an angel to close the lions' mouths."

King Darius was so happy that he made a new law that everyone should worship the God who had saved Daniel from the lions. Then the king had the bad men themselves put into the lions' den!

From *A Child's First Book of Bible Stories* by Wanda Hayes. Standard Publishing, p. 59.

REMEMBERING GOD'S TRUTHS: There are four concepts you will be teaching this session. Remove these picture cards from the *I Pray* section of your file before class. Be prepared to teach them so that your time with the children is fun and instructive.

- The bad king made a law that said the people could not pray to God. We know this is a bad law. Daniel knew it was a bad law. Daniel did not obey the law; he obeyed God.

Can you answer these questions about praying?

When you pray, what are you doing?
<u>When I pray, I am talking to God.</u>
Does God hear you when you talk to Him?
<u>Yes, God always hears me when I talk to Him.</u>
When can you talk to God?
<u>I can talk to God anytime.</u>
Where can you pray?
<u>I can pray anywhere.</u>
When you are very happy, what should you do?
<u>I should thank God for making me happy.</u>

EXPERIENCING GOD'S TRUTHS: Give the children opportunities to make decisions. Bring from home four children's items (Examples, baseball hat, teddy bear, etc.). Ask a parent or teenager to visit your class and help you for this section of the lesson.

Prepare two "cue cards" by making two copies of the chart below—one for you and one for your helper. Tell your helper that in each story he will be helping child A, the child who advocates doing wrong. Suggest that he let the child use his own ideas and words as much as possible.

In class, tell the children, "Daniel had to decide whether to obey the king or to obey God. We often have to decide whether to obey God or to obey other people."

"We are going to pretend some stories in which you will have to decide who to obey."

Have the children go to a different part of the room for each story. Tell them that, for example, "this is a pretend flower garden." Ask for two volunteers who will be actors. Child A will wear or hold one of the items you brought from home, be coached by your helper, and be the actor who advocates mischief.

Child B will be coached by the teacher and will think of Scripture verses that tell him not to do the mean thing that child A advocates.

SUMMARIES OF FOUR STORIES		
Situation	Decision (made by the class)	Scripture
Two children in a garden, tempted to pick flowers	To obey child A, who wants to pick flowers, or to obey God's Word as advocated by child B.	"Do what is right and good." Deuteronomy 6:18, (NIV)
Child A and child B are playing together. Child C knocks at door. Child A says, "Let's not answer the door."	To obey child A or obey a verse from God's Word that child B remembers.	"Love one another." 1 John 4:7, (NIV)
Mother says, "Don't go around the corner. Stay on your own street." Child A entices child B to go around the corner by saying child B is a sissy.	To obey the mother or the playmate.	"Children, obey your parents." Ephesians 6:1, (NIV)
New child (whose skin or accent is different than that of your class) moves into the neighborhood. Child A tells child B, "Don't play with him because his skin (or talking) is different from ours."	To obey child A or obey a verse from God's Word that child B remembers.	"Be kind to one another." Ephesians 4:32, (NIV)

For example, in story 1, child A says, "Let's pick these flowers. The lady who lives here won't see us. And she will not miss them." Child B recalls that God's Word says, "Do what is right and good," in Deuteronomy 6:18 (NIV). So the class must decide to obey child A or God's Word. Let the children discuss and decide. Then go to another area of the room, or to the hall, to act out story two. Change locations and characters with each story.

After role playing these stories, lead the children back to the tables. Give each child an activity sheet, "Deciding" (p. 9, *Through the Bible Activities for Preschoolers, Book 2*). Read the story about Mark. Give each child a brown crayon to color the chocolate popsicle, and a pencil to connect the dots. (You will not have time to color the rest of the paper in class. Encourage the child to finish his picture at home.)

REVIEWING GOD'S TRUTHS: You might want to read, *Obedience,* by Jane Buerger, Standard Publishing (#4926), if it is available.

Play the "Believing God Game" suggested in Lesson 13, page 44.

Review today's Bible verse. Ask the children, "What does the Bible say about doing what is right?" Help them answer with today's verse, "Do what is right and good, Deuteronomy 6, verse 18."

Closing Prayer: "Dear God, please help us to do what You want us to do. We want to obey You. Amen."

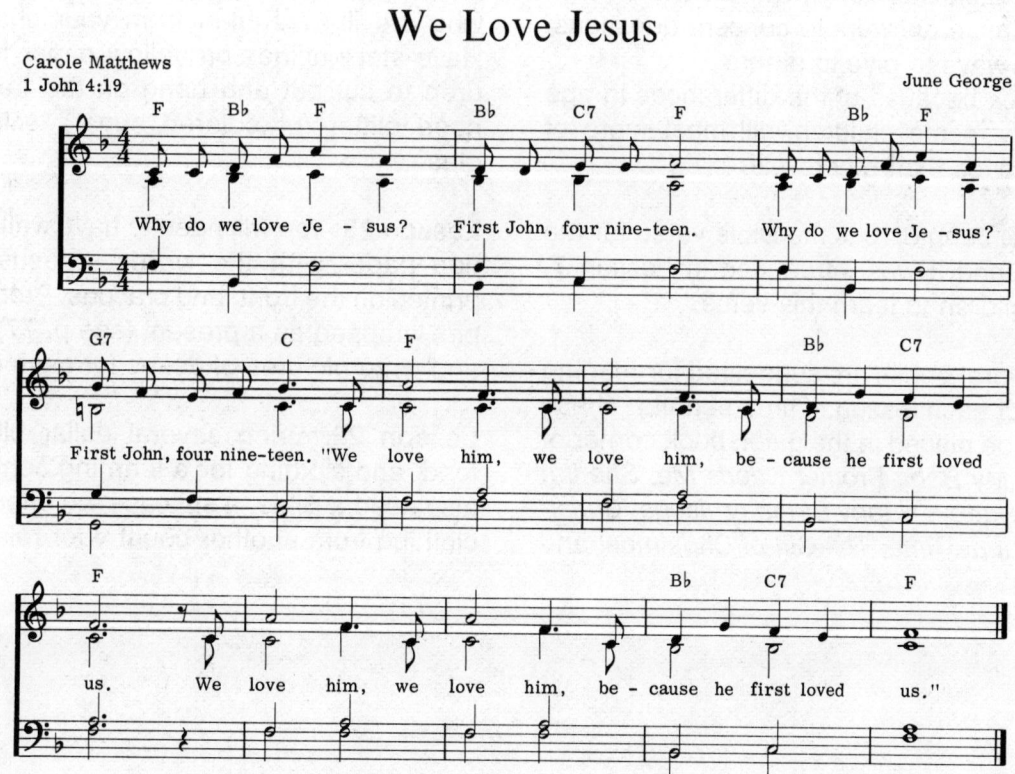

Unit 7—God's Special Son

GETTING READY FOR UNIT SEVEN

The theme of this unit is that God gave us a very special gift—His Son, Jesus. Help the children understand that God loved each one of them so much that He gave His only Son, Jesus, to come to earth to live and tell us about God. God had a special plan for Jesus and us. God wants us to love Jesus.

Learning Objectives: Some things you should expect your children to accomplish in this unit:

The children should know (1) God hears them when they pray to Him; (2) Jesus came to show us that God loves us; (3) Jesus is the best gift God has given us.

The children should feel (1) Glad that God keeps His promises; (2) Love for Jesus; (3) Willing to give to others in need; (4) Willing to tell others about Jesus

The children should be able to (1) Tell the highlights of the Bible stories; (2) Say the Bible verse and state simple answers to concept questions; (3) Think of ways to give to others.

Remember, because of the differences in age and maturity, some children will meet more of these objectives than others will.

Bible Verse: John 3:16 is the Bible verse for the whole unit, and it was introduced in Lesson 7. Help the children to learn this verse.

Books: Several books are suggested for reading at the end of each lesson, if time permits. These books may be placed in the quiet, book corner of your room. *My Baby Brother Needs Me; Sharing Makes Me Happy; Happy Birthday, Jesus; Christmas Is a Happy Time; The Gift of Christmas;* and *The Very Special Night* are suitable for the ages of the children and for the subjects being studied.

Bulletin Board: Display baby pictures of each of the children. Use the heading, "Special Babies." Put a large picture of baby Jesus in the middle.

THINGS TO DO:

Lesson 23: Call the parents the week before class and ask them to bring to class a snapshot of their child when a baby. Make preparations for a new attendance check (see p. 71). You will need a paper lunch bag for each child. Also, bring several dolls, bowls and spoons, diapers, and blankets.

Lesson 24: You will need construction paper, old Christian Christmas cards or greeting cards, marking pens, and glue. Get the names of people who are ill or shut-in from your church office. Have star outlines on yellow paper for the children to cut out and hang on the tree. You will need glitter (or colored sugar), scissors, and glue.

Lesson 25: You will need to have white construction paper with the words, "Jesus Is Born," printed on the front, and crayons. Prepare a large box wrapped as a present (see p. 77). Purchase and wrap pictures of Jesus for each child.

Lesson 26: Bring several dollar bills, canned food, and clothing for a learning center. You will also need a Bible, a suitcase, an offering basket, clothing from another country for role playing.

Read the Picture Bible. Find picture of Baby Jesus.

Unit Seven: God's Special Son

Bible Verse: For God so loved the world that he gave his one and only Son. (John 3:16, NIV)

Luke 1:5-25, 57-66

Lesson 23

GOOD NEWS

AS THE CHILDREN ARRIVE: Greet each child warmly and direct him to one of the learning centers.

Attendance Check Center: Use these suggestions if you use this lesson during the Christmas season. Bring to class a very small Christmas tree or a cardboard Christmas tree cut from large green paper. Each week during the Christmas season you will need to bring an item cut from construction paper for each child to hang or glue to the tree. For example, you might cut out twenty bells for this lesson if you have twenty students. Write the date of this meeting on each bell. As each child arrives, print his name on a bell, and let him attach it to the tree.

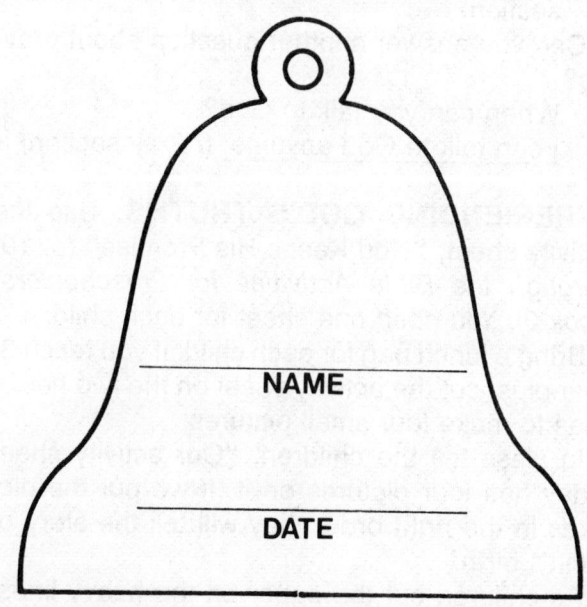

If this lesson is used other than Christmas, help each child place a star or a sticker on his or her attendance chart.

Bible Words Center: Today's verse "For God so loved the world that He gave His one and only Son," John 3:16, NIV, was first introduced in Lesson 7. Bring to class a picture of baby Jesus. Teach this verse as suggested in Lesson 7, page 28, with the following addition: When you say the word, "Son," hold up the picture of baby Jesus.

Special Babies Center: Phone the parents of your students. Tell each parent something you like about his child. Ask each parent to bring a baby snapshot of his child, with the child's name on the back. In class, let each child show his baby picture, and then ask him questions about his family and how he thinks they took care of him when he was little. Display the pictures in the story area and write the child's name underneath his or her picture.

At the sound of music from the cassette tape or piano, have the children go to the story area of the room for singing.

SINGING AND TALKING TO GOD: Sing, "God Loves Me" (p. 36, v. 2, *Songs for Preschool Children*); "I Can Talk to God" (p. 80, SPC); "Rock Baby Jesus" (p. 63, SPC, change "Jesus" to "John"); and "God So Loved" (p. 42 this book).

Have a special time of thanking God for keeping His promises. Let each child pray "Thank You, God, for keeping every promise You make. Amen."

Lead the children in a march around the room for exercise as you sing again, "God Loves Me."

READING ABOUT GOD'S WORD: Read Luke 1:11-14 from your copy of the *International Children's Version*.

Then read or tell the Bible story.

Luke 1:5-25, 57-66

Good News!

Zacharias, the priest, was excited. It was his turn to serve God in the temple. Zacharias' job was to burn incense at a special altar while the people who came to worship stood outside and prayed.

Zacharias entered the special room in the temple and burned the sweet-smelling incense as an offering to God. This was a moment Zacharias had waited for all his life. But something he didn't expect happened. As Zacharias burned the incense, an angel of God stood by the altar. Zacharias was very surprised and afraid.

But the angel said, "Don't be afraid, Zacharias. God has heard your prayer. You and your wife, Elizabeth, are going to have a little baby boy. You will name your little boy John. Many people will be happy that John is born. He will be a special helper for God. Many people will obey God when they hear John preach."

Zacharias didn't know what to think. "This is hard to believe," he told the angel. "My wife and I are old. How can I be sure this will happen?"

"I am Gabriel who stands in the presence of God," the angel answered. "I have been sent to tell you this good news. But because you have not believed my words, you will not be able to talk until these things happen."

Now Zacharias had been in the temple a long time. The crowd of people outside wondered what had happened to him. But when he came out, he could not tell them because he was not able to talk.

When Zacharias finished his work at the temple, he went home to the place where he and his wife, Elizabeth, lived. Several months later, just as Gabriel told him, their baby boy was born.

Elizabeth's relatives and friends were very happy for her. They knew God had blessed her in a special way, because she had been waiting so long for a baby. When the baby was eight days old, relatives and friends of Zacharias and Elizabeth came for a special service for the baby. They wanted to name him Zacharias like his father, but Elizabeth said, "No! He will be called John."

The men and women were surprised. "But no one in your family is named John," they said to Elizabeth. Then they made signs to Zacharias, who still could not talk, to find out what he wanted to name the baby. Zacharias motioned for a tablet and wrote, "His name is John." Everyone was surprised.

Then everyone had a bigger surprise because at that moment, Zacharias could talk. His very first words were words of praise to God. Zacharias was very happy.

The friends and relatives remembered Zacharias' words and talked about them for a long time. They wondered, "What kind of man will this child John be? God must surely be with him." And they were right.

From *A Child's First Book of Bible Stories* by Wanda Hayes. Standard Publishing, pp. 62, 63.

REMEMBERING GOD'S TRUTHS: You will need the following pictures from your file. Be enthusiastic as you teach these concepts to your students.

- Zacharias went to the temple to talk to God, his Heavenly Father.
    Does God hear you when you talk to Him?
    Yes, God always hears me when I talk to Him. (*I Pray* section)
- Zacharias worked at the temple. He knew many things about God. Do you know the answer to this question about God?
    Where is God?
    God is everywhere. (*Heavenly Father* section.
- Zacharias prayed to God. You can pray too.
    When you pray, what are you doing?
    When I pray I am talking to God. (*I Pray* section)
- Can you answer another question about praying?
    When can you talk to God?
    I can talk to God anytime. (*I Pray* section)

EXPERIENCING GOD'S TRUTHS: Use the activity sheet, "God Keeps His Promise" (p. 10, *Through the Bible Activities for Preschoolers, Book 2*). You need one sheet for each child.

Bring a lunch bag for each child. If you teach 3-year-olds, cut the activity sheet on the two heavy lines to make four small pictures.

In class tell the children, "Our activity sheet today has four pictures on it. If we put the pictures in the right order they will tell the story of John's birth."

As children cut the paper on the heavy lines, the teacher should write each child's name on the child's bag and each child's initials on each of the four pieces of paper the child has for telling the story.

Help each child place the four pieces of paper in proper order as you read the words on each paper.

After the children see this done several times,

they will be able to put the pictures in order and tell the story by themselves. *See if picture Bible has pictures that she can tell the story herself.*

Encourage the children to be patient and listen to each other as the story is retold.

You will not have time for the children to color their pictures in class. So, suggest that they color the pictures and tell the story to their parents at home.

Provide an opportunity for the children to role play today's story. Call the parents of several children in your class and ask them to bring dolls to class for use in this activity. Have bowls and spoons, pretend diapers, and blankets ready for use also. *have Krissy do this Eliz.*

With the children gathered together in a group sitting on the floor, give out dolls, diapers, etc. Let the children spend a little time playing that they are Elizabeth and Zacharias caring for baby John. Sing:

"Rock-a-bye baby
God loves you.
Rock-a-bye baby
God loves you.
Rock-a-bye baby
God loves you.
We read in the Bible
God loves you."

REVIEWING GOD'S TRUTHS: Read *My Baby Brother Needs Me* by Jane Belk Moncure, Standard Publishing (#4901) if it is available, or play "Hide the Picture Cards" game as described on page 9.

Ask, "What is a Bible verse that tells us that God loved the world?" Help the children to answer, "For God so loved the world that he gave his one and only Son. John 3, verse 16."

Closing prayer: "Thank You, God, for keeping Your promise to Zacharias. We know You will keep Your promises to us, too. Amen."

Unit Seven: God's Special Son

Bible Verse: For God so loved the world that he gave his one and only Son. (John 3:16, NIV)

Luke 1:26-45

Lesson 24

AN ANGEL VISITS MARY

AS THE CHILDREN ARRIVE: Greet each child warmly and direct him to one of the learning centers.

Attendance Check Center: If you are using this lesson during the Christmas season, have a paper angel ready for each child to write his name on and hang on the tree today.

Bible Words Center: See Lesson 23 for suggestions as to how to teach this verse (p. 71). Have the children use the motions as they say, "For God so loved the world that he gave his one and only Son John 3:16, NIV."

Good News Cards Center: You will need business size envelopes, construction paper, Christian Christmas cards, marking pens, glue, and your church directory. Help the children fold a

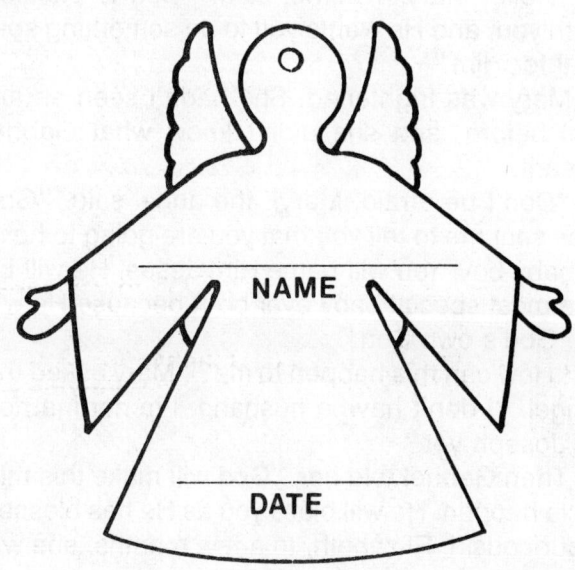

73

sheet of construction paper and glue a picture of their choice on the paper to make a pretty card. Write for the children the greeting they want on the card. (Example, "Jesus is Good News," "Love Jesus," "I love you," etc.) Address each envelope to a sick, elderly, or shut-in person in your church. Mail the cards immediately.

At the sound of music from the cassette tape or piano, have the children go to the story area of the room for singing.

SINGING AND TALKING TO GOD: Sing, "Jesus, the Son of God," (p. 59, v. 1, *Songs for Preschool Children)*; "Rock Baby Jesus" (p. 63, SPC); "See the Star" (p. 66, SPC); "Here We Come To Bethlehem" (p. 66, SPC); and "Jesus Is the Son of God" (p. 56, SPC).

Pray, "Dear God, please help those who are sick or old to have a good Christmas and to enjoy the cards we made for them. In Jesus' name, amen."

Lead the children in a walk around the room for exercise as you sing again, "Jesus Is the Son of God."

READING ABOUT GOD'S WORD: Read Luke 1:26-31 in the *International Children's Version.* Now read or tell the Bible story.

[handwritten: Luke 1:26-45]

An Angel Visits Mary

Several months after the angel Gabriel appeared to Zacharias in the temple, God sent him with a special message to a young woman named Mary.

"Hello, Mary," Gabriel said, "God is pleased with you, and He wants you to do something special for Him."

Mary was frightened. She hadn't seen an angel before, and she didn't know what Gabriel meant.

"Don't be afraid, Mary," the angel said. "God has sent me to tell you that you are going to have a baby boy. You will name Him Jesus. He will be the most special baby ever born because He will be God's own Son."

"How can this happen to me?" Mary asked the angel. "I don't have a husband. I'm not married to Joseph yet."

Then Gabriel told her, "God will make this miracle happen. He will bless you as He has blessed your cousin, Elizabeth. In a few months, she will have a baby too, even though she is much too old. Wonderful things are possible with God's help."

Mary believed the angel. She said, "I love God and want to serve Him. I will do whatever He wants me to do." Then the angel left.

Mary was surprised and pleased that God had chosen her to have this special baby. And she was also very happy for her cousin, Elizabeth. So Mary decided to go visit Elizabeth and tell her what the angel had said.

God's Spirit told Elizabeth that Mary was going to be the mother of Jesus. This news made Elizabeth very excited and happy. And when Mary came into Elizabeth's house she said, "Hello, Elizabeth."

Elizabeth answered, "I am so glad you have come, Mary, because you are going to be the mother of Jesus."

From *A Child's First Book of Bible Stories,* by Wanda Hayes. Standard Publishing, p. 64.

REMEMBERING GOD'S TRUTHS: Use the picture cards that are found in the *Jesus* section of your picture file.

- Can you answer these questions about Jesus' birth?
  Who is Jesus?
  Jesus is the Son of God.
  What is the best gift God has given you?
  Jesus is the best gift God has given me.
  What is Christmas?
  Christmas is the time we celebrate Jesus' birthday.
  Why did Jesus come to earth?
  Jesus came to show us that God loves us.

EXPERIENCING GOD'S TRUTHS: Have the children go to the tables. You will need glitter (or colored sugar), glue, pie plate, and newspapers to cover the table. Give each child an activity sheet, "Good News From an Angel" (p. 11, *Through the Bible Activities for Preschoolers, Book 2).* Read the activity sheet to the children. Print each child's name on his paper.

Help each child apply glue to his angel. Explain that we do not know what angels look like. We are making our angels have sparkled clothes just for fun. Sprinkle glitter (or colored sugar) on each angel. Shake excess off into pie plate. Allow glitter to dry while you are doing the next activity. Help the children cut out the angel after it dries, put thread through the star so they can hang the angel on their tree at home.

Pretend that you are walking with the children to cousin Elizabeth's house. Let one child pretend she is Elizabeth in one corner of the room. Let other children take the long trip to see her. Talk about how excited Elizabeth and Mary must have been as they talked about the little babies that they were going to have. Read **Act It Out** on page 9.

REVIEWING GOD'S TRUTHS: Mary decided to go see her cousin Elizabeth in another town. She wanted to tell her the news about her baby.

We are going on a trip, too. See 'Going on a Trip' game instructions in the *Games* section in the front of the book, page 9.

Do you think that Mary and Elizabeth talked about the babies who were growing inside of them? Maybe they talked about how to take care of a baby after he was born. Read *My Baby Brother Needs Me* by Jane Belk Moncure (if it is available and you have time).

Closing prayer: "We thank You, God, for Jesus. Amen."

LOOKING AHEAD—Please read "A Present From God" in Lesson 25. You will need to begin now preparing this special project.

Unit Seven: God's Special Son

Bible Verse: For God so loved the world that he gave his one and only Son. (John 3:16, NIV)

Luke 2:1-20

Lesson 25

JESUS IS BORN

AS THE CHILDREN ARRIVE: Greet each child warmly and direct him to one of the learning centers.

Attendance Check Center: Have small paper gift boxes cut out and ready for the children to hang on the Christmas tree (see Lesson 23, p. 71). Or, add a star or sticker to each attendance chart.

Bible Words Center: See Lessons 7 and 23 for suggested ways of teaching this verse, pages 28 and 71. "For God so loved the world that he gave his one and only Son" John 3:16, NIV.

Sharing Happy News Center: Bring for each child a piece of white construction paper, folded to form a greeting card, with the words, "Jesus is the Son of God. We love Him," printed on the front. Supply crayons for the children to draw and color a picture of baby Jesus on the card. Center the conversation on the Christian meaning of Christmas and sharing the good news with others.

Encourage the children to give the card to a

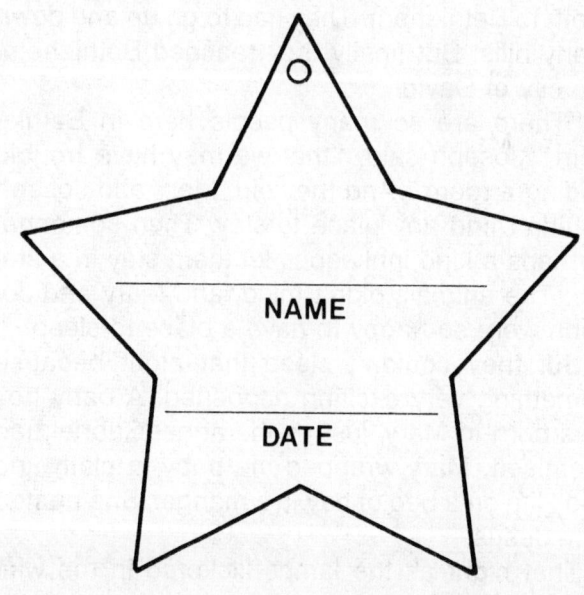

neighbor of theirs who does not have a church home and may not know about Jesus.

At the sound of music from the cassette tape or

piano, have the children go to the story area of the room for singing.

SINGING AND TALKING TO GOD: Sing, "Jesus Is the Son of God" (p. 56, *Songs for Preschool Children);* "Jesus, the Son of God" (p. 59, v. 1, SPC); "See the Star" (p. 66, SPC); "Here We Come to Bethlehem" (p. 66, SPC); "Rock Baby Jesus" (p. 63, SPC); and "Song of Praise" (p. 75, v. 1, SPC).

Pray thanking God for sending baby Jesus to earth. Give each child an opportunity to express his thanks, but don't insist that he pray aloud.

Lead the children in a walk around the room for exercise as they sing "Here We Come to Bethlehem" (p. 66, SPC).

READING ABOUT GOD'S WORD: Read Luke 2:6 from your copy of the *International Children's Version.* Read or tell the Bible story.

Luke 2:1-20 CR p.119, 120 - Bible in Pictures

Jesus Is Born
CR - My Bible Friends

The road from Nazareth to Bethlehem was long. Mary and Joseph traveled slowly. Every once in a while, Joseph probably asked, "Are you tired, Mary?"

"A little," she may have said. "I think the baby will be born soon."

"Then we'll rest awhile," Joseph told her. It probably took them a few days to travel from Nazareth to Bethlehem. They had to go up and down many hills. But finally they reached Bethlehem, the city of David.

"There are so many people here in Bethlehem," Joseph said, "that we may have trouble finding a room." And they did. Mary and Joseph couldn't find any place to stay. Then someone, perhaps a kind innkeeper, let them stay in a stable. The animals didn't mind, and Mary and Joseph were so happy to have a place to sleep.

But they couldn't sleep that night because something very exciting happened. A baby boy was born to Mary, just as the angel Gabriel had promised. Mary wrapped the baby in cloth and laid Him on a bed of hay in a manger. She named Him Jesus.

That night as the lamps flickered in the windows of Bethlehem, stars shone down on shepherds watching their sheep in a field nearby. Perhaps a shepherd boy played his flute softly while the sheep made low "baaing" sounds. Some of the sheep and shepherds were asleep.

Suddenly the shepherds were startled by a bright light from the sky. Then an angel appeared to them, and they were frightened.

"Don't be afraid," the angel told the shepherds. "I have good news for you that will bring a lot of happiness to everyone. A baby has just been born in Bethlehem. And this baby is the Son of God."

The shepherds listened closely as the angel told them where they could find the baby.

"He is in a stable in Bethlehem, sleeping in a manger on some hay," said the angel.

Then suddenly, there were many angels praising God and saying, "Glory to God in the highest, and on earth, peace to men and women because God wants to make them happy."

As soon as the angels left, the shepherds said, "Let's go to Bethlehem right now and see this baby that the angels have told us about."

So the shepherds hurried and found Mary and Joseph and baby Jesus. Jesus was wrapped in cloths and lying in a manger filled with hay. They knew this must be the right baby, and so the shepherds told Mary and Joseph what the angel had told them.

Mary and Joseph were glad the shepherds had come. They were glad to hear what the angel had told them about Jesus. Mary thought about what the shepherds told her. Perhaps she was thinking, too, about Gabriel's visit to her months before.

The shepherds went back to their flocks, praising God and thanking Him for leading them to Jesus, His Son.

From *A Child's First Book of Bible Stories* by Wanda Hayes. Standard Publishing, pp. 66, 67.

REMEMBERING GOD'S TRUTHS: Remove the following picture cards from the *Jesus* section of your picture-card file. Teach the answers in an enthusiastic manner. Keep cards available for use next week.

- We just read about the birth of Jesus.
    Who is Jesus?
    Jesus is the Son of God.

- The Son of God left Heaven. He became a very tiny baby growing inside of Mary. He was God's gift to the world.
    What is the best gift God has given you?
    Jesus is the best gift God has given me.

- We have a special time when we celebrate Jesus' birthday.
  What is Christmas?
  Christmas is the time we celebrate Jesus' birthday.
- Well, then,
  Why did Jesus come to earth?
  Jesus came to show us that God loves us.

EXPERIENCING GOD'S TRUTHS: There are three parts to this section of the lesson.

1. **God's Gift:** Prepare at home a large box wrapped as a Christmas present. Place a large attractive picture of Jesus (framed if possible) in the box.

In class explain to the children that they can open this box that contains a picture of the *best* gift God can give.

Let them have fun tearing the paper and finding the picture.

2. **A Present From God:** This project will require more home preparation than the projects in most lessons. Will you give it your loving attention?

Buy a small picture of Jesus for each child in your class. A Christian bookstore should have these.

Secure enough small gift boxes so that you can give one to each child. The box should be large enough to hold the picture. A local merchant may give them to you if you explain that they will be used for the children of your church. If the boxes are donated, be sure to write a thank-you note to the store manager.

Wrap the *top* of each box or decorate it with a Christian Christmas sticker or ribbon. Write the following words on the back of each picture:
"What is the best gift God has given you?
Jesus is the best gift God has given me."

Wrap each picture in tissue and place it in the box. Write each child's name on the bottom of the box.

In class let the children have fun opening the boxes and answering the question.

3. **Gifts At Christmas** is the name of the activity sheet (p. 12, *Through the Bible Activities for Preschoolers, Book 2),* Give each child one. Read the paper to the children. Write each child's name on his paper. Tell the children that they may color the picture.

REVIEWING GOD'S TRUTHS: Pretend to be Mary and Joseph making the trip to Bethlehem. Walk around the classroom or to another part of your church building if possible. Stop for food and rests and talk. Encourage the conversation to center on the trip and the excitement Mary and Joseph felt as they anticipated Jesus' being born. To add realism you may want to use a bundle of clothes (wrapped and tied in cloth) and real food (Example, small pieces of fruit). If you can walk outside the classroom, end your journey at the church nursery. Look in to see the babies. Talk about how small the babies are and that Jesus was once that small too. Don't let the children touch the babies. Talk about how happy Joseph and Mary must have been when they held baby Jesus.

Closing prayer: "Thank You, God, for Your great gift—Jesus. He came to show us how much You love us. Amen."

Unit Seven: God's Special Son

Bible Verse: For God so loved the world that he gave his one and only Son. (John 3:16, NIV)

Matthew 2:1-12

Lesson 26

WISE-MEN WORSHIP JESUS

AS THE CHILDREN ARRIVE: (See *As the Children Arrive,* p. 7.) Greet each child warmly and direct him to one of the learning centers.

Attendance Check Center: See Lesson 23, page 71 for suggestions. Give each child a paper star, write his name and the date on it, and hang the star on the tree. Or help each child place a star or sticker on the attendance chart.

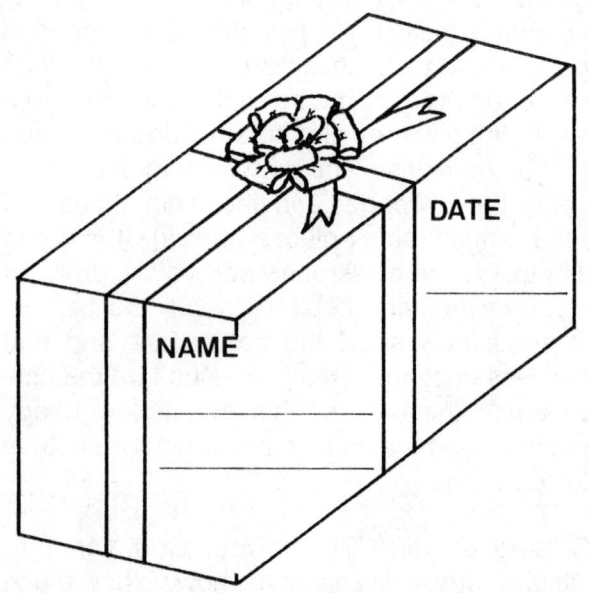

Bible Words Center: Continue to review John 3:16. See Lessons 7 and 23 for a suggested way of teaching this verse.

Giving Center: Bring real money—lots of change and several dollar bills, canned food, and clothing to class with you. Have fun naming and counting the money, picking out favorite foods, and trying on the clothing with the children.

Play a game with them where they have the money, food and clothing, and you are in need. Say, "I am a Christian friend of yours; will you help me?" Encourage them to share what they have with you.

At the sound of music from the cassette tape or piano, have the children go to the story area of the room for singing.

SINGING AND TALKING TO GOD: Sing, "God So Loved" (p. 42, this book); "Jesus Is the Son of God" (p. 56, *Songs for Preschool Children*); "Jesus, the Son of God", (p. 59, v. 1, SPC); "See the Star" (p. 66, SPC); "Here We Come to Bethlehem" (p. 66, SPC) and "Song of Praise" (p. 75, v. 1, SPC).

Have a special time of talking to God. Thank God that Jesus came to show us that God loves us.

Let the children pretend they are the Wise-Men riding on their camels. Let them follow the teacher around the room and back to the story area.

READING ABOUT GOD'S WORD: Read only one verse today, Matthew 2:1, from your copy of *International Children's Version.* "Jesus was born in the town of Bethlehem in Judea during the time when Herod was king. After Jesus was born, some wise men from the east came to Jerusalem."

Read or tell the Bible story.

Matthew 2:1-12 CR p.121, 122

Wise-men Worship Jesus

After Jesus had been born in Bethlehem, some men who studied the stars came looking for Him. They lived far away in the East. These men were not sure where to find Jesus, so they went to Jerusalem. They stopped everyone they met and asked. "Where can we find the King of the Jews? We saw His star shining in the East, and we have come to worship Him." But no one seemed to know where Jesus was.

When King Herod heard that there were men from the East looking for another king, he got very angry. Herod didn't want anyone else to be king. And the people in Jerusalem were worried, too. They didn't know what King Herod might do.

And King Herod did have a plan. He called all the religious leaders and teachers together and asked, "Where will the King of the Jews be born?" They looked in the Bible and found the words of the prophet Micah who wrote that a ruler or king would be born "in Bethlehem."

Then King Herod pretended that he wanted to help the Wise-men find Jesus. So he asked them, "When did you first see the star?" They told him. Then Herod said, "Look for Him in Bethlehem, and when you find Him, come back and tell me exactly where He is. I want to go and worship Him, too."

So the Wise-men left King Herod and started toward Bethlehem. And when they looked up into the sky, they saw the beautiful star. It was the same star they had seen in their own country far away. The Wise-men were happy to see the star. Now they knew for certain that God was leading them in the right direction.

The star moved and led the Wise-men to the exact house where Jesus and His parents were. Then it stopped. Its beams shone down on the house to let the Wise-men know, "Here is where you'll find the baby King."

The Wise-men entered the house and saw Mary and Jesus. They kneeled and worshiped Him. And when they finished worshiping Jesus, they gave Him their gifts—gold, frankincense, and myrrh. The Wise-men had brought expensive gifts because they were for a King.

Before the Wise-men left Bethlehem to go back home, God warned them in a special dream, *Do not tell King Herod where Jesus is. He is mean and wants to kill Him. Go back to your homes by a road that does not go to Jerusalem where King Herod lives.*

From *A Child's First Book of Bible Stories* by Wanda Hayes. Standard Publishing, pp. 70, 71.

REMEMBERING GOD'S TRUTHS: Review the picture cards from Lesson 25 on page 76.

EXPERIENCING GOD'S TRUTHS: Provide an opportunity for the children to learn to give. Bring from home: a man's hat or tie (for missionary); lots of dollar bills (real money or play money can be used but do not use coins); a Bible and suitcase for a pretend missionary to take to another country; an offering basket; and clothes for one of the children to wear in order to look like a child in another country.

Set up your room so that one area is a pretend church building, one area is a pretend missionary's house in the United States, and one area is where a child lives in another country. Be sure the children understand each area before beginning the story. Walk the children to each area as you tell them about it.

Dress one child as a missionary (tie or hat) and put him or her in the pretend house with the Bible and suitcase.

Dress one child as a child from another country and put him or her in the area designated as the place where he lives.

Explain that the teacher and other students will be the church—the people who love and trust Jesus. Put the offering container in the area you call the church building. Give each child several dollar bills.

As the church is seated in the pretend church building, the teacher can act as the person who explains that "We will now give our money for God's work. We are happy to give our money. We give because we love Jesus. We will each be like the Wise-men in our story and give our gifts." Pass offering container.

Then explain that we will all follow the money to the pretend house and talk to the pretend man about his plans to be a missionary. Give him the money and tell him to use the money to buy an airplane ticket.

The man takes his Bible and suitcase and pretends to buy an airplane ticket and fly far away to another country.

In the other country the missionary talks to the child there and tells the child that Jesus loves him. After role playing, lead them to the tables.

Give each child an activity sheet, "Giving" (p. 13, *Through the Bible Activities for Preschoolers, Book 2*).

Let each child find and color the hidden objects as you read the bottom portion of the paper.

REVIEWING GOD'S TRUTHS: Play the game "Going on a Trip" using the picture cards mentioned earlier. See page 9 for instructions. Introduce the game by explaining that the Wise-men went on a trip, and we are going on a trip.

Closing prayer: "We thank You, God, for loving us so much that You sent Your Son, Jesus, to earth as a tiny baby. We love You. In Jesus' name, amen."

Unit 8—Jesus Prepares for His Special Work

GETTING READY FOR UNIT EIGHT

The theme of this unit is that Jesus had a special job to do. As a child, He obeyed His parents and God. He studied the Scriptures and knew them. He was baptized and was then tempted. Yet He did not sin. He chose twelve men to be His helpers. He wants us to love and follow Him.

Learning Objectives: Some things you should expect your children to accomplish in this unit:

The children should know (1) The Bible is God's Word; (2) All people who love and trust Jesus are the church; (3) Jesus is our best friend; (4) All people who love and trust Jesus are in God's family.

The children should feel (1) Happy to read God's Word; (2) Eager to obey; (3) Happy that they can help each other.

The children should be able to (1) Tell the highlights of the Bible stories; (2) Say the Bible verses and answers to concept questions; (3) Tell how Jesus was baptized; (4) Name four disciples.

Remember, because of the difference in age and maturity, some children will meet more of these objectives than others will.

Bible Verses: There is one new Bible verse in this unit. See page 83 for suggestions in introducing it. The other verses are review verses.

Books: Several books are suggested for reading at the end of each lesson. These books may be placed in the quiet, book corner of your room. *The Very Best Book of All; Obedience; Choosing Is Fun;* and *Doing Right Makes Me Happy* are suitable for the ages of the children and for the subjects being studied.

Bulletin Board: Place pictures of the life of Christ on the board and use the unit title for the heading.

THINGS TO DO:

Lesson 27: Prepare new attendance charts (see p. 81). Use lemon juice, cotton swabs, and 3" x 8½" strips of white paper, and write the mystery verse. Take an iron and a heavy terrycloth towel to class. A small suitcase is needed for the game (see p. 83).

Lesson 28: Learn the clapping rhythm for teaching today's verse. This is a long verse and needs to be broken down into smaller parts. Poster board, magazine pictures of people of all races, and glue are needed. Write today's verse at the bottom of the poster board. Arrange for your minister to meet you and the children at the baptistry to explain how a person is baptized. Bring cotton balls for glueing on the activity sheets.

Lesson 29: You will need three or five small animal toys, and five different hats. Be prepared to play the "Obeying Game" (see p. 87).

Lesson 30: See page 88 for the items needed for the "Choosing" Center. Make twelve name tags, one for each disciple. You will also need a six inch paper plate and a tongue depressor, or a craft stick, for each child, and some colored paper, yarn, crayons, buttons, etc., for the children to make a face on the plate (see p. 90).

Unit Eight: Jesus Prepares for His Special Work   Luke 2:41-51

Bible Verse: God is good. (Psalm 73:1, NIV)   Lesson 27

A SPECIAL TRIP

AS THE CHILDREN ARRIVE: (See *As the Children Arrive,* p. 7.) Greet each child warmly and direct him to one of the learning centers.

Attendance Check Center: Prepare an attendance card for each child in your class. Buy stickers with pictures of Jesus (#1736, #1740, or #1943) on them for use each week. The attendance cards should include these statements:

> I am *(child's name.)*
> I love Jesus.
> I want to learn about Him.
> I will come to church each week.

Attach the cards to a wall at the child's eye level. Each week, read the card to each child and let him put a picture of Jesus sticker on his card.

Bible Words Center: Present this familiar verse in a different way today. Before class write the verse, "God is good" on 3" x 8½" strips of white paper, using a Q-tip dipped in lemon juice. Allow the paper to dry. Take an iron and a heavy terry towel to class with you.

Caution the children about the hot iron. Give each child a sheet of paper on which you have written the verse. (The writing should be invisible.) Tell the children, "We are going to make some important words appear on our paper." Let each child take turns using the hot iron (with the teacher's help), and discovering the Bible verse. Say, "God is so good to provide so many fun ways for us to learn."

(You may want to have Q-tips, lemon juice, and paper strips handy for older children to write the verse on the paper to take home to show their family.)

Scroll Bible Center: From light-colored construction paper, cut a piece of 12" x 6" paper for each child in your class. On each piece of paper copy the following Hebrew words which say, "God is good."

In class, help the children glue each end of the paper on to plastic straws, and let them dry while you tell the children that Jesus went to the temple when he was a boy. Remind the children that the temple was the place where God's people gathered to worship God long ago. Show them Psalm 73:1 in your Bible and talk about how the letters look. Then show them Psalm 73:1 written in Hebrew, and talk about the difference in the languages. As you help each child roll each end of his scroll Bible, talk about Jesus going to the temple and reading the Word of God from a scroll Bible.

At the sound of music from the cassette tape or piano, have the children go to the story area of the room for singing.

SINGING AND TALKING TO GOD: Sing, "The Church" (p. 90 this book); "God's Family" (p. 90, this book); "God Is Good" (p. 38, *Songs for Preschool Children,* adding the reference, "Psalm seventy-three, one, God is good."); "Sing, Little Children, Sing" (p. 37, SPC); "J-E-S-U-S" (p. 50, SPC, changing the last line to "Jesus is the Son of God."), and "We're Here in Our Church" (p. 35, SPC, change the title and lines 4 and 8 to "In Our Church Building").

Have a special time of talking to God. Prepare at home by reading the section in the front of this book called *Talking to God.* For this lesson it would be appropriate to thank God for our *church building.*

Lead the children in a march around the room for exercise as you sing "The Marching Song" (p. 11, SPC).

READING ABOUT GOD'S WORD: If you have a copy of the *Frances Hook Picture Book,* show the picture of the boy Jesus, the sixth story in the book.

Read or tell the Bible story.

Luke 2:41-51 CR p. 124.

A Special Trip

While Jesus was still a baby, Mary and Joseph took Him back to Nazareth where they had lived.

Jesus was a good son. Whatever Mary asked Jesus to do, He was glad to do. Perhaps Jesus helped Joseph in his carpenter's shop, too.

Jesus played with His friends in the streets of Nazareth. He learned a lot of Bible verses from Joseph and Mary, too.

When Jesus was twelve years old, He was old enough to worship with the men in the temple at Jerusalem. Joseph and Mary went to the temple every year to remember the Passover, and Jesus was eager to go. The trip took about three days, but it was fun because so many men and women, boys and girls were going from Nazareth and other cities. The people did not want to miss worshiping God in the temple. At the Passover feast, the Jewish people remembered how God helped Moses lead them out of Egypt many years before. This was a way of saying thank you to God.

Thousands of people lived in the city of Jerusalem. Many of them opened their homes to the families who came from far away.

In the homes, the families ate the Passover meal and read Scriptures. At the temple, the men and boys offered their sacrifices.

When the Passover celebration was finished, Mary and Joseph started home to Nazareth, along with the other families. They must have thought Jesus was in the group somewhere. But He wasn't!

After Mary and Joseph and the others had been traveling back home for one day, Mary looked for Jesus. He wasn't with her friends or family. Perhaps she thought, *He is with Joseph and the men.*

Then Joseph looked for Jesus and didn't see Him either. Maybe he thought, *He is probably with His mother or some of the other children.*

But that evening, when Mary and Joseph stopped to rest, they said to each other, "Where is Jesus? I thought He was with you."

Then they asked the people traveling with them, but no one had see Jesus. Now they knew that He was missing!

The next day Mary and Joseph went all the way back to Jerusalem. They were worried. Perhaps they thought, *This isn't like Jesus. He always obeys, and He is always where He is supposed to be.*

In Jerusalem they looked everywhere and asked everyone they saw, "Have you seen our boy, Jesus?" But no one had.

Then the third day, Mary and Joseph found Jesus. They found Him in the temple, talking to some of the teachers of God's Word. Jesus was listening to what the teachers had to say and asking them questions. These men were very, very smart, and they were surprised at how much this twelve-year-old boy understood about God and the Bible.

Mary and Joseph were thankful they had found Jesus, but Mary scolded Him, "Son, why did you do this? Your father and I have looked everywhere for you."

Jesus answered, "Didn't you know that I had to be in my Father's house?" Jesus meant God's house, the temple, because He is God's Son.

Then Jesus went home to Nazareth with Mary and Joseph. He obeyed them, and continued to grow and learn in a way that pleased God.

From *A Child's First Book of Bible Stories* by Wanda Hayes. Standard Publishing, pp. 74, 75.

Then read Luke 2:49 from the *International Children's Version.* "Jesus asked, 'Why did you have to look for me? You should have known that I must be where my Father's work is!'"

REMEMBERING GOD'S TRUTHS: You will need one picture card from the *Heavenly Father* section of your file and three from the *Church* section for today's lesson.

- Jesus and His parents visited the temple. The temple was called God's House. We know that God is everywhere, not just in one house. So we do not go to a temple to worship. We go to a church building. Can you answer this question?

    Where is God?
    God is everywhere.

- Yes, the building we are in is a church building. Can you answer this question?

    Who are the church?
    All people who love and trust Jesus are the church. Be sure to explain to the children what it means to love and trust Jesus.

- We have all come to our church building because we are God's family.

    Who are in God's family?
    All people who love and trust Jesus are in God's family. Be sure to explain to the children what it means to love and trust Jesus.

- Jesus went to the temple. When He was there He read and learned part of the Bible.
  What is the Bible?
  <u>The Bible is the Word of God.</u>

EXPERIENCING GOD'S TRUTHS: Tell the children we are going to explore our church building. Take the children for a walk around your church building. As you walk, talk about the following:
  a. Our church building has many rooms.
  b. Different people go to different rooms. Here is a room for first graders, etc.
  c. God's family meets together in our church building.
  d. God's family comes here to show God that we love Him.
  e. This church building is a place where we come to learn the Bible.
  f. God is happy that we choose to come to our church building instead of staying home and watching T.V.

You may want to stop and sit and talk about these things and then get up and walk again.

Lead the children back to their classroom and to the tables. Give each child the activity sheet, "God's Word" (p. 1, *Through the Bible Activities for Preschoolers, Book 3*). Help them connect the dots on the papers, and print their names on the papers. Let each child take turns holding your Bible and saying, "I love to read God's Word."

REVIEWING GOD'S TRUTHS: Play "Going on a Trip" using the four picture cards from today's lesson. Instructions for this game are found on page 9 of this book. Introduce the game by saying that Jesus, Mary, and Joseph went on a trip to the temple in Jerusalem. So, we are going on a pretend trip too.

When Jesus was in the temple He was talking with the teachers about the Word of God. Read *The Very Best Book of All* by Fran Flournoy, Standard Publishing (#3591).

Closing prayer: "Dear God, thank You for our church building. We like to come here and learn about You. In Jesus' name, amen."

Unit Eight: Jesus Prepares for His Special Work

Matthew 3:13-17

Bible Verse: To those who believed in his name, he gave the right to become children of God. (<u>John 1:12</u>, NIV)

Lesson 28

JOHN BAPTIZES JESUS

AS THE CHILDREN ARRIVE: Greet each child warmly and direct him to one of the learning centers.

Attendance Check Center: Help each child place a picture of Jesus sticker on his attendance chart. Read the sentences on the chart as the child puts on the sticker (see p. 81).

Bible Words Center: Today's verse is new. "To those who believed in his name, he gave the right to become children of God. John 1:12, NIV."

This verse will be taught and reviewed in nine lessons, so don't be anxious if your class needs help saying it the first few times. Prepare to teach this verse by saying it out loud and clapping this rhythm to it (clap on "c"):

```
To those who believed in his name,
   c         c          c
he gave the right to become
              c
       children of God.
         c    c    c
           John 1:12
         c    c    c
```

Bring to class the needed items for a bean-bag

toss game. It will be used eight more times, so you will want to make it sturdy and attractive. Use a picture of a clown with a large hole in his hat for the bean bags to be thrown through, decorate a bucket, or use small hula hoops into which the bean bags are to be tossed.

In class, practice saying and clapping the verse and reference. When the children are familiar with the verse and reference, let them line up for playing the bean-bag toss. Ask, "What people can be children of God?" Let them say the verse and reference and then toss the bean bags in, allowing each child a turn to recite and throw.

Children of God Center: Bring to class a piece of large poster board with the Bible verse printed on the bottom. Cut pictures from magazines or catalogues of people of all ages and races. Glue or paste will be needed also.

In class, talk about the verse as you allow the children to paste the pictures onto the poster board. Introduce the idea that people who are to be in God's family obey Jesus by being baptized.

At the sound of music from the cassette tape or piano, have the children go to the story area of the room for singing.

SINGING AND TALKING TO GOD: Sing, "Children of God" (p. 61, this book); "The Church" (p. 90, this book); "Go to Heaven" (p. 90, this book); "God's Family" (p. 90, this book); "This Is My Beloved Son" (p. 30, *Songs for Preschool Children);* and "J-E-S-U-S" (p. 50, SPC).

Have a special time of talking to God. Thank God that we can love and trust Jesus, and be in God's family.

Lead the children in a march around the room for exercise as you sing "God So Loved" (p. 42, this book).

READING ABOUT GOD'S WORD: Using your copy of the *International Children's Version* show the picture on the top of the page preceding page 27.

Ask the children, "Who is Jesus?" Help them answer, *Jesus is the Son of God."* Tell them you will read some verses from your Bible where the Heavenly Father, God, is talking to Jesus, the Son of God. Read Matthew 3:16, 17. "Jesus was baptized and came up out of the water. Heaven opened and he saw God's Spirit coming down on him like a dove. And a voice spoke from heaven. The voice said, 'This is my Son and I love him. I am very pleased with him.'"

Now read or tell the Bible story.

Matthew 3:13-17 CR P.125

John Baptizes Jesus

While Jesus was growing up in the town of Nazareth, His cousin, John, was growing up in Judea. John was now a man, thirty years old.

And John did not dress like the men in the city. He did not wear nice clothes. His clothes were made of camel's hair, and he wore a leather belt. He did not eat like most people eat either. He ate what he could find in the desert—locusts and wild honey. While John was in the desert, he learned what God wanted him to do.

One day John went to the Jordan River where he began preaching. "Stop doing wrong things," he told the people. "Obey God and get ready for His kingdom."

And many people believed what John said. To show that they were sorry they had not been doing what God wanted them to do, the people were baptized.

One day when John was preaching and baptizing in the river, Jesus came to him. "I want to be baptized," Jesus said to John.

Now John knew that Jesus had not done anything wrong. He knew that Jesus was God's Son. He was not like any of the other people.

"Oh! no," said John. "I should be asking You to baptize me."

But Jesus said, "I want to be baptized because God wants me to." So John baptized Jesus in the Jordan River.

Jesus prayed as John baptized Him. And as He came up out of the water, the skies were opened, and the Spirit of God came down from Heaven in the form of a beautiful dove. Suddenly, a voice from Heaven said, "This is my Son. I love Him, and am pleased with Him."

From *A Child's First Book of Bible Stories* by Wanda Hayes. Standard Publishing, p. 77.

REMEMBERING GOD'S TRUTHS: Use the following picture cards from *The Church* and *About Me* sections of the picture file. Allow the children to stand, sit, or kneel for each picture card to add variety. Clap out the answers rhythmically to aid learning.

- People who get baptized today are people who are in God's family.

Who are in God's family?
<u>All people who love and trust Jesus are in God's Family.</u> Be sure to explain to the children what it means to love and trust Jesus.
- Another name for God's family is the church. Who are the church?
<u>All people who love and trust Jesus are the church.</u> Be sure to explain to the children what it means to love and trust Jesus.
- God's family uses a special book, the Bible. What is the Bible.
<u>The Bible is the Word of God.</u>
- When we are in God's family, God forgives our sin.
When you do something wrong and then say, "I'm sorry, God," what does God say?
<u>I forgive you.</u>

EXPERIENCING GOD'S TRUTHS: If it is possible for the children to see a real baptism, that would be ideal. If not, take the children to see the baptistry. Ask a member of your church staff to be there to explain how a person is baptized. In your discussion include the following:
1) Baptism is only for people who love Jesus.
2) Baptism is a way of showing other people that we are obeying and following Jesus.
3) We are baptized because Jesus told us to do it.
4) We are baptized because the Bible teaches us we should be.

Return to your classroom and have the children go to the tables. Give each child an activity sheet, "Jesus Was Baptized" *(p. 2 Through the Bible Activities for Preschoolers, Book 3).* Help the children glue cotton balls on the clouds. Let each child color only the water by providing a blue crayon for each child. As the children do this, print each child's name on his paper.

REVIEWING GOD'S TRUTHS: Play "Hide the Picture Cards" as described in the *Games* section on page 9.

Closing prayer: "Dear God, thank you for Jesus. We want to obey You as Jesus did. Thank You for letting us be Your children. We love You. Amen."

Unit Eight: Jesus Prepares for His Special Work

Bible Verse: Do what is right and good.
(<u>Deuteronomy 6:18,</u> NIV)

Matthew 4:1-11

Lesson 29

JESUS SAYS NO

AS THE CHILDREN ARRIVE: Greet each child warmly and direct him to one of the learning centers.

Attendance Check Center: Help each child place his sticker on the attendance chart and read the sentences to him. Make each child feel important.

Bible Words Center: See Lesson 12, page 40, for a suggested way of teaching this verse, "Do what is right and good." (Deuteronomy 6:18, NIV)

Saying "No" Center: Bring to class three or five animal toys. They could be stuffed animals or puppets.

Role play some incidents where one character (puppet or animal) tells another to do something that is wrong, and the second character says, "No," and tells why he won't do it. At first the teacher will need to speak both parts. But, as soon as the children understand, let them take turns holding and talking for the characters. Here are some possible sentences for the first characters to say.
a. Let's sneak outside when your mom is not looking.
b. Tell her that the dog ate the cookies. We don't want to get into trouble.

c. It's OK to scribble in the library book.
d. Let's take our clothes off in the swimming pool.

At the sound of music from the cassette tape or piano, have the children go to the story area of the room for singing.

SINGING AND TALKING TO GOD: Sing, "Pleasing God" (p. 26, *Songs for Preschool Children,* adding Ephesians 6:1 and Deuteronomy 6:18 to the tune); "This Is My Beloved Son" (p. 30, SPC); "J-E-S-U-S" (p. 50, SPC, change the last line to "Jesus is the Son of God."); and "Jesus Is the Son of God" (p. 56, SPC).

Read *Talking to God,* page 7. Let the children pray asking God to help them know what is right and do what is right.

Lead the children in a march around the room for exercise as you sing again, "Jesus Is the Son of God."

READING ABOUT GOD'S WORD: Read Matthew 4:1-11 from your copy of the *International Children's Version,* or tell the Bible story which is based on that Scripture.

Matthew 4:1-11 CR p. 126

Jesus Says, "No"

Soon after He was baptized by John, Jesus was led by the Holy Spirit into the desert. A desert is a very lonely place. There are no houses or people. There is only open space with no grass or trees. It is very bare.

While Jesus was there, the devil tried to get Him to disobey God. The Bible says He was tempted. The devil is God's enemy, and that's why he wanted to get Jesus to disobey God. This is what the devil did.

Jesus had not eaten for a long time. This is called fasting. He had been in the desert for forty days and forty nights. That's a long time! He had not eaten at all. He was so hungry!

The devil, knowing how hungry Jesus was, came to Him. He told Jesus, "If you are the Son of God, tell these stones to become bread."

Jesus answered Satan (the devil's other name) by telling him what the Bible said. Jesus knew the Scriptures, and He knew they said that "Man does not live by bread alone, but on every word that comes from the mouth of God." Jesus did not let the devil cause Him to disobey God.

The devil tried again. This time he took Jesus to the holy city, Jerusalem. He had Jesus stand on the highest point of the temple. Then he told Jesus to throw himself down—jump off. He used Bible words, too, this time. He said that God would command His angels to protect Jesus so that He would not get hurt. Jesus understood what the devil was trying to do—to get Him to disobey God. He spoke Scripture, saying, "Do not put the Lord your God to the test." Jesus would not disobey God. He chose to say no.

For the third time Satan tried to get Jesus to disobey God. He just wouldn't give up. This time, Satan took Jesus to a very high mountain and showed Him all the kingdoms of the world and their great beauty. The devil told Jesus that he would give Him all these kingdoms if He would bow down and worship him, the devil. Jesus knew that the Scriptures said He was to worship and serve only God. He told Satan to go away from Him. Jesus again said, "No," to Satan. The devil left Jesus and the angels came and helped Him. Jesus did not disobey God. He said, "No," when the devil tempted Him. He chose to obey God.

REMEMBERING GOD'S TRUTHS: Use these four picture cards from the picture files.
- The devil wanted Jesus to do wrong things, but Jesus would not. Jesus is the only person who has never done any wrong things. He has never done any wrong things because He is a very special person.
  Who is Jesus?
  Jesus is the Son of God. (*Jesus* section)
- Jesus could have turned the stones into bread. But that would have been sin because He would be obeying Satan. Can you answer this question?
  What can God do?
  God can do anything. (*Heavenly Father* section)
- The devil wanted Jesus to disobey.
  Who helps you to obey?
  God helps me to obey. (*About Me* section)
- If Jesus is your friend, He gives you power to obey. Is Jesus your friend?
  Who is your best friend?
  Jesus is my best friend. (*Jesus* section)

EXPERIENCING GOD'S TRUTHS: Play the

"Obeying Game." Bring five different hats with you and a bag of candy. Practice the following skit at home and present it to the children using words similar to those below.

"Sometimes we should *not* obey! Sometimes bad people tell us bad things to do. Should we obey bad people? No! We should always obey God. God has given us parents and teachers, and we should obey them. We are going to play a game where you must decide if you should obey. I will pretend that I am different people. You will not know if I am pretending to be a good person you should obey or a bad person you should say 'No' to. You must watch and decide. Obey me if you decide that it is right to obey. Now, let's all stand up and start our game.

1. (Put on a hat) "Hop on one foot!" (Watch to see if children obey.) "Good! You obeyed. You decided that I am pretending to be a good person because I am telling you a good thing to do."

2. "Now, let's do another one. Remember, when I put on this hat (put on second hat) you pretend you do not know who I am. OK? (Pretend to be driving a car and then stop your car near the children and hand them some candy.) 'Eat this candy, children. Here is candy for you to eat.' (Wait to see if children take and/or eat candy and then take off hat. Congratulate the children who did not take the candy and explain that they should say "No" and run right to their parents because the person giving the candy might be a bad person. (Collect *all* candy.)

3. (Put on third hat.) "Let's all act nasty and mean. It's fun to act nasty and mean. (Wait to see if children say "No." Take off hat.) Good. You remembered to say "No." It is right to say "No" to bad people who are telling you to do bad things."

4. "Now I will be another person. (Put on fourth hat.) Let's all do some exercises. Touch your head, now your shoulders; good, now touch your knees; now touch your toes. Good, you obeyed because I am telling you a good thing to do. You decided to do a good thing."

5. "Now I'm going to pretend to be another person. Maybe I will be a bad person, or maybe I will be a good person (Put on fifth hat.) Now run around the room and scream so that we will bother the people in the other rooms. Go ahead—everybody run and scream real loud." (Wait to see who says "No" and congratulate them. Take off hat.) All sit down at tables and talk about the game.

Give each child an activity sheet, "Deciding to Say 'No'" (p. 3, *Through the Bible Activities for Preschoolers, Book 3*). Read each story and let the children discuss the response. Tell the children to color only the pictures that show that Karen and Andy decided to do what is right. Write each child's name on his paper. Give each child a piece of candy just for fun.

REVIEWING GOD'S TRUTHS: Play a simple game with the children. Have the children get in a line side by side against one wall. The teacher explains the game by saying, "I will tell you what to do and I'll watch to see who obeys. Please do only what I tell you to do."

Say, "You may obey by taking three giant steps." The children obey. Say, "Thank you for obeying."

Say, "You may obey by jumping on one foot until I say stop." The children jump. Say, "Stop! Thank you for obeying."

Repeat the statements, using different actions like the following:
    take two baby steps,
    pat your head,
    stretch your arms up high,
    take one elephant step, and
    take two jumping steps.

Always say, "Thank you for obeying," after each exercise.

Closing prayer: "Dear God, please help us to say, 'No,' when someone tells us to do a bad thing. We need Your help. Amen."

Unit Eight: Jesus Prepares for His Special Work

Bible Verse: We love (him) because he first loved us. (1 John 4:19, NIV)

Luke 6:12-16

Lesson 30

JESUS CHOOSES HELPERS

AS THE CHILDREN ARRIVE: Greet each child warmly and direct him to one of the learning centers.

Attendance Check Center: Help each child put a sticker on her attendance chart. Read the sentences on the chart.

Bible Words Center: See Lesson 19, on page 58, for a suggested way of teaching the verse. Ask, "Why do we love Jesus?" Encourage the children to answer, "We love (Him) because he first loved us, *1 John 4 verse 19.*"

"Choosing" Center: Preschoolers often have difficulty making choices. Here is a fun way to introduce them to a concept taught in this lesson.

Bring to class five to ten items from three or four different categories of items. Examples:
1. Ten different colored crayons
2. Six to eight different animal cookies
3. Five different kinds of fruit
4. Six different small storybooks

Tell the children, "Each of us has times when we can choose what we want. We are going to play a choosing game. You will choose the thing you want to hold. You will not take the item home because it does not belong to you. We will watch to see which child chooses which item."

Spread out the items from one category (example: the crayons) and ask, "Which color do you want to choose?" Give each child a chance to choose, and tell why he chose that item.

Put those items away and repeat with another set of items.

Use expressions like these:
"Your eyes will help you choose."
"Your brain is working hard trying to choose."
"Different people choose different things."
"Sometimes it's hard to choose."
"All of these things are good, but you must choose what you think is best."
"Thanks for choosing."

At the sound of music from the cassette tape or piano, have the children go to the story area of the room for singing.

SINGING AND TALKING TO GOD: Sing, "This Is My Beloved Son" (p. 30, *Songs for Preschool Children*); "J-E-S-U-S" (p. 50, SPC); "The Twelve Apostles" (p. 57, SPC); "My Best Friend Is Jesus" (p. 58, SPC); "God's Family" (p. 90, this book); "Go to Heaven" (p. 90, this book); and "We Love Jesus" (p. 69, this book).

Have a special time of talking to God. For this lesson, it would be appropriate to thank God that we can be His followers.

Lead the children in a march around the room for exercise as you sing "The Twelve Apostles" again.

READING ABOUT GOD'S WORD: Read Mark 3:13-14 from your copy of the *International Children's Version*.

Read or tell the Bible story.

Jesus Chooses Helpers

Jesus had chosen twelve special helpers to be with Him all the time. They traveled with Jesus. They ate when He ate, listened when He talked, and tried very hard to follow Jesus in everything He did.

It had not been easy for Jesus to choose these twelve special workers. He had prayed all night long before He began to choose them.

Jesus had gone up on a mountain to be alone with God. He wanted to pray to His Father in Heaven. He wanted to ask God to help Him choose His helpers.

As Jesus climbed up onto the mountain, He was thinking very hard, *Whom shall I choose to help me? I need twelve special men who will work very hard. They must be the best men I can find.*

Jesus prayed all night long! It was morning when He stopped praying. Jesus had asked God to help Him choose the best men for His special work. Now He was ready to begin selecting the twelve.

No one knows why Jesus decided to have just twelve special disciples. He could have had more. He could have had less. But Jesus chose just twelve.

After the night in prayer, Jesus began to form His special group. The first disciple He asked to help Him was Andrew, a fisherman. Andrew was so excited about helping Jesus, he couldn't wait to tell his brother. He said, "I have a brother named Simon Peter. I know he will want to be a special helper for Jesus, too."

Do you think Peter wanted to be a disciple of Jesus? Yes, he did! In fact Peter became one of the greatest preachers who ever lived.

These were the first two disciples. There were ten more to be chosen. Jesus next asked two more brothers, James and John. They agreed right away to help Jesus. They didn't hesitate or worry about leaving their fishing boats. They wanted to help Jesus most of all.

Now Jesus had four helpers. But He kept choosing more. He asked two men named Philip and Bartholomew.

The seventh was a tax collector named Matthew. Many people were very surprised that Jesus would ask a tax collector to be one of His special helpers. But He did. Jesus knew Matthew would be a good worker.

Jesus continued to choose the twelve. He now had seven. Who would the other five be? The answer came soon. They were Thomas, another James who was the son of Alpheus, and another Simon who was called Zelotes. This made the number ten. Only two left to choose.

The last two men had the same name—Judas. But they were very different from each other. One was Judas the brother of James, and the other was Judas Iscariot.

Now Jesus had completed selecting the twelve. But why had He chosen them? What kind of work do you think Jesus wanted these men to do? He wanted them to be preachers! They were the ones who would preach to the whole world about Jesus. They would start the church when Jesus went back to Heaven.

Jesus taught His twelve special disciples exactly what He wanted them to preach. He lived with them and talked to them every day. He gave them special powers so they could heal sick people just by touching them. This healing power caused people to come to the twelve for help. Then they could tell those people about Jesus and His love for them.

From *A Child's First Book of Bible Stories* by Wanda Hayes. Standard Publishing, pp. 79, 80.

REMEMBERING GOD'S TRUTHS: Use the picture cards from the picture files suggested on page 6. Help the children with the answers to these questions.

- Jesus' special men loved Jesus very much. They were like a family. We have learned about God's family. Can you remember the answer to this question?
    Who are in God's family?
    <u>All people who love, and trust Jesus are in God's family.</u> (*The Church* section) Be sure to explain to the children what it means to love and trust Jesus.
- Jesus had friends when He was on earth. He has friends today, too.
    Who is your best friend?
    <u>Jesus is my best friend.</u> (*Jesus* section)
- Jesus talked to His special men when He was alive on earth.
    Is Jesus alive today?
    <u>Yes, Jesus is alive today.</u> (*Jesus* section)
- Yes, Jesus is alive today in Heaven.
    Who can go to Heaven?
    <u>All people who love and trust Jesus can go to Heaven.</u> (*Heavenly Father* section) Be sure to explain to the children what it means to love and trust Jesus.

EXPERIENCING GOD'S TRUTHS: Give the children an opportunity to role play Jesus choosing twelve helpers. Read *Act It Out* on page 9.

Make twelve name tags numbered and printed in manuscript style: 1) Peter 2) Andrew 3) James 4) John 5) Philip 6) Thomas 7) Bartholomew 8) Matthew 9) Thaddeus 10) James the Less 11) Simon 12) Judas, too

Practice singing the names to the tune of "Ten Little Indians."

   Peter, Andrew, James and John
   Philip, Thomas, Bartholomew
   Matthew, Thaddeus, James the Less
   Simon and Judas, too.

In class tell the children that they are going to pretend to be the special men Jesus called to be His helpers.

Have the children go to different parts of the

room and tell them to sit in that area. Give each child a disciple name tag.

Walk to each child and say, "Come, be my special helper," and tell him his disciple name. (Example—"You are Peter, the fisherman.")

Now, have the children spread out again and gather them to the story circle as you sing the song. Repeat if the children are still interested.

Sing verse one of "The Twelve Apostles" (page 57, SPC), and let the children count each other. Then help the children learn the apostles names by singing the name song above.

Now sing the second verse of "The Twelve Apostles" song (p. 57, SPC), and put actions with it. For example, ask the children what kind of work they can do. Example, sweeping. Pretend to sweep as you sing verse two again. Repeat, using other forms of work.

Have the children go to the tables and provide a paper-plate puppet for each one. Attach a tongue depressor (or craft stick) to the back of a six inch paper plate.

Have the children make a face on the puppet. Use scraps of colored paper, yarn, crayons, or buttons. (Plan the project so that you partially make the puppet at home and leave appropriate parts for the children to complete in class.)

Write this on the back of each plate:
　Why do we love Jesus?
　We love (Him) because He first loved us.
　　　　　　　　　　　　1 John 4:19 NIV
Print each child's name on his or her puppet.

REVIEWING GOD'S TRUTHS: Play "It's a New Day." Pretend to be Jesus' helpers sleeping at night and waking up to a new day. See game instructions on page 10. Use the four picture cards used today plus the four picture cards from last week's lesson.

Review the Bible verse. Ask the children, "Why do we love Jesus?" Encourage them to answer, "We love (Him) because He first loved us, 1 John 4, verse 19."

Closing prayer: "We thank You God for loving us. We sure do love You. Amen."

The Church (tune: "Farmer in the Dell")

All people who love and trust Jesus
Are the church, you see.
All people who love and trust Jesus
Are the church, you see!
(Be sure to explain to the children what it means to love and trust Jesus.)

God's Family (tune: "Farmer in the Dell")

All people who love and trust Jesus
Are in God's family.
All people who love and trust Jesus
Are in God's family.
(Be sure to explain to the children what it means to love and trust Jesus.)

Go to Heaven (tune: "Farmer in the Dell")

All people who love and trust Jesus
Can go to Heaven some day.
All people who love and trust Jesus
Can go to Heaven some day.
(Be sure to explain to the children what it means to love and trust Jesus.)

Unit 9—Jesus' Special Work

GETTING READY FOR UNIT NINE

The theme of this unit is that God had special work for Jesus to do. God's plan for His people was made known through His Son, Jesus. Jesus went about doing good. He healed the sick and the blind, and He taught the people about God. He loved all people. Jesus wants us to love others, too.

Learning Objectives: Some things you should expect your children to accomplish in this unit:

The children should know (1) Jesus wants them to love one another; (2) God will forgive them; (3) All people who love and trust Jesus are in God's family.

The children should feel (1) Thankful that Jesus can help them when they have problems; (2) Thankful that God takes care of them; (3) The need to say "I'm sorry." (4) Happy that they can talk to God anytime.

The children should be able to (1) Tell the highlights of the Bible stories; (2) Say the Bible verses and answers to concept questions; (3) State a way they can help a handicapped person; (4) Tell how they can help hungry people in their community.

Remember, because of the differences in age and maturity, some children will meet more of these objectives than others will.

Bible Verses: All of the Bible verses are review verses. Help the children to understand the meaning of the verses as well as the words. Use the teaching aids suggested in previous lessons.

Books: Several books are suggested for reading at the end of each lesson. These books may be placed in the quiet, book corner of your room. *Nick Joins In; Sharing Makes Me Happy; Zaccheus Meets Jesus; Growing as Jesus Grew;* and *Jesus Is My Special Friend* are suitable for the ages of the children and for the subjects being studied.

Bulletin Board: Make a bulletin board on the life of Jesus. Use the heading *Jesus' Special Work.* Add pictures that relate to this unit's Bible stories. You will want to plan to extend this theme through Unit 10.

THINGS TO DO:

Lesson 31: You will need to borrow a wheelchair, and secure a blindfold. Arrange for a handicapped child or young person to come to class. You will need to have black yarn for the activity sheet.

Lesson 32: Two paper plates and pictures of food cut from magazines are needed for each child. See page 93, **Hungry People Center** for the words you will need to write on each plate. Bring a roll or ¼ of a piece of bread for each child, a can of tuna, and small paper plates for a snack in the *Experiencing God's Word* section (see p. 94). Make arrangements for the children to bring canned food or money for food for poor people. Check the church office to get names of people who need help. Provide a basket for the canned food and money. You will need uncooked rice and small ribbons for the activity sheets.

Lesson 33: You will need a hand puppet for the **My Way Center** (see p. 96). Provide two lunch bags for each child to put the word cards in for the "Yes-No" game. You will need to write "Yes" on one bag and "No" on the other. Staple the bags together so that the words face out.

Lesson 34: You will need scissors, construction paper, and glue for the activity sheet. You will also need lots of pieces of green paper for money, a step ladder and two man-sized shirts—one white and one colored.

Unit Nine: Jesus' Special Work

Mark 2:1-12

Bible Verse: We love (Him) because he first loved us. (1 John 4:19, NIV)

Lesson 31

A CRIPPLED MAN

AS THE CHILDREN ARRIVE: Greet each child warmly and direct him to one of the learning centers.

Attendance Check Center: Help each child place a sticker picture of Jesus on his or her attendance chart. See Lesson 27, page 81.

Bible Words Center: (See Lesson 19 page 58, for a suggested way of teaching this verse.) Ask the children this question, "Why do we love Jesus?" Have the children do the actions as they say, "We love (Him) because He first loved us, 1 John 4:19."

Handicapped Center: Bring to class several baby dolls and long strips of sheet cut one inch wide.

Let the children pretend to be doctors putting bandages on crippled babies. Talk about the problems crippled people encounter and the limitations they have. If you can borrow a wheelchair, let the children take turns sitting in it and being pushed. Discuss limitations they have.

Put a blindfold on a child, and have him or her feel an object and describe it. Ask the child, "How does it feel to be blind?" Discuss their feelings. (You may think of other handicaps to role play.)

At the sound of music from the cassette tape or piano, have the children go to the story area of the room for singing.

SINGING AND TALKING TO GOD: Sing, "We Love Jesus" (p. 69, this book); "J-E-S-U-S" (p. 50, SPC, change the last line to "Jesus is the Son of God."); "My Best Friend Is Jesus" (p. 58, SPC); "JESUS" (p. 58, SPC); and "I Love Jesus" (p. 58, SPC).

Have a special time of talking to God. Pray for a sick or handicapped person whom the children know. Ask the children to name a person. Then pray specifically for that person.

Lead the children in a march around the room for exercise as you sing "We Love Jesus" again.

READING ABOUT GOD'S WORDS: Read Mark 2:10, 11 from your copy of the *International Children's Version.* "Jesus said to the paralyzed man, 'I tell you, stand up. Take your mat and go home.'" Read or tell the Bible story.

Mark 2:1-12

A Crippled Man

Many people were crowded into a house in the city of Capernaum. They wanted to hear what Jesus would say. Some people came because they heard that Jesus had healed people of all kinds of sicknesses.

Four men came to the house carrying a sick friend on a mattress.

"Please let us in," they begged the men and women in the house. "We want Jesus to heal our friend. Please let us through."

But there were too many people. There was no way for them to get into the house.

"I have an idea," said one of the men. "There are steps leading up to the roof. Let's climb them."

Up, up climbed the friends very carefully with their friend. The man was paralyzed. He couldn't even wiggle his toes, much less walk. When the kind men got to the top of the stairs, they laid the mattress down on the flat roof.

Chip, chip, chip. The men worked at loosening the tiles on the roof. Soon there was a hole in the roof big enough for the mattress to go through.

Very carefully the friends fastened ropes around the mattress of the sick man. Even more carefully, they lowered their friend into the room where Jesus was.

Jesus looked at the man who could not move at all and said, "Get up, pick up your bed, and go home." And right away the man did just that. He got up, picked up his bed, and said, "Thank You, God," all the way home.

The people could hardly believe what had happened! They began praising God because Jesus had made the crippled man walk.

From *A Child's First Book of Bible Stories* by Wanda Hayes. Standard Publishing, p. 83.

REMEMBERING GOD'S TRUTHS: Remove these picture cards from your file before class. (See p. 6.) Be prepared to teach them so your time with the children is fun as well as instructive.
- The man in our story had a problem.
    Does Jesus love children who have problems?
    Yes, Jesus loves everyone. (*About Me* section)
- You and I have problems sometimes, too.
    When you have a problem, what should you do?
    I should pray and ask God to help me.
    (*I Pray* section)
- Jesus told the man, "Stand up. Take your mat and go home." The man obeyed Jesus.
    Who helps you to obey?
    God helps me to obey. (*About Me* section)
- Jesus made the man well. He can do anything He wants to do.
    What can God do?
    God can do anything. (*Heavenly Father* section)

EXPERIENCING GOD'S TRUTHS: Help the children understand what it means to be crippled. If you know a crippled child, invite him to visit your class.

In class, talk about how it feels to be crippled and all the things children cannot do if they are crippled. Crippled people need lots of love. Crippled children need us to talk to them and play with them. Say, "Jesus loved crippled people and helped them. We should, too."

Let the crippled child take the lead in demonstrating how to use his medical equipment, and share his feelings. Let the child tell how he or she wants to be treated by others. Thank the child for coming.

Have children go to the tables and give each one an activity sheet, "Crippled Friends" (p. 4, *Through the Bible Activities for Preschoolers, Book 3*). Help the children glue black yarn on the wheels of the wheelchair, and then color the clothes of the child. Read the paper to them as they color.

REVIEWING GOD'S TRUTHS: Role play the Bible story. Use a folding rest mat for the bed. Let the children take turns being the crippled man and the four friends.

Or read the book, *Nick Joins In,* written and illustrated by Joe Lasker, published by Albert Whitman and Co., that can be borrowed from a public library.

Review the Bible verse. Ask, "Why do we love Jesus?" Say with the children, "We love (Him) because He first loved us, 1 John 4:19."

Closing prayer, "Dear God, thank You for loving children who have problems. Please help me to be kind and helpful to people I know who have problems. In Jesus' name, amen."

LOOKING AHEAD—Be sure to make early preparations for the *Experiencing God's Truths* section in the next lesson.

Unit Nine: Jesus' Special Work

Bible Verse: We love (Him) because he first loved us. (1 John 4:19, NIV)

John 6:1-15

Lesson 32

JESUS FEEDS A BIG CROWD

AS THE CHILDREN ARRIVE: Greet each child warmly and direct him to one of the learning centers.

Attendance Check Center: Help the children put a sticker with a picture of Jesus on his attendance card. Read the sentences on the card and say "Jesus loves you, and so do I."

Bible Words Center: Use the suggestions in Lesson 19, page 58, for teaching this verse. But point to a picture of Jesus when you say, "Him" and "He." Ask the question, "Why do we love Jesus?" Answer with the children, "We love (Him) because He first loved us, 1 John 4:19."

Hungry People Center: Bring two paper plates for each of your children and some pictures of food cut from magazines. On one plate (for each child) write, "Some people have no food. I can share with them." On the second plate (for each child), write, "Thank You, God, for giving me food." In class, let each student paste pictures of food on his second plate. Leave the first plate empty. Encourage the children to share the food they have. Let them decide what they will give and tell why. Let them transfer some of the food from the filled plates to the empty plates.

At the sound of music from the cassette tape or piano, have the children go to the story area of the room for singing.

SINGING AND TALKING TO GOD: Sing, "We Love Jesus" (p. 69, this book); "He Careth for You" (p. 32, *Songs for Preschool Children*, change "careth" to cares"); "J-E-S-U-S" (p. 50, SPC, change the last line to "Jesus is the Son of God."); "The Twelve Apostles" (p. 57, SPC); "Jesus" (p. 58, SPC, change the last line to read, "He can feed a crowd."); and "Song of Praise" (p. 75, SPC).

Have a special time of talking to God. Thank God that He makes food grow for us. Ask Him to help us share our food with hungry people.

Lead the children in a march around the room for exercise as you sing again, "We Love Jesus."

READING ABOUT GOD'S WORD: Read Mark 8:1-3, from your copy of the *International Children's Version*. Jesus said, "I feel sorry for these people. They have been with me for three days, and now they have nothing to eat. I cannot send them home hungry."

Explain that Jesus had a problem. There were lots of people and no food. How did Jesus solve the problem? Read or tell the Bible story.

John 6:1-16 CR p. 146

Jesus Feeds a Big Crowd

Jesus wanted to be alone. He was sad because His cousin, John, had been killed by wicked King Herod. So Jesus and His disciples got into a boat to sail across the Sea of Galilee.

While Jesus and His disciples were crossing to the other side of the sea, many people were bringing sick friends and relatives for Jesus to heal. They were waiting by the Sea of Galilee for Jesus to come. After waiting awhile, the people began to worry.

"Where is Jesus?" they asked each other. "We have come a long way to see Him."

Someone said, "I saw Jesus and His disciples go across the sea in a boat. It may be a long time before He comes back here."

The people didn't want to wait a long time to see Jesus. They said, "Let's save time. Let's walk around the lake to where Jesus is. Then we can see Him today, and ask Him to help us."

When Jesus' boat landed on the other side of the sea, He saw a big crowd of people waiting—the old, the young, the crippled, the blind, the very, very sick, and He loved them all. Jesus wanted to help everyone of them and He did. He healed all the sick people. Then He taught everyone there about the love of God.

It must have taken a long time to heal the men and women, boys and girls who wanted Jesus' help. It had been a long day. It would be night soon because the sun was going down.

Jesus looked at the big crowd of people. Then He said to His disciple, Philip, "The people are hungry. Where can we buy bread to feed all of them?"

Philip said, "Master, we don't have enough money to buy bread and give everyone even a small piece."

Jesus knew that, and He knew how He was going to feed the people.

Jesus said, "Go and see how many loaves of bread you can find in the crowd."

And His disciple, Andrew, said, "A young boy has five barley loaves and two fish that he will share. But how can that feed so many people?"

Jesus had a plan, and He was also able to do wonderful things. "Tell the people to sit down in groups on the green grass," Jesus told His disciples. And the people sat down in groups, with fifty in some groups and one hundred in others. The disciples counted more than five thousand men. There were also women and children there who weren't counted.

Jesus took the five barley loaves the little boy gave, looked up toward Heaven and thanked God for them. Jesus also took the two fish, and again looked up toward Heaven and thanked God for them.

Then Jesus began breaking the five small loaves of barley bread and the two fish into pieces and putting them in baskets. Then His disciples passed the baskets of bread and fish among the people seated on the soft, green grass. And all of the men, women, boys, and girls ate until they were full.

When everyone was through eating, Jesus told His disciples, "Gather the food that the people didn't eat so that nothing will be wasted."

And when they had gathered up the bread and fish left over, the disciples counted twelve baskets full. The little boy's lunch had been enough to feed all of the people. Jesus had made it more than enough.

From *A Child's First Book of Bible Stories* by Wanda Hayes. Standard Publishing, pp. 85, 86.

REMEMBERING GOD'S TRUTHS: Use these picture cards from your file.

- Jesus showed us how powerful He is in our story.
  What can God do?
  God can do anything. (*Heavenly Father* section)

- In our story Jesus gave the people food. How about you?
  Who gives you food?
  God makes food grow for me. (*God's Care* section)

- Jesus took care of the people by feeding them. He takes care of you by making food grow for you and taking care of you while you are awake and asleep.
  Who takes care of you when you sleep?
  God takes care of me when I sleep. (*God's Care* section)

- When the people were with Jesus they were very happy.
  When you are happy, what should you do?
  I should thank God for making me happy. (*About Me* section)

EXPERIENCING GOD'S TRUTHS: There are three parts to this section of the lesson.

1. *Eating Together:* Bring from home a small roll or 1/4 of a piece of bread for each child; an open can of tuna or other fish—enough for a taste for each child; a small paper plate for each child; and a box of Wet Ones for washing hands.

In class, ask each child to wash his hands. Let the children help prepare the table and eat fish and bread together after you thank God for the food.

2. *Hungry People:* Consult your minister, church board, outreach committee, or missions committee to get help determining what agency your church works through for feeding hungry people. If there is a mission to the hungry in your city that your church endorses, contact them. If you choose to use an international agency that your church endorses, get their address.

Your children need to be contacted and told to bring either canned food or money for food for poor people. Use the telephone or letter method to convey the following message:

"I am glad your child comes to my class. At our next meeting we are going to talk about hungry people. Please help your child to bring canned goods (or money) to our next meeting so he can have the experience of sharing."

Bring pictures of hungry children to show to the children.

As you clean up from your eating together, begin talking about what it must be like not to have food. Guide the conversation to talk about children who do not have enough food. Show pictures of hungry children. Ask the children to get the canned food or money they brought and place it in a basket that is located at the story circle. Have a time of prayer in which you thank God that you can share with hungry people.

(Be sure to mail the money promptly to the agency, or deliver the canned food to an agency or needy family.)

3. After the children put their food or money in the basket, they are to go to the tables. Give each child the activity sheet, "Hungry People" (p. 5, *Through the Bible Activities for Preschoolers, Book 3*). Have uncooked rice and scraps of rib-

bon on the tables and help the children glue the rice on the bowls and the ribbon on the basket. Read the paper to the children as they do this. Write each child's name on the back of his paper.

REVIEWING GOD'S TRUTHS: Play the "Pop-Up Game" with the picture cards listed for today's lesson, plus last week's picture cards. Game instructions are on page 9.

If the book and extra time are available, read *Sharing Makes Me Happy* by Dot Cachiaras.

Closing prayer: "Dear God, please help us to find ways to help hungry people. We know You love them as You love us. Amen."

Unit Nine: Jesus' Special Work

Bible Verse: Children, obey your parents. (Ephesians 6:1, NIV)

Luke 15:11-32

Lesson 33

THE LOST SON

AS THE CHILDREN ARRIVE: Greet each child warmly and direct him to one of the learning centers.

Attendance Check Center: Look into the eyes of each child as you talk to him, and help him put the Jesus sticker on his attendance card.

Bible Words Center: You will be reviewing two verses today, "Children, obey your parents," (Ephesians 6:1, NIV), and "Do what is right and good." (Deuteronomy 6:18, NIV)

Teach these verses using the song, "Pleasing God," page 26 of *Songs for Preschool Children.* Sing these verses, and then sing them again while using rhythm-band instruments. If you do not have rhythm instruments, Lesson 17, page 54, tells you how to make them.

My Way Center: Bring a puppet (any type) to class with you and introduce it to the children as Miss "My Way" or Mr. "My Way." Play a game with your students (similar to Simon Says) in which you give simple commands for the children to follow. But always have the puppet say, "No, do it my way" and refuse to follow the instructions. After the puppet refuses to follow instructions, he gets himself into trouble. You may want to make up your own stories. Here are some suggestions:

1. The teacher tells the children to hop on one foot. The children obey but the puppet says, "No, I want to do it my way." The puppet tries to hop on one of his hands and falls down on his nose.
2. The teacher gives each child a piece of paper, with one line drawn down the center, and a pair of scissors. The teacher tells the children to cut neatly on the line. The children obey but the puppet says, "No, I'll do it my way!" The puppet tears the paper instead of cutting it and makes a mess.

The teacher should ask the class to explain why the puppet fell on his nose and why he ruined his paper.

Read Proverbs 1:8, "Listen, my son, to your father's instruction and do not forsake your mother's teaching." Talk about this verse with the children.

At the sound of music from the cassette tape or piano, have the children go to the story area of the room for singing.

SINGING AND TALKING TO GOD: Sing, "Pleasing God" (p. 26, *Songs for Preschool Children* add these verses, Ephesians 6:1 and Deuteronomy 6:18); "We're Here in Our Church (p. 35, SPC, change the title and lines 4 and 8 to "In Our Church Building"); "I Can Talk to God" (p. 80, SPC); "Let Us Love One Another" (p. 29, SPC, change the last line to "First John 4, verse 7"); "J-E-S-U-S" (p. 50, SPC, changing the last line to "Jesus is the Son of God."); and "Clap,

Clap Your Hands for Joy" (p. 54, SPC).

Have a special time of talking to God. Ask God to forgive us for being disobedient. (See *Talking to God,* p. 7.)

Lead the children in a march around the room for exercise as you sing again, "Clap, Clap Your Hands for Joy."

READING ABOUT GOD'S WORD: Read or tell the Bible story.

Luke 15:11-32 CR p. 152, 154, 155

The Lost Son

Jesus told a story one day about a father and his two sons. The older son worked hard and did everything his father told him to do. But the younger son was not happy. He wanted to leave home.

"Give me my part of the money now, Dad," he said. "I want to leave home. I'll travel to faraway places, find new friends, and have a lot of fun."

The father was very sad to see his young son leave home. But he gave him the money and watched him go.

The young man traveled to a faraway country. He did find a lot of new friends. They saw how much money he had to spend. They helped him spend it, too.

Then one day the young man looked in his money bag. Do you know what he found? Nothing! It was empty! He had spent all the money his father had given him!

Soon he was hungry. He had no place to sleep. His clothes became old rags. He had no friends now. No one would give him food or help him. Finally, the young man got a job feeding pigs.

"Oh, I wish I'd never left home!" he said.

He thought about home. He missed his father. He missed his brother, too.

"Even my father's servants have more food to eat than they need. If I were one of my own father's servants, I'd at least have food to eat. I know what I'll do. I'll go home! I'll ask my father if I can work for him."

Right then the young man started home. It was a long way back home.

Finally, he could see his home in the distance. He could see a man standing near the house. Was that his father? Yes, it was!

The father had been standing, looking down the road. He, too, saw his son in the distance.

"Is that my son who left home?" asked the father. Yes! It was! The father began to run to meet his son. He couldn't run fast enough. When he reached his son, he hugged him! He kissed him. He hugged him again!

"Father, I did wrong in leaving home," said the son. "I'm sorry now. I am no longer good enough to be your son. Will you just let me work for you as one of your servants?"

"No, no! my son," said the father. "I am so happy to have you back home! You are my son who was lost. You are now found.

"Servants," said the father, "bring some clothes for my son. Put a ring on his finger. Put shoes on his feet. Cook a big dinner for him to eat. Let's all be happy. My son is back home!"

Jesus told this story to show us how much God loves us. He said the father is like God. And the boy who left home is like each one of us when we go away from God and do things we know are wrong. But God always forgives us and welcomes us back, just like the father in the story forgave his son and welcomed him back home.

From *A Child's First Book of Bible Stories* by Wanda Hayes. Standard Publishing, pp. 89, 90.

Then tell the children that this is a story Jesus told. We read this story in the New Testament in the back part of our Bibles. Let's read part of it from the Bible. Use the *International Children's Version* to read Luke 15:20-24.

REMEMBERING GOD'S TRUTHS: Remove these picture cards from the *I Pray* section of your file; and use them to teach these four concepts.

- The boy in our story did something wrong. His father did not want him to leave home, but the boy left anyway. Then the boy did something else wrong. He spent his money for the wrong things. You and I do wrong things sometimes, too.

    When you do something wrong and then say, "I'm sorry, God," what does God say?
    <u>I forgive you.</u>

- Yes, talking to God about the good and bad things we do is important.
    When can you talk to God?
    <u>I can talk to God anytime.</u>

- You can talk to God anytime. But can you tell God about your problems?
    When you have a problem, what should you do?

I should pray and ask God to help me.
Does God hear you when you talk to Him? Yes, God always hears me when I talk to Him.

EXPERIENCING GOD'S TRUTHS: Go on a walk around your classroom or the hallway to pretend you and the children are the son walking and talking as you leave home. Stop at a spot (not the usual story spot) and pretend you are taking care of pigs. Discuss the following with the children:

a. How bad it smells and how hard the son had to work.
b. How did the son feel?
c. Did he wish he had obeyed his father and stayed home?
d. Is it better to obey parents or disobey parents?
e. Children are always happier if they obey. Ask, "Who helps you obey?" Let the children answer, *"God helps me to obey."*

Now, let's pretend we are the son walking back home. (Return to story-telling area).

a. Are we glad to see our father?
b. Do we ask him to forgive us?
c. Should we ask God to forgive us for disobeying?

Sit and all fold hands. Have children repeat this prayer phrase by phrase after you.

Dear God/Please forgive us/for all the times we disobey./ Please help us/to always obey our parents/and always obey you./ We love you, God/In Jesus' name,/amen.

d. We just talked to God. Does God hear you when you talk to Him? *Yes, God always hears me when I talk to Him.*

Have the children go to the tables and give each child an activity sheet, "Yes-No Game" (p. 6, *Through the Bible Activities for Preschoolers, Book 3*). Bring two lunch bags for each child in your class. For each child paste bright paper on one side of his lunch bag and print the word **YES** on it. On another bag, paste a piece of dull unattractive paper on one side and write **NO** on that bag. Then staple the plain sides of the two bags together so that the words face out on opposite sides. If you teach 3-year-olds who can not cut, you will need to cut out the individual question cards at home. For older children, let them cut out the question cards in class.

Give each child his double bags and explain the words **NO** and **YES**. With each child, ask each question and let him put the question card in the **YES** bag or the **NO** bag. Then go to the next child at the table and do the game with him. Let other children listen and participate as you play the game with each child at the table. If your class is large, each teacher or helper should play the game with several children.

REVIEWING GOD'S TRUTHS: The son left home and did bad things. He disobeyed God. He spent his money on bad things. Do you think he made new friends while he was away from home? Maybe these new friends told him to do sinful things. Sometimes bad people tell us bad things to do, and we should say, "No, I won't do that." Play the "Obeying Game" described in the *Experiencing God's Truths* section of Lesson 29, on page 87.

Closing prayer: "We thank You, God, that You always love us. Please forgive us when we do disobey You like the boy in our story. In Jesus' name, amen."

(When parents pick up the children, encourage them to play the bag game at home.)

Unit Nine: Jesus' Special Work

Luke 19:1-10

Lesson 34

Bible Verse: To those who believed in his name, he gave the right to become children of God. (John 1:12, NIV)

JESUS FINDS A FRIEND IN A TREE

AS THE CHILDREN ARRIVE: Greet each child in a friendly way and direct him to one of the learning centers. Help the child to place any toy he or she may have brought with him or her in the Safe-Keeping box till after class.

Attendance Check Center: Help each child put pictures of Jesus stickers on the attendance chart. Tell the child, "I'm glad you are my friend. Jesus is your friend, too."

Bible Words Center: See Lesson 28, page 83, for a suggested way of teaching this verse. Help the children recall this verse. Ask, "What people can be children of God?" Help them to reply, "To those who believed in his name, he gave the right to become children of God, John 1, verse 12."

Picture Cards Center: Introduce the picture cards listed in this lesson under *Remembering God's Truths*. Use the game called, "Hide the Picture Cards," described on page 9. Play this game briefly with your students.

At the sound of music from the cassette tape or piano, have the children go to the story area of the room for singing.

SINGING AND TALKING TO GOD: Sing, "Children of God" (p. 61, this book); "God's Family" (p. 90, this book); "This Is My Beloved Son" (p. 30, *Songs for Preschool Children*); "My Best Friend Is Jesus" (p. 58, SPC); "J-E-S-U-S" (p. 50, SPC, change the last line to "Jesus is the Son of God."); and "Clap, Clap Your Hands for Joy" (p. 54, SPC).

Have a special time of talking to God. For this lesson, it would be appropriate to thank God that He forgives us when we say we are sorry.

Lead the children in a march around the room for exercise as you sing "Clap, Clap Your Hands for Joy" (p. 54, SPC).

READING ABOUT GOD'S WORD: Read or tell the Bible story. The *International Children's Version* has a picture of Zaccheus on the page following page 186. Luke 19:1-10

Jesus Finds a Friend in a Tree

Jesus and His disciples were walking toward the city of Jericho. This was the city where Joshua and his army had once marched around the city walls, and God had made the walls fall down.

As Jesus and His twelve helpers entered Jericho, a crowd was already waiting along the streets. One of the men waiting to see Jesus was a tax collector named Zaccheus. Zaccheus had heard about the wonderful things Jesus did—like making a blind man see—and Zaccheus wanted to see Jesus. But Zaccheus was not very tall, and he couldn't get through the crowd.

"Excuse me, sir. Pardon me," Zaccheus may have said. But as Jesus came closer and closer to Zaccheus, the people crowded closer and closer to each other and to the path where Jesus was walking.

Zaccheus wanted to see Jesus. But how could he? He looked around and quickly came up with an answer to his problem.

I know what I'll do, he said to himself. *I will run farther down the road and climb into a tree so I will be above the people. Then no one will be in my way, and I can see Jesus.*

And that's exactly what Zaccheus did. He grabbed a limb and pulled himself up and climbed until he was high enough to see Jesus.

"Here He comes," people were saying. "Jesus is coming this way."

Zaccheus was all ready. He shaded his eyes with his hand so he could see Jesus better. Jesus and His friends walked closer and closer. Zaccheus could feel his heart beating faster and faster. Suddenly, the little man got a big surprise. Jesus stopped right under the tree where Zaccheus was sitting.

Zaccheus wondered what was going to happen next, but he didn't have to wait long. Jesus looked right up at him and said, "Zaccheus, hurry and come down. Today I must stay at your house."

And that's exactly what happened. Zaccheus hurried down from the tree and took Jesus to his house. Zaccheus was very, very happy.

Now, a lot of people in Jericho did not like Zaccheus because he collected tax money for the Roman government, and because he was rich. Most of the tax collectors were very rich because they cheated people. The people knew the tax collectors often took more money for taxes than the people really owed. Then they kept the extra money for themselves.

Or maybe they were jealous because Jesus was going to Zaccheus' house. So when they saw Jesus going with Zaccheus, they grumbled and said, "Jesus is going to stay at the house of a bad man. We don't think Jesus should do that."

Zaccheus did not worry about what people were saying. At his house, he stood and said, "I will give half of what I have to the poor, and if I have taken too much tax money from anyone, I will give back four times as much to that person." Zaccheus wanted to do what was right. He was very happy and very thankful.

"Today, Zaccheus," Jesus said, "you have learned what it means to be saved. You have learned how to live. I came to earth to help people like you. I came to find people who need my help and show them how to live."

From *A Child's First Book of Bible Stories* by Wanda Hayes. Standard Publishing, pp. 92, 93.

REMEMBERING GOD'S TRUTHS: Remove these picture cards from your picture file before class. Be prepared to teach them so your time with the children is fun as well as instructive.

- Zaccheus was sorry for doing wrong.
  When you do something wrong and then say, "I'm sorry, God," what does God say? "I forgive you." (*I Pray* section)
- Zaccheus learned about being in God's family. Who are in God's family?
  All people who love and trust Jesus are in God's family. (*The Church* section) Be sure to explain to the children what it means to love and trust Jesus.
- You can learn about God's family from the special book God's family uses.

What is the Bible?
The Bible is the Word of God. (*The Church* section)

- When Jesus left Zaccheus' house, Zaccheus was happy because Jesus had become his friend.
  Who is your best friend?
  Jesus is my best friend. (*Jesus* section)

EXPERIENCING GOD'S TRUTHS: Have the children go to the tables and give each child an activity sheet, "Holy Bible" (p. 7, *Through the Bible Activities for Preschoolers, Book 3*).

Help the children cut along the black lines and fold the large piece of the paper in half like a book. Provide construction paper and fold in half to form the cover. Let each child glue the white paper to the inside of the colored paper and "Holy Bible" on the outside of the paper.

Teach forgiveness in the following way: Kneel down beside each child to write his name on his paper. But either call or write his name incorrectly. Then say, "I'm sorry I called (or wrote) your name wrong. Will you please forgive me?" Then help the child say, "I forgive you." Then teacher says, "I will try to not do that again." Be sure to correct your mistakes.

Read the inside page to the children and help them learn the verse.

REVIEWING GOD'S TRUTHS: (See *Act It Out* on p. 9.) Give the children an opportunity to role play the Bible story. Bring lots of small pieces of green paper to represent money, a step ladder and two man-size shirts (one white and one colored).

Have your *International Children's Version* open to Luke 19:1-8. Choose a child to be Zaccheus and put a colored shirt on him. Choose a child to be Jesus and put a white shirt on him. Scatter the other children around the room and give several green "money" papers to each child.

Begin telling the story of Zaccheus.

Explain to the children that Zaccheus was sorry for his sin and asked Jesus to forgive his sin. Jesus did forgive Zaccheus, and Zaccheus became part of God's family. Zaccheus then gave the money back to the people.

Closing prayer: "Dear God, thank You for forgiving us when we say we are sorry. We love You. Amen."

Unit 10—Jesus Shows God's Love

GETTING READY FOR UNIT TEN

The theme of this unit is that Jesus showed God's love and power to the world. He loved little children, and the children loved Him. Jesus showed His disciples how to serve one another. He loved us so much He willingly died on the cross so that we could be saved from our sins. He overcame death and lives again in Heaven. We are to tell others of God's love as Jesus did.

Learning Objectives: Some things you should expect your children to accomplish in this unit:

The children should know (1) Jesus is their best friend; (2) Jesus died for them; (3) Jesus is alive today; (4) Jesus will live forever.

The children should feel (1) Thanks to God for His gift, Jesus; (2) Glad that Jesus came to show us that God loves us; (3) Sad that Jesus had to die; (4) Happy that Jesus is alive.

The children should be able to (1) Tell the highlights of each Bible story; (2) Say the Bible verses and state simple answers to concept questions; (3) Tell another person that God loves him or her.

Remember, because of the differences in age and maturity, some children will meet more of these objectives than others will.

Bible Verses: There are no new Bible verses this unit. Each verse has been presented before. Help your children review each verse and remember it. Use the teaching aids or actions suggested in previous lessons.

Books: Several books are suggested for reading at the end of each lesson. These books may be placed in the quiet, book corner of your room. *Kindness* and *The Happiest Day* are suitable for the ages of the children and for the subjects being studied.

Bulletin Board: Continue to use the pictures and theme from the last unit entitled "Jesus Special Work". Add pictures of Jesus that correspond to the stories in each lesson.

THINGS TO DO:

Lesson 35: You will need construction paper and a picture of each child. (Take instant pictures of the children with your camera.) A short-sleeve man's shirt and ten small stones are needed for role playing the story. Gather these items for each child: small feathers, ball fringe, small buttons, cloth squares, and ribbon for the activity sheet.

Lesson 36: Make palm leaves. You will need two large crepe-paper palm leaves and a balloon stick for each child. Cut small sandpaper strips for placing on the activity sheet (two per child).

Lesson 37: Make new attendance charts by cutting out construction-paper crosses (see p. 106). You will need flower seals. For one of the centers, you will need two adult people-type dolls, a small container (jar top) and a tiny towel (¼ of a washcloth). A light snack is suggested, buttered rolls, grape juice, slices of apple, and raisins. You will also need small cups, plates, napkins, a pitcher of water, a basin, and a towel. Have small pieces of terry cloth ready to glue on the activity sheet.

Lesson 38: Potting soil, green-bean seeds, paper cups, newspaper, watering can and tray are needed. Small receiving blankets or pieces of sheet are needed for each child.

Lesson 39: On folded sheets of construction paper (one for each child) draw two large ovals. You will need crayons. Obtain a list of shut-ins from the church office. Get a poster board for each shut-in, and write the words "Jesus Is Alive" at the top. Glue pictures of Jesus in the center, and add pictures of flowers and birds, cut from magazines or old greeting cards.

Unit Ten: Jesus Shows God's Love

Luke 18:15-17

Lesson 35

Bible Verse: To those who believed in his name, he gave the right to become children of God. (John 1:12, NIV)

JESUS AND THE CHILDREN

AS THE CHILDREN ARRIVE: Be enthusiastic as you greet each child and direct him to one of the learning centers.

Attendance Check Center: (See Lesson 27, p. 81.) Help each child place a sticker on his attendance card. Read the sentences on the chart to each one. Say, "Jesus loves you. You are special."

Bible Words Center: (See Lesson 28, p. 83, for a suggested way of teaching this verse.) Ask the children, "What people can be children of God?" Let them answer, "To those who believed in his name, he gave the right to become children of God, John 1, verse 12."

Jesus Loves Me Center: Ask a parent with a Polaroid camera to come to your class to take a picture of each child. Remember to reimburse him for the cost of the film from money your church has set aside for class expenses.

Prepare a brightly-colored piece of construction paper for each child with these words printed on the top:

Jesus loves *(child's name)*.

Let each child have fun having his picture taken. Attach his picture to his paper and write in his name. Tell the children to take the pictures home and hang them in their bedroom.

At the sound of music from the cassette tape or piano, have the children leave the centers and go to the story-circle area of the room for singing.

SINGING AND TALKING TO GOD: Sing, "Children of God" (p. 61, this book); "Let Us Love One Another" (p. 29, *Songs for Preschool Children,* change the last line to "First John 4, verse 7"); "J-E-S-U-S" (p. 50, SPC, change the last line to "Jesus is the Son of God."); "Come to Me" (p. 51, SPC); "My Best Friend Is Jesus" (p. 58, SPC); and "I Love Jesus" (p. 58, SPC).

Have a special time of talking to God. For this lesson it would be appropriate to thank God that Jesus loves children.

Let the children skip around the room and back to the story area.

READING ABOUT GOD'S WORD: Read Luke 18:15-16 from your copy of the *International Children's Version.* "Some people brought their small children to Jesus so that he could touch them. When the followers saw this, they told the people not to do this. But Jesus called the little children to him and said to his followers, 'Let the little children come to me. Don't stop them, because the kingdom of God belongs to people who are like these little children.'"

Then read or tell the Bible story.

Luke 18:15-17   CR p. 150

Jesus and the Children

Jesus talked about God in such a loving way that mothers wanted Him to hold their children and ask God to bless them. One day after Jesus had been teaching, the women started bringing their babies and other young children to see Jesus.

Some women carried babies in their arms, and some children walked beside them. This was exciting to the mothers and children.

"There He is!" they said. "I see Jesus."

The children were smiling and laughing. Jesus was smiling because He loved them so. But Jesus' helpers were not smiling.

They may have thought that Jesus was too tired to welcome the babies and children. They said to the mothers, "Stop! Go away. Jesus does not have time for children. He has more important work to do. Leave Him alone."

The mothers and children stopped. They were so disappointed. They couldn't talk to Jesus.

But before they could say anything, the mothers and the children heard a kind voice saying, "Let the children come to me. Don't stop them." It was Jesus.

Then He said, "God's kingdom is for people like these children. They love me and are happy to do what I ask."

Jesus loved the children. He picked them up and held them in His arms.

He touched each child and prayed to God. Perhaps He said, "Father, bless these children. Keep them healthy. Help them to be good and obey You. May they love You as You love them." The Bible says that Jesus blessed the children that day.

From *A Child's First Book of Bible Stories* by Wanda Hayes. Standard Publishing, p. 94.

REMEMBERING GOD'S TRUTHS: Prepare for this section by removing these five picture cards from the *Jesus* section of your file.

- When Jesus was on earth, some of the children thought He was a very special friend.
  Who is your best friend.
  Jesus is my best friend.
- Yes, Jesus is such a good friend. He left Heaven and came to earth especially for you.
  What is the best gift God has given you?
  Jesus is the best gift God has given me.
- When Jesus was on earth, He showed us He was a friend who loves us.
  How did Jesus show you that He loved you?
  Jesus died for me.
- Yes, Jesus died for each of us.
  Will Jesus every die again?
  No, Jesus will live forever.
- If Jesus will live forever, does that mean He is alive today?
  Is Jesus alive today?
  Yes, Jesus is alive today.

EXPERIENCING GOD'S TRUTHS: Let the children role play today's story (see *Act It Out,* on p. 9). You will need a man's short-sleeve shirt for each child in your class and ten small stones.

Tell the children they are going to each put on a shirt to dress up like children in Jesus' day. Let some of the children pretend to be children in Jesus' time who are gathered together counting stones.

Let one of the children (who is not in the counting game) run to the group and say, "Jesus is coming. Hurry, let's go see Him." The playing children answer, "Hurray! Jesus. Let's go see Jesus!" Children then leave their game and run to see Jesus.

The teacher pretends to be Jesus and enthusiastically greets each child by name and hugs him. Repeat the acting out several times letting other children be the child who announces as Jesus is coming.

Have the children go to the tables and give each child an activity sheet, "Jesus Loves All Children" (p. 8, *Through the Bible Activities for Preschoolers, Book 3).* Have objects such as small feathers, small pieces of cloth, ball fringe, ribbon, and small buttons for the children to glue on their pictures. Use this opportunity to say things like, "Jesus loves children with brown skin. Jesus loves children with red skin," etc. As the children glue the items on the pictures, talk about how much Jesus loves them too!

REVIEWING GOD'S TRUTHS: Play "Hide the Picture Cards" (as described on p. 9,) just like the children in Jesus' day used to play hide-and-seek games.

We are happy that Jesus loves us too. We show our happiness by praising God.

Closing prayer: "Dear God, thank You for loving each one of us. Please help us to share Your love with others. Amen."

Unit Ten: Jesus Shows God's Love

Bible Verse: Give thanks to him and praise his name. (Psalm 100:4, NIV)

Matthew 21:1-17

Lesson 36

CHILDREN PRAISE JESUS

AS THE CHILDREN ARRIVE: Be sure to praise the children for a special quality you see in them today. Tell them how happy you are to see them. Direct each one to one of the learning centers.

Attendance Check Center: Use the attendance cards made in Lesson 27. Add a Jesus sticker to the card, and let each child take his card home after class.

Bible Words Center: (See Lesson 4, p. 21, for a suggested way of teaching this verse.) Ask the children, "What does the Bible say about giving thanks?" Lead them in doing the actions suggested on page, as they answer, "Give thanks to him and praise his name, Psalm 100:4." Repeat till you think the children know the verse. Sing the song, "Give Thanks," on page 23.

Making Palms Center: Buy palm branches from a florist. Also bring other signs of spring—pussy willow, a tulip, a daffodil, etc. Show the children each item, and teach them the name of each. Break apart each frond of the palm branch, and give one frond to each child. Or provide two green crepe-paper palm leaves for each child. You will need to cut these out before class. Make the leaves 20 to 30 inches long and six to eight inches wide. Glue one leaf to a balloon stick, or heavy strip of cardboard, and glue the other leaf to the back. Let the children practice waving their palm branches as they say the Bible verse. Collect the palm branches and save them for use later in the lesson.

At the sound of music from the cassette tape or piano, have the children go to the story area of the room for singing.

SINGING AND TALKING TO GOD: Sing, "Go to Heaven" (p. 90, this book); "Praise Ye the Lord" (p. 28, *Songs for Preschool Children*); "Sing, Little Children, Sing" (p. 37, SPC); "Please Him, Please Him" (p. 39, SPC, change the words to "Praise Him"); "In His Bible Book" (p. 41, SPC, use "praise"); and "Come To Me" (p. 51, SPC).

Have a special time of talking to God. Read *Talking to God* on page 7. For this lesson it would be appropriate to lead the children in praying thank-you prayers.

Sing "Head and Shoulders" (p. 5, SPC).

READING ABOUT GOD'S WORD: Read the verse for this lesson from your *New International Version*. "Give thanks to him and praise his name, Psalm 100:4." Then read or tell the Bible story.

Matthew 21:1-17

Children Praise Jesus

Jesus was a king. But He was not the kind of king who sits on a throne and rules a country. Jesus was the King of everyone who would love and obey God.

The Jewish people had waited a long time for the kind of king Jesus was. They had waited a long time for the Savior God would send.

God had promised Abraham, Isaac, and Jacob that He would bless everyone through Someone born into their family. Hundreds of years later, that special person was born. He was Jesus, God's own Son.

Jesus knew that it was time to let the people know that He was the King God had promised to send. He told two of His disciples, "Go to the town near you, and there you will find a mother donkey and her baby colt. Tell whoever speaks to you that the Lord needs them, and right away that person will send the donkeys with you."

Jesus knew that the Bible said, "Your king is coming to you, riding on a donkey."

The disciples went to the town and got the donkeys just as Jesus told them. They spread their coats on the young donkey so Jesus could ride on it. Then Jesus began His slow, bumpy ride up the hill to Jerusalem.

It was Passover time again—time for the people to worship at the temple. The city was crowded, and many people were so sure that Jesus was going to be their king that they greeted Him in a special way. They cut palm branches from the trees and spread them in the road for Jesus' donkey to walk on. Many people put their outer coats in the road, too, so the donkey carrying Jesus could walk on them.

When the people saw Jesus coming into the city of Jerusalem riding on the donkey, they waved palm branches and praised Him saying, "Hosanna to the Son of David. Blessed is He who comes in the name of the Lord. Hosanna in the highest."

What a sight! Jesus riding on the donkey and hundreds of people on the streets and in the windows, waving branches and shouting.

In Jerusalem Jesus got off the donkey and walked into the temple where he healed people who could not see or walk. And even in the temple, children were shouting to Jesus, "Hosanna to the Son of David!"

Some of the teachers in the temple did not want Jesus to be their king, and they did not believe God had sent Him. It made them angry to hear the children praising Jesus. They said to Him, "Do you hear what the children are saying?"

"Yes," Jesus said, "God is letting these children praise me with these words. He is happy with them." And Jesus was pleased with the children, too, because He loved them very much.

From *A Child's First Book of Bible Stories* by Wanda Hayes. Standard Publishing, pp. 96, 97.

REMEMBERING GOD'S TRUTHS: Use the pictures from your picture files suggested on page 6. You will need four for today's lesson. Help the children learn the answers to the questions.

- The people were happy to welcome Jesus as a He rode into Jerusalem. God had promised to send a Savior for the people.
  Who is God?
  God is our Heavenly Father. (*Heavenly Father* section)
- Some people who waved palm branches did not know who Jesus really was. But you know. Who is Jesus?
  Jesus is the Son of God. (*Jesus* section)
- The people were happy to see Jesus. We would like to see Jesus, too. He is living in Heaven.
  Who can go to Heaven?
  All people who love and trust Jesus can go to Heaven. (*Heavenly Father* section) Be sure to explain to the children what it means to love and trust Jesus.
- Jesus loved his friends in Jerusalem. He loves you very much too.
  How did Jesus show you that He loved you?
  Jesus died for me. (*Jesus* section)

EXPERIENCING GOD'S TRUTHS: Give the children an opportunity to praise Jesus. Use the palm branches from the learning center. You will also need to gather rhythm-band instruments or other play instruments like kazoos or boxes for play drums. Bells sewn to elastic bands are fun to shake. Plastic containers with beans or rice inside are good shakers. Be sure the top is taped on securely. Provide an instrument for each child.

Sing "Please Him, Please Him" (p. 39, SPC, changing the words to "Praise Him.") as you wave the palm branches.

Sing "Give Thanks" (p. 23, this book) while using the instruments. Sing "J-E-S-U-S" (p. 50, SPC, change last line to "Jesus is the Son of God.") as the children march around the room, using the rhythm instruments. Have the children place the instruments in a box when you are finished with this song.

Sing "Clap, Clap Your Hands for Joy" (p. 54, SPC) as the children clap. Sing the previous song using "stamp, stamp your feet for joy."

Lead the children to the tables and give each an activity sheet, "Praising Jesus" (p. 9, *Through the Bible Activities for Preschoolers, Book 3*). Help the children glue sandpaper strips on the rhythm blocks. Let the children color the instruments on the paper as you write each child's name on his paper.

REVIEWING GOD'S TRUTHS: Play "Going on a Trip" (see p. 9) because Jesus and His friends were taking a trip to Jerusalem.

Closing prayer: "We are glad that we can praise You, Jesus, as we clap, march, and sing songs of praise. We love You. Amen."

Unit Ten: Jesus Shows God's Love

Bible Verse: I will trust and not be afraid. (Isaiah 12:2, NIV)

John 13:1-17

Lesson 37

A SPECIAL SUPPER

AS THE CHILDREN ARRIVE: Greet each child warmly and direct him to one of the learning centers.

Attendance Check Center: Help the children make new attendance charts for use in Lessons 36-41.

Before class, draw a cross for each child on a piece of construction paper

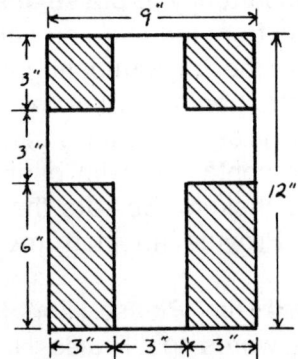

Print each child's name on the top.

In class, help each child carefully cut out his cross. If you have three- and young four-year-olds in your class, you will probably have to cut for them. Tape the crosses to the wall at the children's eye level. Each week provide each child with a flower sticker to glue onto his cross.

Bible Words Center: See Lesson 8, page 30, for a suggested way of teaching this verse. Ask, "What should you do when you are afraid?" Let the children take turns answering, "I will trust and not be afraid, Isaiah 12:2."

Foot Washing Center: Later in this lesson you will be doing real foot washing. This idea is new to the children. In order to prepare them for the experience so that they will not be silly about it, give them a chance to play some foot washing with dolls.

Bring to class at least two adult people-type dolls (Example, like Barbie and Ken). Dress these dolls in robes which you can make from scraps of cloth. Also bring a very small container of water (example: small jar top) and a tiny towel (perhaps ¼ of a washcloth).

In class, describe the following to the children:

"When Jesus was on the earth, people wore sandals, not tennis shoes and socks like you wear. Sandals do not cover up feet very well. So when people like Jesus and His disciples walked down the dusty road, their feet got dirty. It was polite in Jesus' time to wash the feet of a person who came to visit you. Sometimes a servant washed the feet of each guest.

"I have brought some doll people, dressed like Jesus' friends used to dress. You may pretend you are the servant and wash this pretend person's feet."

Let the children do the washing and drying.

At the sound of music from the cassette tape or piano, have the children go to the story area of the room for singing.

SINGING AND TALKING TO GOD: Sing, "Let Us Love One Another" (p. 29, *Songs for Preschool Children,* change last line to "First John 4, verse 7"); "He Careth for You" (p. 32, SPC, change "careth" to "cares."); "God Loves Me," (p. 36, v. 1, SPC); "I Will Trust in God" (p. 38, SPC, change lines 2, 3 and 5 to "Isaiah twelve, two"); "The Twelve Apostles" (p. 57, SPC); and "Jesus, the Son of God" (p. 50, v. 3, SPC).

Have a special time of talking to God. For this lesson, it would be appropriate to ask God to help us show love to each other just like Jesus showed love.

Lead the children in singing "The Twelve Apostles" (p. 57, SPC).

READING ABOUT GOD'S WORD: Read or tell the Bible story. (There is an excellent picture of the foot washing in the thirteen story of *Frances Hook Picture Book,* and the *International Childrens Version,* p. 218.)

John 13:1-17   CR p.163

A Special Supper

Jesus and His twelve disciples were all together for the last time. And everything was ready for them to eat the Passover meal together.

Jesus knew that He would not be with His disciples much longer. So that evening, Jesus took a towel and tied it around His waist. Then he poured water into a bowl, kneeled down on the floor, and washed His disciples' feet. Then He dried them with the towel. Jesus went around the table and washed and dried the feet of each of His disciples.

When He finished, He sat back down at His place at the table. Then Jesus said, "I am your Teacher and Lord, and I have washed your feet. If I am willing to be a servant to you, then you should be willing to be a servant to others."

And while they were eating, Jesus did something else for the disciples to remember. He took a piece of bread, thanked God for it, and broke it into pieces. Then He gave the pieces to His friends and said, "This bread is like my body which well be nailed to the cross and broken for you. Eat the bread to remember me."

Then Jesus took a cup of grape juice and thanked God for it. He passed it around for His disciples to drink.

"This juice is like my blood that I will shed on the cross," Jesus said. "Drink the juice to remember me."

Peter and Andrew, James and John, and the other disciples did not understand that Jesus would die soon. But after He died, arose, and went back to Heaven, they ate the bread and drank the grape juice just as Jesus told them. They remembered everything Jesus had said and what He had done for them.

From *A Child's First Book of Bible Stories* by Wanda Hayes. Standard Publishing, p. 98.

Now read from your copy of the *International Children's Version*. Read John 13:3-5, 34, 35.

REMEMBERING GOD'S TRUTHS: Remove the following picture cards from your picture file. You will need four for this lesson.

- In our story, Jesus ate supper with His best friends. We read this story in our Bibles.
  What is the Bible?
  <u>The Bible is the Word of God.</u> (*The Church* section)
- You know another answer that is almost like that.
  Who made you?
  <u>God made me.</u> (*About Me* section)
- Jesus told His friends that He had to go away from them. You know the answer to another question about going far away.
  If you go far away, who will take care of you?
  <u>God will take care of me.</u> (*God's Care* section)
- Jesus ate this special supper with His friends. He gave them bread and other things to eat.
  Who gives you food?
  <u>God makes food grow for me.</u> (*God's Care* section)

EXPERIENCING GOD'S TRUTHS: Guide the children into thinking about Jesus' Supper. Try to convey these three truths to your class:
1. Jesus showed love by washing the disciples' feet.
2. Jesus ate a special supper with His friends.
3. Jesus told His friends that He would have to leave them. He would be killed on a cross.

Center the conversation around these three truths. Do *not* talk about the bread representing Jesus' body and the cup His blood. Preschoolers do not understand symbolism.

Provide a special supper time by bringing a small basin, a pitcher for water, and a towel, and preparing the following for *each* child:
  a buttered roll
  a small cup of grape juice
  a small piece of peeled apple
  a few raisins
  a paper plate and napkin

If there are more than eight children in your class, ask someone to help you. Supply your helper with a pitcher, basin and towel.

Take the children to the nearest rest room and have them wash their hands in preparation for Jesus' special supper. Fill the water pitcher while you are there. Return to the classroom and ask each child to remove his shoes and place them near the door. They are to leave on their socks.

Gather the children in the story area and tell them about the time when Jesus asked His apostles to get a special supper ready. Assign a different table-setting job to each child. Let only a few work at a time while others watch, to save confusion.

Ask the children to take off their socks. Talk to the children about how Jesus washed each of His disciple's feet, as you wash and dry each child's feet. If you have a helper, let him wash the feet of half the class in the other end of the room so each of you can have meaningful personal conversation with each child. Be sure the children are seated and calm during the foot washing.

Then invite the children to sit at the table. Let each child say "Thank You, God, for this food."

All may eat together as you explain, "This food is like the food Jesus ate. Jesus ate the special supper with His helpers. Jesus wants us to remember that He died for us while we eat this special supper. When they were eating, Jesus told the apostles that He would have to leave them soon. He would be killed soon. But Jesus told them He would come back."

Have the children clean their places at the table and come back to their seats. Give each child an activity sheet "Jesus Shows Love" (p. 10, *Through the Bible Activities for Preschoolers, Book 3).* From an old wash cloth cut 1" x 1" pieces. Plan one piece per child. Read the paper to them. Help each child glue the piece of towel to the picture on Jesus' hand. Write the child's name on his paper.

REVIEWING GOD'S TRUTHS: Review today's Bible verse. Be sure each child knows it.

Read *Kindness* by Jane Belk Moncure if it is available. Introduce the book by talking about Jesus' kindness to His disciples.

Closing prayer: Dear God, I am glad that Jesus is my friend. Please help me to be kind to others as Jesus was. Amen."

Unit Ten: Jesus Shows God's Love

Bible Verse: We love (Him) because he first loved us. (1 John 4:19, NIV)

Luke 22:39—23:56

Lesson 38

THE SADDEST DAY

AS THE CHILDREN ARRIVE: Greet each child warmly and direct him to one of the learning centers.

Attendance Check Center: (See Lesson 37, on p. 106.) Help the children put a flower sticker on their crosses.

Bible Words Center: (See Lesson 19, p. 58, for a suggested way of teaching this verse.) Ask, "Why do we love Jesus?" Encourage the children to answer, "We love (Him) because he first loved us, 1 John 4:19." Do the motions suggested in Lesson 19. Repeat.

Planting Seeds Center: You will need potting soil, green-bean seeds, paper cups (to plant the seeds in) with a small hole in the bottom of each, small pitcher (for watering the seeds), newspaper to cover the table, and a paper-covered tray for the teacher to carry the plants home.

In class, let the children fill the cups with soil, plant the seeds, and water them. Tell the children you will place each cup on your tray and write the child's name on the paper covering of the tray close to his cup. Tell them you will take the seeds and cups home, and you will bring them to next week's meeting. Be sure each child present has an opportunity to plant seeds.

At home, plant several additional seeds in cups for any additional children next week and a few extra cups in case some of the seeds do not germinate. Keep the tray of seed cups in a warm place and water midweek.

At the sound of music from the cassette tape or piano, have the children go to the story area of the room for singing.

SINGING AND TALKING TO GOD: Sing, "Trust in the Lord" (p. 25, *Songs for Preschool Children);* "I Will Trust in God" (p. 38, SPC, change line 2, 3 and 5 to "Isaiah twelve, two"); "Hallelu" (p. 53, SPC); "Jesus Is the Son of God" (p. 59, v. 3, SPC); "Song of Praise" (p. 75, v. 2, SPC); and "We Love Jesus" (p. 69, this book).

Have a special time of talking to God. Thank God that Jesus died for each child.

Sing "Song of Praise" again as the children march around the room.

READING ABOUT GOD'S WORD: Read Luke 23:32-34 from your copy of the *International Children's Version*. (See the picture on the page before p. 219.)

Then read or tell the Bible story.

Luke 22:39-23:56   CR p. 165, 166, 167, 168, 169, 170

The Saddest Day

Jesus' friends were sad. They could hardly believe what was happening. Jesus was sad, too. He knew that some bad men wanted to kill Him. They were looking everywhere for Jesus. Soon they would find Him.

So after their time together at the Passover supper, Jesus and His disciples went to a garden to pray. Jesus wanted to pray in a quiet place because He was so sad. Jesus knew where a nice quiet place was—a garden where olive trees grew. Jesus had been in this garden before. The garden was called Gethsemane.

While Jesus was praying in the garden, Judas Iscariot came with the bad men. He pointed out Jesus by kissing Him and some soldiers arrested Him like He was a criminal. They grabbed Jesus and took Him away.

Jesus had not done anything wrong, but some people did not like Him. They did not believe He was God's Son. So they told lies about Jesus. Then they got the Roman governor, Pilate, to say Jesus must be crucified. He must be nailed to a cross like a criminal to die.

The Roman soldiers beat Jesus. They made fun of Him because He said He was a king. They put a crown of thorns on His head and a purple robe around His shoulders. They spit on Him and slapped Him.

Jesus walked down the street, carrying a wooden cross on His back. He was so weak and the cross was so heavy that He fell down. Then the soldiers made a man named Simon carry Jesus' cross the rest of the way.

A lot of people followed Jesus. Some of them cried. They knew what the soldiers were going to do. At the top of a hill, Jesus was nailed to a cross. Two other men, both of them bad men, were nailed to crosses too. One was on a cross to the right of Jesus, and the other on a cross to the left of Him. Above Jesus' head on the cross was a sign that read *King of the Jews.*

Jesus' disciples, His mother, and other friends stood watching. They were very sad to see Jesus hanging there. They did not want to leave Him alone. Jesus had done nothing wrong, but He looked at the soldiers and said, "Father, forgive them because they do not know what they are doing." Jesus was not angry.

One of the men on a cross beside Jesus said, "Jesus, remember me when You come into Your kingdom."

Jesus said, "Today you will be with me in Paradise."

Jesus was not afraid to die. He knew what God was going to do. He knew that after He died, no one who believed in God would need to be afraid to die. But His friends did not understand this yet. They felt very sad.

While Jesus was on the cross, He did something else for someone. He had already asked God to forgive the soldiers who crucified Him. He had already forgiven the robber and promised that He would be with Him when he died. Now Jesus did something special for His mother, Mary. He looked at her and His disciple, John, who were standing near the cross with some women.

Then Jesus said, "Woman, look at your son." But Jesus did not mean himself. Then He said to John, "Look at your mother." They knew what Jesus meant. From that time on, John took care of Mary as a member of his own family.

When Jesus had done everything God wanted Him to, He said, "It is finished." Then He died.

Later, two men, Joseph of Arimathea and Nicodemus, took Jesus' body, wrapped it in nice linen cloth with sweet-smelling spices and laid it in a new grave in a garden.

From *A Child's First Book of Bible Stories* by Wanda Hayes. Standard Publishing, pp. 102, 103.

REMEMBERING GOD'S TRUTHS: Remove the following picture cards from your picture file. The first four are from the *Jesus* section of your file, the last one is from the *God's Care* section.

- God sent Jesus as a gift to us.
    What is the best gift God has given you?
    <u>Jesus is the best gift God has given me.</u>
    Why did Jesus come to earth?
    <u>Jesus came to show us that God loves us.</u>

- When Jesus was on earth, He surely showed His love for you.
  How did Jesus show you that He loved you?
  <u>Jesus died for me.</u>
  Will Jesus ever die again?
  <u>No, Jesus will live forever.</u>
- When Jesus died, the disciples were sad. When you are alone and sad, what should you do?
  <u>I should ask God to help me.</u>

EXPERIENCING GOD'S TRUTHS: Children can identify with feelings. Help them understand how Jesus felt when He was arrested and put on the cross. Below is a list of feelings Jesus might have had. The list on the right gives corresponding feelings children might have and the possible situations children might be in when they have those feelings.

Jesus Might Have Felt	I Feel
Angry at soldiers	Angry at my mother sometimes
Afraid of the soldiers	Afraid of big noises
Worried when with Pilate	Worried about punishments
Forgiving toward His enemies	Forgiving toward enemies
Love for others and God	Love for family, friends, and God.

Guide children in acting out the part of the story about the actual arrest. (Do not act out the crucifixion.) Talk about how Jesus felt. Use the chart to guide the discussion. Let the children tell of times when they have felt afraid, etc. Do not plant negative pictures in their minds by telling them of bad situations. Let the children take the lead in describing their ideas.

Have the children go to the tables and give each child the two pages to make the booklet, "Who Loves Me?" (pp. 11 and 12, *Through the Bible Activities for Preschoolers, Book 3*). Help the children fold and staple their booklets. Write each child's name on his book.

Let the children color the cover picture. Let them gather around you at the story circle so that you can read the book to them.

REVIEWING GOD'S TRUTHS: Let the children inspect their seeds. Tell them they may take the seeds home next week. Then have them pretend to be seeds. Use the pieces of sheet or blankets for the "It's a New Day" game, page 10, or bring covers from home for each child. Talk about seeds being put in the ground and covered with soil (cover child with blanket). Talk about the rain and sun and how the seed slowly grows (child slowly stands up).

Closing prayer: "Thank You, God, for helping seeds to grow. Everything You make is good. Thank You for Jesus. Amen."

Unit Ten: Jesus Shows God's Love

Bible Verse: To those who believed in his name, he gave the right to become children of God. <u>(John 1:12, NIV)</u>

John 20:1-18; Luke 24:1-12

Lesson 39

THE HAPPIEST DAY

AS THE CHILDREN ARRIVE: Greet each child warmly and direct him to one of the learning centers.

Attendance Check Center: (See Lesson 37, p. 106.) Help the children put flower stickers on the cross-shaped charts.

Bible Words Center: (See Lesson 28, p. 83, for a suggested way of teaching this verse. Ask the children, "What people can be children of God?" Help them answer, "To those who believed in his name, he gave the right to become children of God, John 1:12."

Sad-Happy Center: Supply for each student a piece of drawing paper folded in half with large ovals drawn on each half.

In class, talk about the emotions of happy and sad. Let the children draw a sad face on the oval on the left side of their paper and a smiling face on the oval on the right side of their paper. Remind them about the sadness of the disciples when Jesus died. Tell them that in today's story the disciples will be happy.

Let each child tell of one time when he was sad this week, and one time when he was happy. As they tell the event, let them show the appropriate face on their paper.

At the sound of music from the cassette tape or piano, have the children go to the story area of the room for singing.

SINGING AND TALKING TO GOD: Sing, "Children of God" (p. 61, this book); "Sing, Little Children, Sing" (p. 37, *Songs for Preschool Children*); "In His Bible Book" (p. 41, SPC, use "praise"); "Hallelu" (p. 53, SPC); "Jesus" (p. 58, SPC, change last line to "He rose up from the dead."); "I Love Jesus" (p. 58, SPC); and "Jesus, the Son of God" (p. 59, v. 3, SPC).

Have a special time of talking to God. For this lesson it would be appropriate to thank God that Jesus is alive.

To celebrate how happy we are that Jesus is alive, lead the children in a march around the room as they sing "Hallelu" again.

READING ABOUT GOD'S WORD: Read from your copy of the *International Children's Version*, Matthew 28: 1, 5-9. (If you have a copy of the *Francis Hook Picture Book*, show the picture of Jesus and the women found in story fourteen.) Ask the children to stand up and clap because they are happy that Jesus is alive. Have them sit down to listen as you read or tell the Bible story.

John 20:1-18 Luke 24:1-12 CR p. 171, 172, 173, 174

The Happiest Day

After Jesus died, His friends buried His body. Then Pilate had the grave opening covered with a big stone, and put Roman soldiers by the grave to guard it. Pilate was afraid that someone would steal Jesus' body and then say that He had risen from the dead. Pilate thought Jesus had caused a lot of trouble, and he didn't want any more trouble.

Peter and Andrew, James and John, and the other disciples were so sad because Jesus had been crucified. And the women who followed Jesus were sad too. Everyone who loved Him knew He had done nothing wrong. He didn't deserve to die. Jesus had loved and helped everyone.

Sunday morning came, and Mary Magdalene went to the garden where Jesus was buried. She was bringing sweet-smelling spices to put by His body. But when she got to the grave, she was surprised. The big stone had been rolled away from the door to the grave.

Oh, no! Mary thought. *Jesus' body has been moved. Where could it be?* Then she hurried away to tell Simon Peter and John.

While Mary was gone, several other women came to the grave and found it empty. They didn't know what could have happened to Jesus' body either.

Then suddenly, the women saw two men standing beside them in shining white clothes. They were so afraid that they couldn't look at the men.

One of the angels said, "Why are you looking for Jesus here among the dead people? He is not here. He has risen. Remember what He told you? He said that bad men would crucify Him, but on the third day He would rise again." Now the women remembered. They hurried to tell the disciples what the angels said.

Mary Magdalene came to Simon Peter and John before the other women and said, "They have taken Jesus out of the grave, and we don't know where they have put Him."

Peter and John were surprised, too. They ran as fast as they could to the garden where Jesus had been buried. John got to the grave first, but he didn't go in. When Peter arrived, he went in and saw the cloths that had been wrapped around Jesus. But there was no body.

Then John went inside the tomb, too, and saw that it was empty. Then they both knew what Mary Magdalene had said was true.

Mary Magdalene was so sad. She stood outside the empty grave crying. While she was crying, she bent down and looked into the tomb. She was surprised to see two angels dressed in white. One angel was sitting where Jesus' head had been; the other angel where His feet had been. The angels asked Mary, "Woman, why are you crying?"

"Because they have taken Jesus away, and I don't know where they have put Him," she said, still crying.

Then Mary turned around. A man was standing there.

The man asked, "Woman, why are you crying? Who are you looking for?"

Mary thought He might be the gardener, so she said, "Sir, if you have taken Jesus away, tell me where He is."

The man spoke again. "Mary!" He said. Now Mary knew who He was.

She turned to Him and said, "Teacher!"

Mary wasn't sad any more. She had seen Jesus. He was alive!

From *A Child's First Book of Bible Stories* by Wanda Hayes. Standard Publishing, pp. 105, 106.

REMEMBERING GOD'S TRUTHS: Remove the following picture cards from your picture file and be prepared to teach them.

- Jesus died and came back to life. He could do this because He is so special.
  Who is Jesus?
  Jesus is the Son of God. (*Jesus* section)
- Jesus' friends were so happy to find out that Jesus was alive.
  Is Jesus alive today?
  Yes, Jesus is alive today. (*Jesus* section)
- We, too, are happy that Jesus is alive.
  When you are happy, what should you do?
  I should thank God for making me happy. (*I Pray* section)
- Yes, Jesus is alive, but
  Will Jesus ever die again?
  No, Jesus will live forever. (*Jesus* section)
- The Bible says that Jesus died so that our sins could be forgiven.
  When you do something wrong and then say, "I'm sorry, God," what does God say?
  I forgive you. (*I Pray* section)

EXPERIENCING GOD'S TRUTHS: Help the children share the good news that Jesus lives! Select a sick or shut-in person from your local church and try to get a picture of that person. If your class has more than five children, choose one shut-in for each group of children.

Bring to class one piece of poster board for each shut-in and lots of happy pictures (people, flowers, birds, etc.) and pictures of Jesus.

Show the picture of the shut-in to the children and talk about how we can show that we love Jesus by helping this person. (Call the shut-in by name.)

Write on the top of the poster, "Jesus Is Alive. We Love Jesus." Paste the picture of Jesus in the center of the poster and draw a circle around it. Let the children paste the pretty pictures on the poster. Older children could cut out the pictures and/or draw their own pictures.

During the week, deliver the poster to the shut-in. If possible, plan to take several children from your class with you. Be sure to make an appointment with the shut-in in advance so he or she will be prepared for your coming.

After making the poster, give each child an activity sheet, "Jesus Is Alive" (p. 13, *Through the Bible Activities for Preschoolers, Book 3*.) Write each child's name on the back of his paper as you say, "(*child's name*) is happy that Jesus is alive." Let each child color the picture. As the children color, say, "Jesus was killed on the cross. His heart stopped beating. His brain stopped working. His body was dead. All the people who loved Him were very sad. They put His dead body into a tomb. But Jesus did not stay dead. God made Jesus come back to life. His heart started beating again. His brain started working again. He walked out of the tomb. When His friends saw Him, they were full of joy. We are joyful, too, because Jesus is alive."

REVIEWING GOD'S TRUTHS: (This is a follow-up on the seed planting in last week's lesson). Show the children how the seeds have started growing and are now tiny plants that have come up out of the ground. Explain that this plant reminds us of Jesus. He was dead and put into a tomb. Then He came out of the tomb just like the plant has come out of the earth. The plant is alive. Jesus is alive. Let each child take his plant home.

Closing prayer: "We thank You, God, that You turned a sad day into a happy day. We are glad that Jesus is alive today! Amen."

Unit 11—Jesus' Special Friends Do His Special Work

GETTING READY FOR UNIT ELEVEN

The theme of this unit will be that Jesus' special friends carried on His special work after He returned to Heaven. Jesus walked and talked with His disciples after He arose from the dead. He ate with them. After Jesus went back to Heaven, they were given power to be His witnesses. They were eager to tell others that Jesus had overcome death and was alive. They knew He could save them, and they obeyed Him. Jesus wants us to tell others about Him, to love Him, and to obey Him.

Learning Objectives: Some things you should expect your children to accomplish in this unit:

The children should know (1) Jesus really came back from the dead; (2) Jesus lives in Heaven today; (3) God answers their prayers; (4) God's church is people.

The children should feel (1) Happy that Jesus is alive; (2) Eager to tell someone about Jesus; (3) Thankful for the people who are the church.

The children should be able to (1) Tell the highlights of the Bible stories; (2) Say the Bible verses by memory; (3) State simple answers to concept questions; (4) Pray for a new missionary friend.

Remember, because of the differences in age and maturity, some children will meet more of these objectives than others will.

Bible Verses: There are no new Bible verses presented this quarter. Continue to review the ones suggested in each lesson.

Books: Several books are suggested for reading at the end of each lesson. These books may be placed in the quiet, book corner of your room. *God Made Everything; My Book of Prayers; I Can Pray to God;* and *God Made Me* are suitable for the ages of the children and for the subjects being studied.

Bulletin Board: Put the paper on the board and write the heading, *Our Church Is People.* Let the children add drawings of people they know in the church to the mural each week. If your church has an extra pictorial directory, cut pictures of people known to the children and let them paste the pictures on the paper.

THINGS TO DO:

Lesson 40: You will need twelve Bible-times people (see p. 114, **The Eleven Disciples Center** for this week and next. On 3" x 5" index cards write big numbers 1-11. For a snack, provide fish-shaped crackers (or a loaf of uncut bread) and tuna fish, small plates and napkins. Other items needed are reinforcements, envelopes, U-shaped magnet, paper clips, and dowel-rod fishing poles.

Lesson 41: You will need pictures of all types of people—all races—cut from magazines. You will also need the twelve Bible-times people from Lesson 40 and small blankets for each child.

Lesson 42: Make new attendance charts, and use Children-of-the-World stickers (see p. 118). You will need posterboard, shelf paper with rough drawings of continents on it, and the magazine pictures of people of the world used in Lesson 41.

Lesson 43: For one of the learning centers, you will need play people and a toy house. On a piece of poster board write this heading, *"When We Pray."* Glue six pictures, cut from magazines, of things we pray about—include thanks and petition prayers. Be sure to add the picture of a missionary your church supports.

Unit Eleven: Jesus' Special Friends Do His Special Work

Bible Verse: Give thanks to him and praise his name. (Psalm 100:4, NIV)

John 21:1-14

Lesson 40

BREAKFAST WITH JESUS

AS THE CHILDREN ARRIVE: (See *As the Children Arrive* on p. 7.) Greet each child warmly and direct him to one of the learning centers.

Attendance Check Center: (See Lesson 37, p. 106.) Help the children place flower stickers on their cross-shaped attendance charts.

Bible Words Center: (See Lesson 4, p. 21, for a suggested way of teaching this verse.) Ask the children, "What does the Bible say about giving thanks?" Do the actions with them as they answer, "Give thanks to him and praise his name, Psalm 100:4."

The Eleven Disciples Center: You will need twelve pretend people to represent Jesus (who should look special) and the eleven remaining disciples. These pretend people could be Fisher-Price play people, people made from pipe cleaners, or Bible-time people cut from old pictures. You will also need eleven 3" x 5" cards with the numbers 1-11 written, one number per card. Be sure to make numbers large and clear.

In class let the children spread out the cards in numerical order. Let them put one pretend person on each card and have fun counting the people and cards. Then sing this song to the tune of "Ten Little Indians":

Peter, Andrew, James and John,
Philip, Thomas, Bartholomew,
Matthew, Thaddeus, James the Less, and
Simon were with Jesus.

Let the children point to the pretend people as they sing. (Don't be surprised if a bright student informs you that Judas is not there because he turned against Jesus.) Save these twelve Bible-times people for use in Lesson 41.

At the sound of music from the cassette tape or piano, have the children go to the story area of the room for singing.

SINGING AND TALKING TO GOD: Sing, "Give Thanks" (p. 23, this book); "Praise Ye the Lord" (p. 28, *Songs for Preschool Children*); "He Careth for You" (p. 32, SPC, change to "cares"); "Hallelu" (p. 53, SPC); and "Jesus, the Son of God" (p. 59, v. 3, SPC).

Have a special time of talking to God. For this lesson it would be appropriate to thank God that Jesus is alive today.

Let the children pretend to be rowing a boat for exercise.

READING ABOUT GOD'S WORD: Mark John 21:2-14 in your copy of the *International Children's Version* so that you can read directly from it or tell the Bible story.

Breakfast With Jesus

Some of the followers of Jesus were together. They were Peter, Thomas, Nathanael, James, John, and two other followers. They were by the Sea of Tiberias.

Peter said, "I am going fishing."

The others decided they would go with him. So they got into the boat and went out to sea. They fished all night. They caught no fish.

Early the next morning, Jesus stood on the shore, but His disciples did not know it was Jesus.

"Friends, haven't you caught any fish?" Jesus called to them.

"No," they answered.

He then told them to throw their net into the water on the right side of the boat, for they would find fish there. They did what He said to do. They caught so many fish that they could not pull their net back into the boat.

"It is the Lord!" John said to Peter.

As soon as Peter heard him say this, he wrapped his coat around himself, for he had taken this outer garment off while he was fishing. Then he jumped into the water. The other men went to shore in the boat, dragging the net which was full of fish.

They were only about 100 yards from the shore. (That is the length of a football field.)

When they got out of the boat and were on the land, they saw a fire of hot coals. On the fire were some fish cooking, and some bread was there, too.

"Bring some of the fish you have caught," said Jesus.

Simon Peter climbed back into the boat and pulled the heavy net to the shore. It was full of large fish—153 fish to be exact! Even though that many fish are very heavy, the net was not torn.

"Come and eat," said Jesus.

None of the followers dared ask Him who He was. They knew it was Jesus.

Then Jesus came, took the bread, and gave it to His followers. He also shared the fish with them.

This made the third time Jesus had been with His followers since He was raised from the dead.

REMEMBERING GOD'S TRUTHS: Use these four picture cards from your picture file.

- In our story Jesus had gone away. He was not with His friends.
    - If you go far away, who will take care of you?
    - <u>God will take care of me.</u> (*God's Care* section)
- But Jesus' friends knew that Jesus loved them.
    - How did Jesus show you that He loved You?
    - <u>Jesus died for me.</u> (*Jesus* section)
- Jesus kept His promise. He came back. He ate with His friends.
    - Who gives you food?
    - <u>God makes food grow for me.</u> (*God's Care* section)
- Jesus' friends were so glad He was alive.
    - Is Jesus alive today?
    - <u>Yes, Jesus is alive today.</u> (*Jesus* section)

EXPERIENCING GOD'S TRUTHS: Plan a pretend breakfast with Jesus. Bring food to class for your meal. Some suggestions: a loaf of uncut bread, tuna fish, and grape juice (small portions for each child). Don't forget plates and napkins.

Let the children help you get the pretend breakfast ready. Thank God for the food. Talk about the fact that Jesus ate with His disciples. He was alive.

When everyone finishes eating, help the children clear the table. Give each one an activity sheet, "Fish" (p. 1, *Through the Bible Activities for Preschoolers, Book 4).* You will need a piece of string or cord about eighteen inches long for each child, four reinforcements for each child. Put one reinforcement on the nose of each fish and punch a hole in the paper where the reinforcement is.

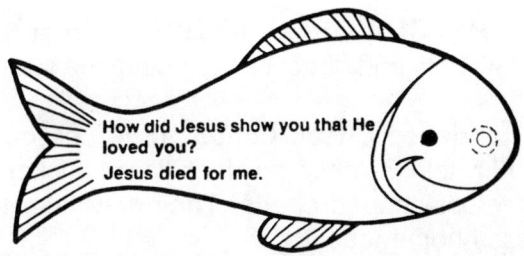

(If you teach three-year-olds, cut out each fish from the take-home paper and put each child's fish in a different envelope.)

Let the children cut out the fish. Help the children string the fish (through the reinforced hole) onto the string. Review the questions and answers on each fish several times with the children as they work. Print each child's name on one of his fish.

REVIEWING GOD'S TRUTHS: Let the children go fishing. You will need a U-shaped magnet, four paper clips, and a dowel-rod fishing pole with string. If you have more than five children in your class, you will need another set. Tie the magnet to the string of a dowel-rod pole. Put a paper clip onto each of the fish that you cut from one of the activity sheets used earlier in this lesson. Check to be sure that the magnet picks up each fish.

Place the four fish (with paper clips on them) on the floor. Let the children take turns catching one fish and answering the question you read from the fish. After all four fish are caught, put them back on the floor and give another child a turn.

Closing prayer: "We thank You, God, that Jesus is alive today. You are so powerful! You brought Jesus back to life. We love You. Amen."

Unit Eleven: Jesus' Special Friends Do His Special Work Acts 1 and 2

Bible Verse: To those who believed in his name, he gave the right to become children of God. (John 1:12, NIV).

Lesson 41

JESUS RETURNS TO HEAVEN

AS THE CHILDREN ARRIVE: Greet each child warmly and direct him to one of the learning centers.

Attendance Check Center: (See Lesson 37, p. 106.) Help the children place flower stickers on their cross-shaped charts. They may take their crosses home today.

Bible Words Center: (See Lesson 28, p. 83, for a suggested way of teaching this verse.) Ask the children, "What people can be children of God." Help the children clap as they say, "To those who believed in his name, he gave the right to become children of God, John 1:12."

Saying Good-bye to a Friend Center: The purpose of this learning center is to give the children a feeling of what it must have been like for the apostles to say good-bye to Jesus. Use the twelve pretend people figures from Lesson 40. In class talk about how we feel when we say good-bye to a friend who is moving away. Let the children play with the figures on the floor, name them, and sing the song from Lesson 40. Let the table top be the pretend Heaven. As the Jesus figure goes up into Heaven, let the children decide what the apostles might have said, and how they might have felt.

At the sound of music from the cassette tape or piano, have the children go to the story area of the room for singing.

SINGING AND TALKING TO GOD: Sing these songs: "Go to Heaven" (p. 90, this book); "Children of God" (p. 61, this book); "Clap, Clap Your Hands for Joy" (p. 54, *Songs for Preschool Children);* "The Twelve Apostles" (p. 57, SPC); and "Jesus, the Son of God," (p. 59, v. 4, SPC).

Have a special time of talking to God. Prepare at home by reading the section in the front of this book called *Talking to God.* For this lesson, it would be appropriate to thank God for Heaven.

Lead the children in a march around the room for exercise as you sing "Children of God" again.

READING ABOUT GOD'S WORD: From your copy of the *International Children's Version* read Luke 24:50-52. "Jesus led his followers out of Jerusalem almost to Bethany. He raised his hands and blessed them. While he was blessing them, he was separated from them and carried into heaven. They worshiped him and then went back to the city very happy."

Now read or tell the Bible story. Stop reading where indicated. *Acts 1 and 2 CR p. 177, 178, 179*

Jesus Returns to Heaven and His Church Begins

Jesus knew it was time for Him to leave the earth. He had not planned to stay with His friends very long. He had come to work, and now His work was all done. It was time for Him to go back to His Father in Heaven. It was also time for Jesus' disciples to do their special work.

Jesus told Peter and the other disciples, "After I leave you, I will ask God to send the Holy Spirit to help you. But you must wait in Jerusalem until God sends you this power from Heaven."

Jesus took His friends to the top of a mountain. They knew something was about to happen. They watched Jesus closely. Then He raised His hands and asked God to bless them. And as the eleven disciples watched, Jesus began to go up into the air, right off the ground! He was going up and up, higher and higher. Nothing was picking Him up. His body was just rising up and up. Jesus was going back to Heaven.

The disciples watched until they could not see Him anymore. And while they were staring into the sky, two men in white appeared and said, "Why are you men standing here looking into the sky? Jesus has gone back to Heaven. Someday He will come back from Heaven in the same way." (Stop reading here, continue reading later in lesson.)

The eleven disciples went back to Jerusalem and chose a twelfth disciple to take Judas Iscariot's place. Then they waited for God's power to come as Jesus had promised.

On a special day called Pentecost, many of Jesus' friends were together in Jerusalem. Peter and the other disciples were there too. Suddenly, three surprising things happened. A very loud noise that sounded like a strong wind filled the house where they were. Then a small flame of fire was in the air over each disciple's head, and each of them began speaking in other languages. God's Holy Spirit had given them the power that Jesus promised before He went back to Heaven.

Many men and women from different countries were staying in Jerusalem. They had come for a special worship time to remember God's law. They heard the loud noise, too, and came to where the apostles were. The people were very surprised.

"How can we hear what they are saying in our own languages?" they asked. "These men are not from our countries. They are from Galilee. What does this mean?"

Then Peter stood up and told everyone what the loud noise and the flames and the speaking in other languages meant. Peter said, "God has sent this power just as He sent Jesus. Although bad men nailed Jesus to a cross, God made Him alive again. Jesus is at the right hand of God now. He is the Lord and King that the Bible said was coming. And if you are sorry for the things you have done wrong, God will forgive you. Then He will give you the power of the Holy Spirit to help you. God has made this promise to you and to your children and to everyone who loves and obeys Him."

When the people heard what Peter said, they wanted to obey God. They wanted to have their sins forgiven. That day, three thousand people were baptized.

This was the kingdom Jesus had talked about. He was King in Heaven. The people who obeyed Him and were baptized were called His church.

From *A Child's First Book of Bible Stories* by Wanda Hayes. Standard Publishing, pp. 107-109.

REMEMBERING GOD'S TRUTHS: Use these three picture cards from your picture file. Show them to the children and discuss each concept stated on the back of the card.
- Jesus had died. Then Jesus had come back to life.
  Will Jesus ever die again?
  No, Jesus will live forever. (*Jesus* section)
- How about today?
  Is Jesus alive today?
  Yes, Jesus is alive today. (*Jesus* section)
- Jesus is now in Heaven. Would you like to be with Him?
  Who can go to Heaven?
  All people who love and trust Jesus can go to Heaven. (*Heavenly Father* section) Be sure to explain to the children what it means to love and trust Jesus.

EXPERIENCING GOD'S TRUTHS: Lead the children to the tables by playing Follow the Leader. Give each child activity sheets "A Book for You" (pp. 2-3, *Through the Bible Activities for Preschoolers, Book 4*). Help each child assemble and staple her book. Let the children color the cover picture.

While the children are still at the story circle, have them lie down on the floor and cover with small blankets. Read the remainder of the Bible story (beginning at "The eleven disciples....") Show the children the pictures on the page after page 250 of the *International Childrens Version*.

REVIEWING GOD'S TRUTHS: From the section of your picture file called "The Church" remove this picture card:
  Who are the church?
  All the people who love and trust Jesus are the church. (*Church* section) Be sure to explain to the children what it means to love and trust Jesus.

Talk about the fact that people are the church. They are more important than the building.

Closing prayer: "Dear God, You began Your church many years ago. Thanks for giving us Your Word, the Bible, as our guide for the church. Please help us to love one another. In Jesus' name, amen."

Unit Eleven: Jesus' Special Friends Do His Special Work　　　Acts 10

Bible Verse: To those who believed in his name, he gave the right to become children of God. (John 1:12, NIV)

Lesson 42

CORNELIUS UNDERSTANDS

AS THE CHILDREN ARRIVE: Greet each child warmly and direct him to one of the learning centers. Be sure every child goes to the **All People Center** today.

Attendance Check Center: Make a new attendance chart for your class. Use a piece of cardboard or tag board for drawing enough lines to accommodate all the names of the children in your class, plus possible newcomers. Leave space for eleven stickers after each child's name. Buy Children-of-the-World stickers from your Christian bookstore for your class to use the next eleven weeks. Write these words on the top of the chart: "We love and trust Jesus"

Bible Words Center: (See Lesson 28, p. 83, for a suggested way of teaching this verse.) Ask the children, "What people can be children of God." Help them clap in rhythm as they say, "To those who believed in his name, he gave the right to become children of God. John 1:12."

All People Center: The purpose of this learning center is to introduce the idea that God wants all people to love and trust Him. Bring to class a roll of plain wrapping paper or shelf paper. Cover the top of the table with paper, and draw some lines and circles on it to represent pretend countries. Also bring crayons.

Show the children how to draw stick figures on one of the countries. Tell the children these are pretend Jewish people, God's chosen people. Then let them draw stick people in other countries. Explain that when Jesus was on the earth, the people who knew Him were almost all Jewish people. Help the children get a visual picture of the Jews only as believers in Jesus. This will prepare them for the story later.

At the sound of music from the cassette tape or piano, have the children go to the story area of the room for singing.

SINGING AND TALKING TO GOD: Sing: "Let Us Love One Another" (p. 29, *Songs for Preschool Children,* change last line to "First John 4, verse 7"); "Children of God" (p. 61, this book); "God's Family" (p. 90, this book); "Jesus" (p. 58, SPC, change last line to "He wants everybody to know."); "Hallelu" (p. 53, SPC); and "Jesus Is the Son of God" (p. 56, SPC).

Have a special time of talking to God. For this lesson it would be appropriate to thank God that Jesus loves all children.

Lead the children in a march around the room for exercise as you sing "The Marching Song" (p. 11, SPC).

READING ABOUT GOD'S WORD: Mark <u>Acts 10</u> in your copy of the *International Children's Version* so that you can read directly from it, or tell the Bible story.

<u>Acts 10</u>

Cornelius Understands

Cornelius was a soldier. He was the leader of one hundred men. He and all the people who lived at his house worshiped God. The Bible says Cornelius was a religious man. He gave much of his money to the poor and prayed often to God.

Cornelius knew about God, but not God's Son, Jesus.

One afternoon, Cornelius had a dream. In his dream an angel of God told Cornelius to send some of his men to another town to get Peter.

"God has heard your prayers," said the angel. "He knows what you have given to the poor. He remembers you, Cornelius."

The angel gave Cornelius instructions for finding Peter. Then the angel left.

Cornelius called three of his men and sent them to find Peter. He instructed them to bring Peter to him.

The next day, Peter had a dream, too. (This happened before Cornelius' messengers got to the house where Peter was staying.) It was at noon, and Peter was on the roof of the house, praying. In the dream, God told Peter that all kinds of people (all colors, and all ages) can be in God's family.

Peter was still thinking about his dream when the men arrived.

"Three men are coming for you," the Holy Spirit told Peter. "Go with them. I have sent them to you."

Peter went down from the rooftop and said to the three men, "I'm the one you are looking for. Why have you come?"

The men told Peter about Cornelius and asked him to go with them to Cornelius' house. The next day, Peter and some of his Christian friends went with the messengers to visit Cornelius.

Peter taught Cornelius and his family and friends about Jesus.

"I really understand now that every person is the same to God," Peter said. "God accepts everyone who worships Him and does what is right. It does not matter what country a person comes from. Jesus is the Lord of all people!"

Cornelius and the others who heard Peter's message about Jesus believed in Jesus. Peter ordered them to be baptized in the name of Jesus Christ. They obeyed. They were a part of God's family.

REMEMBERING GOD'S TRUTHS: Remove the following picture cards from your picture file. In class, be enthusiastic as you teach these concepts.
- At the beginning of our story Cornelius did not know who Jesus was. But he did know who God is. Do you?
  Who is God?
  God is our Heavenly Father. (*Heavenly Father* section)
- Cornelius also knew who made the world.
  Who made the world?
  God made the world. (*Heavenly Father* section)
- Peter visited Cornelius and told Cornelius about Jesus.
  Who is Jesus?
  Jesus is the Son of God. (*Jesus* section)
- Cornelius believed in Jesus and became part of God's family.
  Who are in God's family?
  All people who love and trust Jesus are in God's family. (*Church* section) Be sure to explain to the children what it means to love and trust Jesus.

EXPERIENCING GOD'S TRUTHS: Sing the song, "Jesus Loves the Little Children" as you march around the room. Stop at the map drawing done in the **All People Center**.

You will need pictures of people from all over the world and poster board.

Ask the children, "Do you remember what Peter learned in our Bible story? Peter said, 'I really understand now that to God, every person is the same. God accepts everyone who worships him and does what is right.'" (Acts 10:34, *International Children's Version*)

Show the children one of the pictures of a child from another country. Talk about the fact that this child lives far across the ocean; talk about his skin, eyes, and hair color. Ask the children, "Does Jesus love this child? Yes, Jesus loves everyone." Repeat with each picture. Write on the poster "God wants all people to love and trust Jesus, and do what is right." Read the words to the children several times, remembering that they cannot read themselves. Let the children glue pictures of people of the world on the poster.

Use the activity sheet, "Many People" (p. 4, *Through the Bible Activities for Preschoolers, Book 4)*. Give each child one crayon, and tell him to hold it under the table. Help each child point to the picture in the top, left corner of his paper. Read the words, and ask, "Does God want this person to love and trust Him?" If the child says. "Yes," let him put a circle around that child. Use this procedure for each picture. Have the child draw his picture in the blank square.

REVIEWING GOD'S TRUTHS: Play the "Pop-Up Game," using the picture cards listed above. Directions are found on page 9.

Closing prayer: "We are glad, dear God, that You love all people. We know You want them to love You, too. Please help us to tell them about Your love. In Jesus' name, amen."

Unit Eleven: Jesus' Special Friends Do His Special Work   Acts 12:1-17

Bible Verse: Be kind . . . to one another.   Lesson 43
(Ephesians 4:32, NIV)

A PRAYER MEETING

AS THE CHILDREN ARRIVE: Greet each child warmly and direct him to one of the learning centers.

Attendance Check Center: (See Lesson 42, p. 118) Have "Children-of-the-World stickers for the children to place on their attendance chart. Talk about the country the child on the sticker represents.

Bible Words Center: (See Lesson 2, page 14, for a suggested way of teaching this verse.) Use the jigsaw puzzle made in Lesson 2 to review this verse. Help the children put the puzzle together. Ask, "What does the Bible say about being kind?" Help them answer, "Be kind . . . to one another, Ephesians 4:32." Talk about the kind things people are doing in the pictures on the puzzle.

Missionary Center: Cover the table with plain paper (shelf paper or wrapping paper) and draw a picture of a house on one corner, or place a toy house on the table corner. Provide several play people (toy people or pictures of people cut out of magazines and glued to cardboard).

In class, place one of the pretend people in or near the house and the other pretend people at the other end of the table.

Teach the concept that *a missionary is a person who goes to another place to help people learn about Jesus.*

Say the words of the definition as you walk the pretend person across the table to the group of people. Then let each child take a turn walking the pretend person and saying the words of the definition.

At the sound of music from the cassette tape or piano, have the children go to the story area of the room for singing.

SINGING AND TALKING TO GOD: Sing, "Pleasing God" (p. 26, v. 2, *Songs for Preschool Children);* "Trust in the Lord" (p. 25, SPC); "God's Friends" (p. 86, SPC, change "Noah" to "Peter"); and "We're Here in Our Church" (p. 35, SPC, change the title and lines 4 and 8 to read, "In our church building").

Have a special time of talking to God. Prepare at home by reading the section in the front of this book called *Talking to God.* For this lesson, it would be appropriate to thank God for letting us talk to Him.

Lead the children in the "Action Song" (p. 5, SPC).

READING ABOUT GOD'S WORD: Read from your copy of the *International Children's Version* the following verses, Acts 12:12-14. Then read or tell the Bible story.

Acts 12:1-17   CR p. 183

A Prayer Meeting

John Mark, his mother, and their Christian friends were having a prayer meeting. They were asking God to protect Peter and keep him safe, because a wicked king had put Peter in jail.

Was Peter afraid? Was he worried? No, not at all. He was sound asleep between two guards in his prison cell.

While Peter was sleeping and his friends were praying, God was doing His work. Suddenly, an angel appeared and a light shone into Peter's dark cell. The angel touched Peter's side, woke him up, and said, "Get up, quickly."

The guards did not move. They did not see the angel or the light. They did not see the chains fall off Peter's hands, or hear the angel say, "Put on your clothes and your sandals. Wrap your coat around you, and follow me." God had closed the eyes of the guards so none of them saw Peter follow the angel out of the prison.

Peter did what the angel asked. Peter kept following the angel. He followed the angel outside of the prison and into a street. Then suddenly the angel was gone.

Peter hurried to the house of John Mark and his mother, Mary. He knocked on their door.

Rhoda, the servant girl, heard Peter. But she was so excited, she didn't open the door. She ran to tell the others the good news and left Peter standing outside.

Rhoda ran right into the prayer meeting and said, "Peter is standing at the door!"

The Christians were happy to hear how God had sent His angel to save Peter. They said, "Thank You, God, for hearing our prayers. Thank You for taking care of our friend, Peter."

From *A Child's First Book of Bible Stories* by Wanda Hayes. Standard Publishing, p. 110.

REMEMBERING GOD'S TRUTHS: Help the children learn the answers to these questions found on the picture cards in the *I Pray* section of your picture file.

- The title of the story today is "A Prayer Meeting." I know you pray, too.
  When you pray, what are you doing?
  When I pray, I am talking to God.
- The people in our story were praying in a house.
  Where can you pray?
  I can pray anywhere.
- When Rhoda opened the door and saw Peter, she was very happy.
  When you are very happy, what should you do?
  I should thank God for making me happy.
- When you pray, you often thank God for things. Sometimes you ask God to forgive you.
  When you do something wrong and then say, "I'm sorry, God," what does God say?
  I forgive you.

EXPERIENCING GOD'S TRUTHS: Make a poster of pictures of things we pray about when we pray.

At home, prepare a piece of large poster board or shelf paper by printing these words at the top, **When We Pray.** Cut out from a magazine pictures of things we can pray about. Include "thank you" and "petition" items. (Example, Picture of a teacher—"Thank You, God, for our teachers"; picture of rain—"God, please send us rain," etc.) You will need about six pictures, including a picture of a missionary (preferably one the children know).

In class, ask the children to hide their eyes while you hide the pictures in various parts of the room. Have the children leave the story area when you say, "Go," and try to find the pictures. When one picture is found, tell all the children to stop looking and return to the story area. Discuss the picture and then have the children close their eyes and fold their hands and repeat the prayer after you. Example, "Dear God, please send us rain to help our food grow. In Jesus' name, amen." Then paste the picture on the poster board or shelf paper. Repeat until all the pictures are found.

Say, "It is important that we pray for missionaries. Who is a missionary?" The children who were in the **Missionary Center** will be able to answer, "A missionary is a person who goes to another place to help people learn about Jesus." Have the children return to the tables and give each one an activity sheet, "Praying for Missionaries" (p. 5, *Through the Bible Activities for Preschoolers, Book 4*). Point to the picture of a missionary your church supports whose picture is on the prayer poster. If this missionary has a child, the teacher can talk to the class about the missionary's child. If pictures of the missionary family are available, the teacher might want to get copies for each student. These pictures could be attached to the back of the take-home paper.

Read the paper and write in the name of the missionary and encourage the children to pray for this missionary each day. Write each child's name on the back of his paper.

REVIEWING GOD'S TRUTHS: Let the children draw pictures to send to your missionary family. Write on each picture, "We pray for you!"

If your church does not have a missionary family to feature, you can select a mission home for children that is nearby and pray for the children and adults there.

Review today's Bible verse by saying, "We did a kind thing today when we drew pictures for our missionary friend and told him or her that we will pray for him or her. So we are doing what the Bible tells us to do. What does the Bible say about being kind?" Help the children say, "Be kind . . . to one another, Ephesians 4, verse 32."

Closing prayer: Pray for the missionary family mentioned earlier, and thank God for letting us help them.

Unit 12—New Friends Become Jesus' Followers

GETTING READY FOR UNIT TWELVE

The theme of this unit is that after Jesus returned to Heaven, people were needed to carry on His work. There were many new people who believed and obeyed Jesus' teachings and became a part of the church. They became His helpers. The Ethiopian took the Good News about Jesus to his country. Saul became a friend of Jesus, received a new name, Paul, and told many people about Jesus. Dorcas used her talents and skills to help others. She loved others because she loved God. These new followers eagerly told of their love for God and His Son, Jesus, wherever they went. God wants us to tell others about Him, too.

Learning Objectives: Some things you should expect your children to accomplish in this unit:

The children should know (1) The Bible is the Word of God; (2) That God can change people; (3) Prayer is talking to God.

The children should feel (1) Confident that God helps them when they are afraid; (2) Happy that God will help them change their behavior; (3) Willing to share with others.

The children should be able to (1) Tell the highlights of the Bible stories; (2) Say the Bible verses and state simple answers to concept questions; (3) Tell what a missionary is.

Remember, because of the differences in age and maturity, some children will meet more of these objectives than others will.

Bible Verses: All Bible verses in this unit are review verses. There are ten verses taught and reviewed in this curriculum. Use the teaching aids from previous lessons to help the children commit these verses to memory.

Books: Several books are suggested for reading at the end of each lesson. These books may be placed in the quiet, book corner of your room. *Helping Makes Me Happy; When I Grow Up; The Very Best Book of All;* and *Choosing* are suitable for the ages of the children and for the subjects being studied.

Bulletin Board: Display pictures of the people in each of the Bible lessons.

THINGS TO DO:

Lesson 44: You will need Children-of-the-World stickers, a toy cash register, play money, five or six Bibles, a variety of books, and shopping bags.

Lesson 45: You will need to bring newspapers, eight juice glasses, and four colors of food coloring (see p. 125). For the activity sheets, you will need to cut small yellow construction-paper "suns" for each child, and construction paper "cookies." Prepare notes to send home to the parents telling them of the sharing activity for Lesson 46 (see p. 129).

Lesson 46: Make small construction-paper name tags, 2" x 5" in size, with these words written on them, "I am happy to share with you." Attach these tags to the gifts the children bring to share. Arrange with the teacher of another class to visit her class. Ask how many children are in the class. Ask your children to bring that number of items for sharing. Plan to have extra items in case someone forgets or you have a visitor. Provide paper bags for each child you will be sharing with (see p. 129, *Experiencing God's Truth*). You will need small pieces of cookies to glue on the activity sheet.

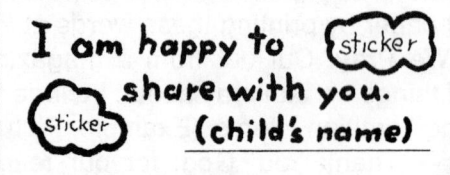

Lesson 47: You will need a medical kit, Bible, picture books, and a play print set or a typewriter for a learning center. See *Experiencing God's Truths,* page 131. Items you will need are a suitcase, a Bible, and a child's Bible storybook. You will need only red, green, yellow, and blue crayons for each child for the activity sheet.

Unit Twelve: New Friends Become Jesus' Followers

Bible Verse: To those who believed in his name, he gave the right to become children of God, (John 1:12, NIV)

Acts 8:26-38

Lesson 44

AN ETHIOPIAN READS GOD'S WORD

AS THE CHILDREN ARRIVE: Greet each child warmly and direct him to one of the learning centers.

Attendance Check Center: (See Lesson 42, p. 118.) Help the children place a Children-of-the-World sticker on the attendance chart. Let the children choose a sticker and talk about the country the child on the sticker represents.

Bible Words Center: Use the song, "Children of God," page   of this book to review John 1:12.

God's Word Center: This learning center will prepare the children for the *Experiencing God's Word* section of the lesson which will use the same items. You will need a cash register, play money, five or six Bibles.

In class, give each child five pretend dollar bills. Let the children take turns coming to your pretend bookstore. They will ask to buy a Bible, count out the five dollar bills for you and take a Bible. After the children understand, one child might like to be the clerk and the others buy Bibles from the clerk.

At the sound of music from the cassette tape or piano, have the children go to the story area of the room for singing.

SINGING AND TALKING TO GOD: Sing these songs: "The Church" (p. 90, this book); "Let Us Love One Another" (p. 29, *Songs for Preschool Children,* change last line to "First John 4, verse 7"); "Thank You, God" (p. 40, SPC); "In His Bible Book" (p. 41, SPC, use "trust"); "Jesus, the Son of God" (p. 59, v. 4, SPC); and "God's Friends" (p. 86, SPC, change "Noah" to "Philip").

Have a special time of talking to God. Thank God for the Bible.

Lead the children in a march around the room for exercise as you sing "God's Friends" again.

READING ABOUT GOD'S WORD: Mark Acts 8:26 in your copy of the *International Children's Version* so that you can read directly from it or tell the Bible story.

Acts 8:26-38   CR p.185

An Ethiopian Reads God's Word

Philip was one of Jesus' followers. One day, an angel of the Lord told Philip to go south on a road that led from Jerusalem to Gaza. This was a lonely desert road.

Philip did not know why God wanted him to go to this road, but he obeyed God. He was alone on the dusty road. Suddenly he saw a chariot (a two-wheeled cart pulled by a horse or horses) on the road. A man was sitting in the chariot. He was an Ethiopian—a man from the country of Ethiopia. The man had dark skin, and he was wearing beautiful clothes. He was a very important and wealthy man. The man was reading.

Do you know what he was reading? He was reading the Bible. It was Isaiah 53:7, 8. Isaiah is in the Old Testament of the Bible.

Philip ran to the chariot.

"Do you understand what you are reading?" Philip asked the man.

"How can I understand unless someone explains it to me?" answered the Ethiopian.

He invited Philip to climb into the chariot and sit with him. Philip told the Ethiopian about how Jesus died for him. He told him about how much Jesus loved him and all people. The Ethiopian was so glad to hear this good news about Jesus.

Philip traveled along the road with the officer. Soon they came to some water.

"Look, here is water!" said the Ethiopian. "What is keeping me from being baptized?"

"If you believe with all your heart you may," said Philip.

"I believe that Jesus Christ is the Son of God," said the officer.

He ordered the chariot to stop. Both Philip and the Ethiopian got out of the chariot. They both went down into the water, and Philip baptized him.

REMEMBERING GOD'S TRUTHS: Use the picture cards from your picture file. In class, be enthusiastic as you teach these concepts.

- When the Ethiopian was reading the Bible by himself, he had a problem. He did not understand what he was reading. God saw the Ethiopian with the problem and God loved him and sent him help.
    Does Jesus love children who have problems?
    <u>Yes, Jesus loves everyone.</u> (*About Me* section)
- Philip got into the chariot with the Ethiopian and helped the Ethiopian understand the part of the Bible he was trying to read. Philip told the Ethiopian that the Bible says that God loves us all.
    Why did Jesus come to earth?
    <u>Jesus came to show us that God loves us.</u> (*Jesus* section)
- The Ethiopian was reading part of the Bible.
    What is the Bible?
    <u>The Bible is the Word of God.</u> (*The Church* section)
- When the Ethiopian understood the Bible, he decided to start to love and obey Jesus. Then he was part of God's family. Another name for God's family is the church.
    Who are the church?
    <u>All people who love and trust Jesus are the church.</u> (*The Church* section) Be sure to explain to the children what it means to love and trust Jesus.

EXPERIENCING GOD'S TRUTHS: Give the children an opportunity to buy a Bible. In addition to items used in the **God's Word Center,** you will need fairy-tale books, adult books, attractive children's Christian books, a children's Bible with modern, attractive pictures like the *International Childrens Version,* and shopping bags.

The purpose of this experience is to show the children that God's Word is the most important book of all.

Tell the children, "We are going to make a pretend bookstore. How shall we move the tables and chairs to make our room look like a bookstore?" When children have helped you arrange the room, let them lay out the books in the pretend bookstore. Tell the children that the teacher will be the bookstore salesperson, and one of the children may be a child buying a book. Let one of the children volunteer to be the book buyer and give him some money. Tell him he is going to pretend to go to the store to buy a new Bible.

The pretend salesperson should take the initiative in the conversation, offering to help the child. If a helping teacher is available, he or she should help the child act out the part of the child buying the book. The clerk should use these words as much as possible:

"God's Word"

"We love the Bible."

"The Bible is the special book God's family uses."

"The Bible tells us all the special things God wants us to know."

"The Bible is the Word of God."

Let different children take the part of the bookstore salesperson and the book buyer. Help them keep the conversation constructive.

One child may ask to buy a fairy-tale book. The clerk could say, "Why don't you also buy a Bible? The Bible is the Word of God." If the child refuses the Bible, don't force him. Ask him for the money to pay for his book and thank him for his purchase.

Have the children return to the tables and give each one an activity sheet, "The Best Book" (p. 6, *Through the Bible Activities for Preschoolers, Book 4*). Print each child's name on the back of his paper. Let each child color the picture of the Bible only. Put a happy face on the paper of those who follow your directions. Now let the children color the whole picture if time permits.

REVIEWING GOD'S TRUTHS: Read *The Very Best Book of All,* by Fran Flournoy (#3591) if it is available. Or play the "Going on a Trip" game (see p. 9).

Have a closing prayer. "Dear God, thank You for giving us the Bible. We want to learn more about You. We love You. Amen."

Unit Twelve: New Friends Become Jesus' Followers

Bible Verse: Children, obey your parents.
(Ephesians 6:1, NIV)

Acts 9:1-22

Lesson 45

SAUL BECOMES A FRIEND

AS THE CHILDREN ARRIVE: Greet each child warmly and direct him to one of the learning centers.

Attendance Check Center: Help the children place Children-of-the-World stickers on the attendance chart by their names. Talk about the country the sticker represents. Stress that God loves the people of this country.

Bible Words Center: (See Lesson 3, p. 17, for a suggested way of teaching this verse.) Use the picture and word cards to review the verse. Help the children to put the verse in order. Then ask, "What does the Bible say about obeying?" Say with the children, "Children, obey your parents, Ephesians 6:1." Sing the verse to the tune of "Pleasing God" (p. 26, SPC), and use the same song to review the Bible verse, "Be kind ... to one another." (Ephesians 4:32, NIV).

Change Center: Bring to class newspapers to cover the table, eight juice glasses, four colors of food coloring, and a pitcher of water. Put two drops of food coloring in the bottom of each of four glasses to make four different colors. Hide the bottles of food coloring so that the children do not get them and ruin their clothes.

When the children arrive, help them pour water into an empty glass. Talk about how the water has no color. Change the color of the water by pouring it into a glass containing the food coloring. Use the word, *change,* as often as possible as you assist the children in pouring water into various glasses to change the color of it. Remember that red and yellow make orange, blue and yellow make green, and blue and red make purple.

Ask the question, "What makes the water *change* color?" The food coloring does! Tell the children that we will hear a story later about a man who changed. God changed him!

At the sound of music from the cassette tape or piano, have the children go to the story area of the room for singing.

SINGING AND TALKING TO GOD: Have fun singing these songs: "Pleasing God" (p. 26, v. 2, *Songs for Preschool Children,* put Ephesians 6, verse 1, to the music.); "My Best Friend Is Jesus" (p. 58, SPC); "Song of Praise," (p. 75, v. 2, SPC); "Jesus' Helpers" (p. 87, SPC); and "Pleasing God" (p. 26, SPC, put Deuteronomy 6:18 to the music).

Have a special time of talking to God. For this lesson it would be appropriate to thank God that He wants people to love and trust Him.

Lead the children in a march around the room for exercise as you sing "The Marching Song" (p. 11, SPC).

READING ABOUT GOD'S TRUTHS: Read Psalm 95:3, "The Lord is the great God." Then say, "Is God great enough to change a person from hating Jesus to loving Jesus? Let's read a story about that." (If you teach 3-year-olds, leave out the first, third and fourth paragraphs of the story, and tell the last half of the story in words they can understand.

Acts 9:1-22 CR p.186, 187, 188

Saul Becomes a Friend

Saul was angry, *Who do those Christians think they are?* he thought to himself. *They really believe that Jesus is the Son of God. And that preacher, Stephen, had the nerve to call the Jewish leaders killers and betrayers! He deserved to die. He was an enemy of God.*

Saul was a young man who knew a lot about the Bible, but he did not understand that Jesus is the Savior the Bible talked about.

"I want the names of all Christians," Saul said. "I want to arrest them and put them into prison."

Then a preacher named Stephen was stoned to death for teaching about Jesus. Saul held the coats of the men while they threw big rocks at Stephen and killed him. Saul believed he was doing the right thing. He thought that Stephen was bad and deserved to die.

Saul was so angry with the Christians that he

went to the high priest of the temple in Jerusalem and asked permission to look for Christians in the city of Damascus. He wanted to arrest them and bring them back to Jerusalem. Saul really believed that the Christians were enemies of God, but Saul himself was the real enemy of God.

Saul started on his trip to Damascus with some of his friends. Suddenly, a bright light from the sky flashed around him, and Saul fell to the ground. Then he heard a voice, saying, "Saul, Saul, why are you hurting me?"

"Who are you, Lord?" Saul asked. And the voice said, "I am Jesus, and you are hurting me. Get up and go into the city, and you will be told what you must do."

Saul got up from the ground and opened his eyes. He couldn't see anything! Saul was blind. His friends had to take him by the hand and lead him into the city of Damascus.

Saul had a lot to think about while he was blind. Before he lost his sight, he had seen and heard Jesus. Saul may have thought about Stephen, too, and all of the other Christians he had arrested. Now he knew that Jesus was alive.

God had plans for Saul to work for Him. So He spoke in a vision to a Christian named Ananias, who lived in the city of Damascus.

"Ananias," Jesus called.

"What do You want, Lord?" Ananias answered.

Jesus told Ananias, "Get up and go to the house of a man named Judas on Straight Street. Ask to see a man named Saul because Saul has been praying. This man Saul has seen a vision of a man coming to touch him and make him see again. Ananias, you are that man."

Ananias said, "Lord, I have heard that Saul did a lot to hurt the Christians in Jerusalem. He has come here to Damascus with permission to arrest everyone who prays in Your name."

Jesus said, "Do what I tell you because I have chosen Saul to teach about me. He will preach in my name to Jews, to people who are not Jews, and even to kings. And he will have to suffer because he believes in me."

Ananias obeyed Jesus. He went to the house of Judas and put his hands on Saul's head. Ananias said, "Brother Saul, Jesus has sent me to you so that you can see again and have the help of the Holy Spirit."

And right away, flakes of skin fell from Saul's eyes, and he could see. Then Saul got up and let Ananias baptize him. Saul was now a Christian. He began to teach in the Synagogues in Damascus. Saul told the people, "Jesus is the Son of God."

From *A Child's First Book of Bible Stories,* by Wanda Hayes. Standard Publishing, pp. 112-114.

REMEMBERING GOD'S TRUTHS: Remove the following picture cards from your picture file, and be prepared to teach them in a positive, funlike way:

- When Saul saw the bright light on the road to Damascus, he was probably frightened.
  Who can help you when you are afraid?
  <u>God can help me when I am afraid.</u> (*God's Care* section)
- The bright light made Saul blind. When Saul was blind, other people had to take care of him and give him food.
  Who gives you food?
  <u>God makes food grow for me.</u> (*God's Care* section)
- Saul changed from hating Jesus to being a friend of Jesus.
  Who is your best friend?
  <u>Jesus is my best friend.</u> (*Jesus* section)
- Saul changed. He became Paul and he became part of God's family.
  Who are in God's family?
  <u>All people who love and trust Jesus are in God's family.</u> (*The Church* section) Be sure to explain to the children what it means to love and trust Jesus.

EXPERIENCING GOD'S TRUTHS: Emphasize the fact that God can change people. Bring from home a dark colored blanket and a bright or pastel blanket. Spread the blankets out on opposite sides of the room. Have the children sit on the dark blanket as they talk about the sinful part of the story. Let them walk to the bright blanket as you say, "God can change people," and sit on the bright blanket to talk about the new non-sinful behavior.

Retell the part of the Saul story where Saul is hurting Christians. The teacher says, "God can change people. (Walk) God changed Saul from hating Christians to loving Christians. (Sit on bright blanket.) When Saul started loving Jesus, his name was changed to Paul. He decided to help Christians." (Go back to dark blanket.)

"God can help us change. I'm going to tell you a story of a little girl who was changed by God. This little girl used to tell her mother and father the wrong story. Instead of telling the right story, she told her parents pretend stories, called 'lies.' When her mother said, 'Who ate the cookies?' the little girl said, 'The dog ate them.' or 'I didn't.' The little girl was telling a lie. So the parents were sad, and the little girl was sad." (Go to the middle area.)

"The little girl prayed and asked God to help her change. She was sorry. (Go to the bright blanket.) God can change people. God changed the little girl from telling lies to telling the truth."

"After God helped the little girl change, she remembered to tell only the right story. She was much happier and her parents were very pleased with her."

You may want to make up other stories to tell with the blankets.

Have the children return to the tables and give them an activity sheet, "God Can Change People" (p. 7, *Through the Bible Activities for Preschoolers, Book 4*). Read the activity sheet to the children. Print each child's name on the back of his paper. Using bright yellow construction paper, let each child cut out a beaming sun, and let the children paste the sun above Saul's head. Then let them cut out several small cookies from tan construction paper (or use small animal crackers) to paste on the floor at Stephanie's feet.

As the children work on their activity sheet, say to them, "Saul hated Christians. He even hurt them. But God can change people. God changed Saul. He even changed his name from Saul to Paul. God changed Saul's hatred into love."

Direct the children's attention to the other picture. "Let's look at the picture of the little girl. Her name is Stephanie, and she used to tell lies. Stephanie asked God to help her to tell the truth. One day Stephanie dropped the cookie jar. She asked her mother to come look. She said, 'I did it.' Stephanie was happy that she had told the truth. Her parents were pleased with her. God was honored by the new way Stephanie acted.

REVIEWING GOD'S TRUTHS: Read *Choosing Is Fun* by Mary Backman (#3580) if it is available and you have extra time.

Have a closing prayer, "Dear God, thank You for having the power to change us. When we do wrong, please help us to say 'I'm sorry.' Thank You for forgiving us and loving us. In Jesus' name. Amen."

LOOKING AHEAD—Send notes home to the parents telling them about the special sharing activity for the next lesson. (See Lesson 46, p. 129, *Experiencing God's Truths* section.)

Unit Twelve: New Friends Become Jesus' Helpers

Bible Verse: Be kind ... to one another. (Ephesians 4:32, NIV)

Acts 9:36-43

Lesson 46

DORCAS HELPS OTHERS

AS THE CHILDREN ARRIVE: Greet each child warmly and direct him to one of the learning centers. It is best not to have more than five children to a center, and it is necessary for each child to go to the **Preparing Presents Center** today.

Attendance Check Center: Help the children place a Children-of-the-World sticker on the attendance chart. Say, "God loves all the children of the world. God loves you."

Bible Words Center: (See Lesson 2, p. 14, for a suggested way of reviewing this verse.) Use the jigsaw puzzle made in Lesson 2 and help the children work it. Ask, "What does the Bible say about being kind?" Help the children answer, "Be kind ... to one another, Ephesians 4:32." Sing the verse to the tune on page 26, SPC. Say, "When we are kind to one another, it shows we love one another."

Preparing Presents Center: Make many small tags for the children to attach to the gifts that they will be bringing in for the "Sharing" activity described in the section of this lesson called *Experiencing God's Truths*. Determine the number of tags needed. Each tag should say

I am happy to share with you.

You may want to use a duplicating machine to make the 2" x 5" construction-paper tags and a paper cutter to cut them out in order to save time. You will need a stapler and a box of sandwich-size plastic bags. In class, place each gift in a plastic bag (if the parents have not done this at home), and let each child tie the tag to the bag. Talk about how pleased Jesus is when we share.

At the sound of music from the cassette tape or piano, have the children go to the story area of the room for singing.

SINGING AND TALKING TO GOD: Have fun singing, "I'm Giving" (p. 67, *Songs for Preschool Children);* "Help Me to Forgive" (p. 71, SPC); "I Can Talk to God" (p. 80, SPC); "Let Us Love One Another" (p. 29, SPC, change the last line to "First John 4, verse 7"); and "God's Family" (p. 90, this book).

Have a special time of talking to God. For this lesson it would be appropriate to thank God for people in our church who help others. Name specific people.

Lead the children in a march around the room for exercise and back to the story area as you sing "God's Family" again.

READING ABOUT GOD'S WORD: Mark Acts 9:36-42 in *International Children's Version* so that you can read directly from it, or tell the Bible story.

Acts 9:36-43

Dorcas Helps Others

In the city of Joppa there lived a lady named Tabitha. She was also called Dorcas. She loved Jesus very much and was one of His followers. Dorcas was always doing good. She helped the poor. She was loved by all whom she helped.

Dorcas became very sick and died. How sad everyone was! Her body was carefully washed and made ready for burial. Her Christian friends heard that Peter was at a town near Joppa, and they sent two men to get him. They knew Peter could help them in their grief.

"Hurry, please come with us!" the two messengers begged Peter when they found him.

Peter got ready and went with them. When he arrived, he was taken to the upstairs room where they had placed Dorcas. The widows were crying. They showed Peter the clothing that Dorcas had made and given to them while she was alive.

Peter kneeled and prayed. Then he turned to Dorcas' body.

"Tabitha, get up!" he said.

Dorcas opened her eyes. She sat up when she saw Peter. He took her by the hand and helped her to stand up. Then he called her Christian friends into the room. He showed them Dorcas. She was alive!

They were all so happy once again and thankful to God for this great thing He had done through Peter.

REMEMBERING GOD'S TRUTHS: Use the following picture cards from the *I Pray* section of your picture file.

Dorcas was a kind Christian who helped others. When she died, her friends were very sad. Then Peter, one of Jesus' helpers, came to Dorcas' house and knelt down to pray for Dorcas. We pray just like Peter did. Can you answer these questions about praying?

When you pray, what are you doing?
<u>When I pray, I am talking to God.</u>
Does God hear you when you talk to Him?
<u>Yes, God always hears me when I talk to Him.</u>
When can you talk to God?
<u>I can talk to God anytime.</u>
When you have a problem, what should you do?
<u>I should pray and ask God to help me.</u>

EXPERIENCING GOD'S TRUTHS: In this section of the lesson the children will experience the joy of sharing—just giving, not receiving. Much preparation is required by the teacher, and the parents' assistance is needed for this activity.

Arrange with the teacher of an older class (example, 1st or 2nd grade), a younger class (example, two-year-olds) or a senior citizens class for your students to visit the class and share with them during the class hour. Ask the teacher of the class you will visit how many students he or she usually expects.

Call the parents of each child in your class to ask them to let their child bring items to give away. Each child should bring the number of items that correspond to the number of children in the class to be visited.

Ask the parent to be sure each item is put in an individual plastic baggie. For example, one child might bring ten baggies of pretzels, or ten pictures he or she has colored. Here are other suggestions: crackers, cookies, gum, magic markers, small pads of paper, homemade play dough cupcakes, small toys (like party favors), or raisins. (Keep in mind the age of the people who will be receiving these gifts when you suggest things to bring.)

Explain to each parent that he should tell his child at home that the items he brings to class **will be given away.**

You should take extra small plastic bags and a brown bag for each child you will be sharing with. This will help the child get the items home conveniently. You should also take items for at least two children in your class whose parents might have forgotten, or for a child who might be a visitor.

In class talk about Dorcas and how she shared. Take the children (each carrying his items to share) to the room of the class you will be sharing with. DO NOT let the children share with each other within your class. That would not teach sharing. Instead, it would be a gift-getting party. Share with another age group.

Help each child share his items and say, "I'm sharing my _____ with you."

If one child in your class refuses to share his item, handle it this way: Let the teacher of the other class take over the class and help the children give out their items. You then can talk to the distraught child in private. Tell him you will put his items with his coat for him to take home later.

Take the class back to your classroom and thank God for giving us so many things that we can share. (If there are leftover items, gather them in a bag and talk about someone you might give them to, or let each child take his own leftover items home.)

As the children return to their own classroom, have them sit at the tables, and give each child an activity sheet, "Sharing" (p. 8, *Through the Bible Activities for Preschoolers, Book 4*). (Bring a box of plain cookies from home.) While the children are coloring the picture, read the paper. Then give each child a cookie when he says the correct answer. Print each child's name on the back of his paper.

REVIEWING GOD'S TRUTHS: Ask the children how they feel now that they have shared with others. Let the children share their feelings individually.

Read *Sharing Makes Me Happy* by Dot Cachiaras (#3589) if it is available.

Have a closing prayer: "Dear God, we thank You that we can share with others. Sharing makes us happy. Amen."

Unit Twelve: New Friends Become Jesus' Followers

Bible Verse: To those who believed in his name, he gave the right to become children of God. (John 1:12, NIV)

Acts 18:1-6

Lesson 47

PAUL THE MISSIONARY

AS THE CHILDREN ARRIVE: Greet each child warmly and direct him to one of the learning centers.

Attendance Check Center: (See Lesson 42, p. 118.) Help the children put Children-of-the-World stickers on the attendance chart.

Bible Words Center: (See Lesson 28, p. 83, for a suggested way of reviewing this verse.) Ask the children, "What people can be children of God?" Clap to the rhythm of the verse and say, "To those who believed in his name, he gave the right to become children of God, John 1:12."

What is a Missionary? Center: Let the children role play being a missionary. Ask, "What is a missionary?" (This question was answered in Lesson 43, p. 120. See the **Missionary Center**.) Let the children answer, "A missionary is a person who goes to another place to help people learn about Jesus."

Point out that there are missionaries who are doctors (medical kit), preachers (Bible), teachers (picture books), nurses (medical kit), and printers (print set or typewriter). Let each child choose which he will be and say where he will go to tell others about Jesus. (Let the children use the items that identify their skills.)

At the sound of music from the cassette tape or piano, have the children go to the story area of the room for singing.

SINGING AND TALKING TO GOD: Sing these songs, "We Love Jesus" (p. 69, this book); "The Church" (p. 90, this book); "God's Friends" (p. 86, Songs for Preschool Children); "Help Me to Forgive" (p. 71, SPC); and "Jesus, the Son of God" (p. 59, v. 4, SPC).

Have a special time of talking to God. Thank God for one of the missionaries known by the children.

Lead the children in a march around the room for exercise as they sing "We Love Jesus," page 69 of this book.

READING GOD'S WORD: Before class, mark your copy of the *International Children's Version* so that you can quickly find the verses in Acts. It is very important to use your Bible each week with your class. There are four pictures after page 346 of this version which you should show during this lesson. Show only the appropriate picture as you talk about that subject. If you do not have this version, you will need to find a picture of Paul the Missionary in your church picture files.

Sing the "Bible Song" (p. 41, SPC), substituting "Paul" for "Jesus" in the second line. Tell the children, "Our story today is about a man named Paul. He lived after Jesus lived on earth. Should I look in the Old Testament or the New Testament of my Bible for this story? Right! I should look in the New Testament, or the back part of my Bible, to read about Paul. I will open my Bible to the book of Acts. Can you say 'Acts'?"

"You remember the story of the man who used to hate Christians. Remember, God changed him. He started loving Jesus and loving Christians." Read from your Bible or tell the Bible story.

Acts 18:1-6

Paul the Missionary

Paul lived after Jesus lived on earth. He used to hate Christians, but God changed him. Paul started loving Jesus and loving Christians. He became a missionary. A missionary is a person who goes to another place to help people learn about Jesus. Paul sometimes walked to other cities. Sometimes, he sailed in a boat to other cities. Wherever Paul went, he would tell the people about Jesus.

One time Paul went to the city of Corinth. He visited Aquila and his wife Priscilla. They were tentmakers, and so was Paul. He stayed with them and worked making tents with them.

Every Sabbath day, Paul went to the synagogue and talked with the Jews and Greeks.

Paul tried to persuade them to believe in Jesus.

"God sent Jesus to earth to show you that He loves you," said Paul. "God has made a way through Jesus Christ for you to have your sins forgiven and live with God forever."

Paul told the people to say they were sorry for their sins and to ask Jesus to forgive them. Some people believed in Jesus and became members of God's family.

Other people did not believe. Sometimes these people were mean to Paul. They chose not to listen to Paul's teachings. So Paul no longer went to the synagogue, but kept on teaching about Jesus in the home of Titius Justus. His home was next door to the synagogue.

God gave Paul a dream. In the dream, God spoke to Paul.

"Don't be afraid!" God said. "Continue talking to people and don't be quiet! I am with you. No one will hurt you because many of my people are in this city."

God's words gave Paul the strength and courage he needed to keep on telling others about Jesus. Paul stayed in Corinth for a year and a half, teaching God's word to the people, before going to another place.

REMEMBERING GOD'S TRUTHS: Use the following picture cards from your picture file.

- A missionary is a person who goes to another place to help people learn about Jesus. Can you answer three questions about Jesus?
    Who is your best friend?
    Jesus is my best friend.
    What is Christmas?
    Christmas is a time when we celebrate Jesus' birthday.
    Will Jesus ever die again?
    No, Jesus will live forever. (*Jesus* section)
- God made missionaries to be very special people. God made you special, too.
    Who made you?
    God made me. (*About Me* section)
- A missionary is a person who goes to another place to help people know about Jesus.
    If you go far away, who will take care of you?
    God will take care of me. (*God's Care* section)

EXPERIENCING GOD'S TRUTHS: You will need a small suitcase, a medical kit, and a child's Bible storybook. Ask the children to tell you how missionaries travel. Let them act out the transportation named—by car, plane, train, boat, motorcycle, etc. Let the children have fun moving about the room as they pretend.

Choose two children to be missionaries. The other children will be their family. Let the children place the chairs like an airplane and let them act out carrying their suitcase to the pretend airport and riding on the plane to another country. When they arrive, they can walk to their new house. Then the daddy can take his Bible and preach to the people.

Let the children repeat the story with other children as the missionary parents and another type of ministry emphasized such as medical doctor. Some of the children can be sick children in another country who are helped by the missionary doctor and nurse. If the role playing is going well, you might let the children do the story again. Use different children as missionaries, children, etc., and let some children be waiting in the "other" country for the missionary family who arrives and shows them pictures of Jesus.

Following this role playing and discussion, have the children go to the tables. Give them an activity sheet, "The Missionary Goes" (p. 9, *Through the Bible Activities for Preschoolers, Book 4*). Write each child's name on the back of his paper. Give each child a red crayon. Tell the children to color the path the missionary takes to get to the Indian child to tell him about Jesus. Collect red crayons as you give each child a green crayon. Tell them to trace the path the missionary family could take to reach the Mexican boy to tell him about Jesus. Follow this procedure for reaching the other people, using four more colors.

REVIEWING GOD'S TRUTHS: Remind the children that a missionary studies God's Word and wants to help people to believe and obey Jesus. Ask, "What people can be children of God?" Help the children answer, "To those who believe in his name, he gave the right to become children of God, 1 John 4:19."

Have a closing prayer. "Thank You God, for missionaries who help people learn about You. Thank You for being with them. Please help them in their work. In Jesus name, amen."

Unit Thirteen—More Friends Tell the Good News

GETTING READY FOR UNIT THIRTEEN

The theme of this unit will be that God uses people all the time to carry on His work. There are many who need the Good News. When a person receives the Good News, it is important to share it with others so they can know about Jesus, God's Son. Barnabas traveled with Paul, and he did many kind things. Timothy, a young man, loved God and studied His Word. Lydia heard of Jesus and was obedient to His command to be baptized and be faithful. Paul, a prisoner, was taken to Rome and while there was able to share the Good News with those in power. We can tell the Good News about Jesus, too.

Learning Objectives: Some things you should expect your children to accomplish in this unit:

The children should know (1) God wants them to be kind; (2) The Bible is God's Word; (3) Jesus died for them, but He is alive today.

The children should feel (1) Glad they can show kindness to someone; (2) Willing to help; (3) Safe, knowing God will take care of them.

The children should be able to (1) Minister to a shut-in; (2) Tell a friend about Jesus; (3) Tell the highlights of the Bible stories; (4) Say the Bible verses by memory and state simple answers to concept questions.

Remember, because of the differences in age and maturity, some children will meet more of these objectives than others will.

Bible Verses: Continue to review the Bible verses using the teaching aids and actions suggested in previous lessons.

Books: Several books are suggested for use with these lessons. These books may be placed in the quiet, book corner of your room. *What Is Love?; God Knows You; Jesus Is My Special Friend;* and *Kindness* are suitable for the ages of the children and for the subject being studied.

Bulletin Board: Gather pictures of Barnabas, Timothy, Lydia and Paul from your church's picture file. Arrange these pictures attractively on the board or wall, and write their names on strips of paper for the children to see and associate with each person. Attach these strips to the pictures.

THINGS TO DO:

Lesson 48: You will need Children-of-the-World stickers for the attendance charts each week. Make arrangements to visit a shut-in (see p. 134, *Experiencing God's Truths*). You will need permission slips for the children's parents to sign, drivers (one per four children), a snack to take to share with the shut-in, and camera for taking pictures. Place the heading, *"We Are Kind"*, on a piece of poster board, and tape the pictures taken on the visit.

Lesson 49: Provide small buckets, sponges, and dust cloths for the children to help clean the room. You will need costumes or clothing from other countries to show the children. If there is a person from another country attending your church, invite her to dress in her native dress and visit your class.

Lesson 50: Provide as many of these items as possible: newspaper, letter, TV, cassette tape, telegram, radio, book, video tape, movie, advertizing circular, magazine, telephone, and a large box.

Lesson 51: Several children's raincoats, hats, umbrellas, and boots are needed.

Unit Thirteen: More Friends Tell the Good News

Acts 9:27; 11:19-26; 13:1-3

Bible Verse: Love one another. (1 John 4:7, NIV)

Lesson 48

BARNABAS, A KIND HELPER

AS THE CHILDREN ARRIVE: Greet each child warmly and direct him to one of the learning centers.

Attendance Check Center: (See Lesson 42, p. 118.) Help the children place Children-of-the-World stickers on the attendance chart. Stress the truth that Jesus loves the children of the world.

Bible Words Center: (See Lesson 18, p. 56, for a suggested way of reviewing this verse.) Use the needle and yarn to put the cards in correct order. Ask, "Whom should you love?" Say with the children, "Love one another, 1 John 4:7."

Preparing to Visit Center: Prepare your students for the visit described in the *Experiencing God's Word* section of this lesson. Act out manners, like shaking hands and saying, "Hello," "Thank-you," and "Good-bye." Let the children practice these polite gestures with you and with each other. Talk to them about visiting a sick or old person. Explain that we do this in order to show love. Do not say that we visit to make the person happy. We have no control over others emotions. If the motive is happiness and the shut-in does not smile very much, the children may feel that their trip was in vain.

At the sound of music from the cassette tape or piano, have the children go to the story area of the room for singing.

SINGING AND TALKING TO GOD: Sing these songs: "The Church" (p. 90, this book); "Pleasing God" (p. 26, v. 2, *Songs for Preschool Children);* "Let Us Love One Another" (p. 29, SPC, change last line to "First John 4, verse 7"); "Bible Song" (p. 41, SPC, substitute "Barnabas"); and "Jesus' Helpers" (p. 87, SPC).

Have a special time of talking to God. Ask God to help us find ways to show love as we visit today.

Lead the children in a march around the room as you sing "The Marching Song" (p. 11, SPC).

READING ABOUT GOD'S WORD: Read <u>1 John 4:7</u> and <u>Ephesians 4:32</u> from your copy of the *New International Version.* Then allow several children to take turns holding the Bible and pretending to read the verses as a way of teaching the two Bible verses for this lesson.

Then read or tell the Bible story.

<u>Acts 9:27, 11:19-26, 13:1-3</u>   CR-188

Barnabas, a Kind Helper

Wonderful things happened when Jesus' helpers started His church. Many people believed in Jesus and were baptized. Then the new Christians stayed in Jerusalem to learn all they could from Peter and John and the other men who had been with Jesus. Some of them did not have enough money to stay for a long time in the city, so the Christians who lived in Jerusalem said, "We will take care of you. You may stay with us."

These first Christians shared what they had. Some of them came to Peter and the other apostles with money and said, "We sold our houses and our land. Take this money and share it with the people who need help." One of the men who sold a field he owned and brought the money to the church leaders was Barnabas.

Barnabas was a good man. He had always obeyed the laws of God. And when he learned that Jesus was the Savior promised by God, Barnabas was baptized and became a Christian.

Then Barnabas went to Antioch where he found many new Christians. This made Barnabas happy.

There were more and more Christians all of the time, which made a lot of work for Barnabas. He needed help and so he went to the city of Tarsus to find Saul. Saul agreed to help Barnabas and they worked together in Antioch for a year, helping the new followers of Jesus.

The Christians in Antioch were like the Christians in Jerusalem. They were helpful and loved each other. When they heard that there was not enough food in Judea, and the Christians there were hungry, they gave money to help them. They sent the money to the leaders of the church in Jerusalem by Barnabas and Saul.

From *A Child's First Book of Bible Stories* by Wanda Hayes. Standard Publishing, p. 117.

REMEMBERING GOD'S TRUTHS: Use the following picture cards from your picture file.

- Our story says, "Wonderful things happened when Jesus' helpers started His church."
    Who are the church?
    All people who love and trust Jesus are the church. (*The Church* section) Be sure to explain to the children what it means to love and trust Jesus.
- Jesus loved you even before you were born.
    Who made you?
    God made me. (*About Me* section)
- Our story tells us that the people who loved Christ shared their food with other people who loved Christ.
    Who gives you food?
    God makes food grow for me. (*God's Care* section)
- We read about Barnabas in the part of our Bible called the New Testament.
    What is the Bible?
    The Bible is the Word of God. (*The Church* section)

EXPERIENCING GOD'S TRUTHS: Providing an actual experience of showing love is much more valuable than just talking about it. So for this lesson you are going to leave your church building in order to visit shut-ins. Here are some suggestions of how to do it:

1. The shut-in should be contacted and the idea of visiting him or her should be discussed thoroughly. He should agree to the number of children coming, the length of the visit, and what the children will do while there. Tell him that your class will bring a snack to share with him and ask him not to feed the children anything else during the visit.

2. Plan for a group of four children and one adult to each visit a different shut-in. (Depending on the amount of travel time involved, you might need to take the entire meeting time to do this project and read the Bible story at the shut-in's house.)

3. Some parents should be recruited as drivers. You should especially ask parents of young or shy children to be part of this experience with their children. Plan one teacher or parent for each group of four children. Be sure to tell all parents about this project during the week prior to this meeting.

4. You might want to take your camera. Pictures of your visit displayed later in your church building might encourage others in your church family to visit shut-ins. Include names and addresses of shut-ins on the display if you do this.

5. Each parent should be contacted by letter or phone to tell him of your plans. One student in each group should be asked to bring plain vanilla cookies for his group to share.

6. As each parent brings his child to the class room, be sure he signs a permission paper giving consent for his child to make the trip with the class.

7. Prepare the children by dividing them into their appropriate groups (approximately four children per adult) and describing exactly what they will be doing. Tell them what the person will look like if he is bed-ridden or uses a special aparatus like a wheelchair.

8. Enjoy your visit. Keep the children calm. Lead them as they talk to the shut-in, sing, hear a story, eat cookies, or whatever you plan.

9. Return to your church building in time to meet your time commitment to the parents.

Note: There is no activity sheet for this lesson. Instant snapshots can be taken of the children with their shut-in friends and placed on a poster board as they return to the classroom. Write, **We Are Kind,** for the heading.

REVIEWING GOD'S TRUTHS: If you arrive back at your church building early, let each group tell about their visit.

Have a closing prayer: "Dear God, we thank You for all who helped us share our love with our shut-in friends. Please help them to feel better and know You love them. In Jesus' name, amen."

Unit Thirteen: More Friends Tell the Good News

Bible Verse: To those who believed in his name, he gave the right to become children of God. (John 1:12, NIV)

Acts 16:1-5

Lesson 49

A YOUNG HELPER

AS THE CHILDREN ARRIVE: Greet each child warmly and direct him to one of the learning centers.

Attendance Check Center: (See Lesson 42, p. 118.) Help each child place Children-of-the-World stickers on the attendance chart. Talk about the country the sticker represents.

Bible Words Center: (See Lesson 28, p. 83, for a suggested way of reviewing this verse.) Ask the children. "What people can be children of God?" Say with the children, "To those who believe in his name, he gave the right to become children of God, John 1:12."

Helpers Center: Provide several small sponges and a small bucket or basin of water. Tell the children that they may be helpers by washing the table, shelves, chalkboard ledge and/or baseboard.

As they work, tell them what a good job they are doing. Then explain that later they will hear a story about Timothy who helped in another way.

At the sound of music from the cassette tape or piano, have the children leave the centers and go to the story-circle area of the room for singing.

SINGING AND TALKING TO GOD: Have fun singing "God's Friends" (p. 86, *Songs for Preschool Children,* change name in song to "Timothy"); "The Church" (p. 90, this book); "God's Family" (p. 90, this book); "Clap, Clap Your Hands for Joy" (p. 54, SPC); and "We're Here in Our Church" (p. 35, SPC, change the title and lines 4 and 8 to read "In our church building").

Have a special time of talking to God. Prepare at home by reading the section in the front of this book called *Talking to God.* For this lesson, it would be appropriate to thank God for the people who started our congregation.

Lead the children in a march around the room for exercise as you sing "The Marching Song" (p. 11, SPC).

READING ABOUT GOD'S WORD: Read or tell the Bible story.

Acts 16:1-5

A Young Helper

Saul and Barnabas began traveling to many cities and countries, teaching about Jesus. Then Saul's name was changed to Paul. From then on he was called Paul.

One of the cities Paul visited was Lystra. There he met a young man named Timothy. Timothy had been taught the stories in the Bible from the time he was a very young boy. His mother, Eunice, and his grandmother, Lois, taught him about God. And when Paul came to Lystra, Timothy learned about Jesus.

Later, when Paul came back to Lystra, he was looking for a helper. He wanted someone to travel with him and help him tell people about Jesus. Paul said to Timothy, "I want you to come with me, Timothy. The Christians here at Lystra and those in Iconium have told me how much you love Jesus. You are the kind of person I am looking for. You can help Jesus' church to grow." So Timothy traveled with Paul to many different cities, teaching and helping in whatever way he could.

Later, when Paul was put in prison for teaching about Jesus, Timothy kept on working for Jesus. And Paul wrote letters to Timothy to help him.

In his letters to Timothy, Paul said, "Pray for everyone, because God wants everyone to be in His church. Teach the people what I have taught you. Be a good example to the other Christians by what you say and by the way you live. Love others and always believe in God and Jesus. Keep teaching and studying, and you will save yourself and the people who listen to you."

Timothy remembered what his mother and grandmother and Paul had taught him. He grew up to be a good helper for Jesus.

From A Child's First Book of Bible Stories by Wanda Hayes. Standard Publishing, p. 118.

Read a verse from your *International Children's Version*. Paul the missionary tells Timothy in 2 Timothy 1:3, "I always remember you in my prayers, day and night. And I thank God for you in these prayers."

REMEMBERING GOD'S TRUTHS: Use the picture cards from your picture file. You will need four.
- When Timothy was a little boy, he used to listen to his grandmother as she read the Bible to him.
  What is the Bible?
  The Bible is the Word of God. (*The Church* section)
- When his grandmother read to him, Timothy learned that God made all people.
  Who made you?
  God made me. (*About Me* section)
- And he learned that God loves everyone.
  Does God love children with problems?
  Yes, God loves everyone. (*About Me* section)
- When Timothy grew up, he learned about Jesus from the missionary Paul. Then Timothy helped to start new churches.
  Who are the church?
  All people who love and trust Jesus are the church. (*The Church* section) Be sure to explain to the children what it means to love and trust Jesus.

EXPERIENCING GOD'S TRUTH: Bring from your home, and ask others to bring from their homes, costumes or outfits worn by people from other countries. If the supply is short, use a man's shirt as a pretend Japanese kimono and a child's heavy coat as an Eskimo coat.

If you have Christians from other countries in your church, invite them to visit your class for a few minutes. Ask them to wear clothes native to their home land or to tell the children about the clothes worn in their country. In class let the children dress in the clothes you brought. Have them to join hands in a circle and swing hands back and forth as you chant,
"We are God's children.
We are God's children.
God want us to love Him and His Son, Jesus.

Still holding hands, march in place as you repeat the chant. Tell the children that you are going to pretend you are Timothy, and they will pretend they are ladies and men who lived a long time ago. As Timothy, you go to each child and tell him about Jesus. Say, "God wants you to love and trust Jesus and do what is right."

Pray together as you thank God that we are all God's children.

Have the children return to the tables and give each child an activity sheet, "Who Are the Church?" (p. 10, *Through the Bible Activities for Preschoolers, Book 4*).

Read the paper to the class. Talk about each picture on the page. Ask the children to draw a circle around each picture that answers the question, "Who are the church?" When you talk about the church *building,* explain that the building is not as important as the people. If a church *building* burns down, the people are still a church.

Have the children point to each of the people on the page as you say, "This person loves, trusts, and obeys Jesus. Is she or he the church?" Let the children answer yes and draw a circle around that person.

REVIEWING GOD'S TRUTHS: Play the "Pop-Up Game" as described on page 9, in the *Game* section of this book. Use the picture cards for this lesson and last week's lesson.

Have a closing prayer: "We thank You, dear God, for the people who love and trust You here. Please help us to love and be kind to one another. Amen."

LOOKING AHEAD—Send a note home with the children asking them to wear something purple to the next class meeting.

Unit Thirteen: More Friends Tell the Good News

Bible Verse: To those who believed in his name, he gave the right to become children of God. (John 1:12, NIV)

Acts 16:11-15

Lesson 50

LYDIA TELLS OTHERS

AS THE CHILDREN ARRIVE: Greet each child warmly and direct him to one of the learning centers.

Attendance Check Center: (See Lesson 42, p. 118.) Help the children place Children-of-the-World stickers by their names on the attendance chart. Count the number of stickers. Say, "I'm so glad you came ____ times. I'm always glad to see you. I like your purple ____." (The children were told to wear something purple in Lesson 49.)

Bible Words Center: (See Lesson 28, p. 83, for a suggested way of teaching this verse.) Ask, "What people can be children of God?" Say with the children, "To those who believed in his name, he gave the right to become children of God, John 1:12."

See if each child can say the verse by himself. Praise the ones who can, and help the ones who need help.

Telling Center: Bring to class a box containing as many means of communication as possible: a newspaper, letter, TV, cassette tape, telegram, radio, book, video tape, movie, advertising circular, magazine, and telephone.

Remove these items from your box one at a time and let the children identify them. Then tell the children that they will be hearing a story about Lydia, who lived after Jesus went to Heaven. Did people in Bible times have TV's? No! (Put TV in box.) Did people like Lydia in Bible times have newspapers? No! (Put newspaper in box.) Repeat the question with each item. Conclude by saying that Lydia had only her mouth for telling people good news.

At the sound of music from the cassette tape or piano, have the children go to the story area of the room for singing.

SINGING AND TALKING TO GOD: Sing these songs: "Children of God" (p. 61, this book); "God So Loved" (p. 42, this book); "J-E-S-U-S" (p. 50, *Songs for Preschool Children*); "Jesus Is the Son of God" (p. 56, SPC); "Hallelu" (p. 53, SPC); and "Bible Song" (p. 41, SPC, using "Lydia" instead of "Jesus").

Have a special time of talking to God. Prepare at home by reading *Talking to God, p. 7*. For this lesson it would be appropriate to ask God to help us tell other people about Jesus.

Lead the children in a march around the room for exercise as you sing the "Bible Song" again. Lead the children back to the story area of the room.

READING ABOUT GOD'S WORD: Ask, "Do you like the color purple? I can see lots of purple clothing on you. Our Bible story is about a lady who sold purple cloth. Her name was Lydia. Mark Acts 16:13-15 in your copy of the *International Children's Version* so that you can read directly from it, or tell the Bible story.

Acts 16:11-15

Lydia Tells Others

Lydia lived in the city of Philippi. She was a busy woman. She sold her purple cloth at the market. Lydia worked hard every day of the week except the Sabbath day. That was the day to pray. Lydia worshiped and loved God. She obeyed His command to keep the Sabbath holy.

One day Paul traveled to Philippi. On the Sabbath day, he and the men traveling with him went outside the city gate. They were looking for a special place for prayer. They came to a river, and saw some women gathered there. The men sat down and talked with the women. Lydia was with the women.

Lydia listened carefully to what Paul was saying. The Lord had opened her mind to pay attention to him. Lydia loved God, but had never heard of Jesus until Paul came to her town to tell her about Him.

Lydia believed Paul's teachings. All the people

137

in her house believed the good news Paul preached. Lydia and all the people in her house were baptized.

They were happy to be Christians.

REMEMBERING AND EXPERIENCING GOD'S TRUTHS: Have the children go to the tables and give each child an activity sheet, "Telling Our Friends" (p. 11, *Through the Bible Activities for Preschoolers, Book 4).* Write each child's name on the back of his paper. Let each child color Jeff's clothes.

Use the picture cards from the *Jesus* section of your picture file.

Who is Jesus?
<u>Jesus is the Son of God.</u>
Why did Jesus come to earth?
<u>Jesus came to show us that God loves us.</u>
How did Jesus show you that He loves You?
<u>Jesus died for me.</u>
Is Jesus alive today?
<u>Yes, Jesus is alive today.</u>

You will also need a book that has a picture of Jesus in it.

Tell the children that we are going to practice telling each other about Jesus. Practice the four answers on the picture cards listed above.

Ask one child to volunteer to be your friend who will listen as you tell him about Jesus. Hold up one card and tell the child the statement that is the *answer* to the question. For example, "Did you know that Jesus is the Son of God?"

Repeat, using another child and another picture card. Let the children takes turns being the listener and the teller, using the other cards.

When everyone who wishes to do so has had a turn, change the format by using the Jesus story book. The teacher should ask another child to volunteer to be her friend. The teacher should then open the book and show her friend a picture of Jesus and say, "This is Jesus. Jesus died for me," or "Jesus is alive today."

Let the children take turns pretending to be the friend and the teller as long as interest lasts.

REVIEWING GOD'S TRUTHS: Tell the children that God wants us to tell our friends about Jesus, just as Lydia did.

Review the Bible verses. Ask, "What is a Bible verse that tells us that God loved the world?" Help the children answer, "For God so loved the world that he gave his one and only Son, John 3:16." This is the good news we are to share so others can become children of God. Ask, "What people can be children of God?" Say with the children, "To those who believe in his name, he gave the right to be children of God, John 1:12."

Show the items used in the **Telling Center,** and tell the children we can use all these items to tell people about Jesus today. If time allows, let the children use the telephone to tell someone about Jesus.

Closing Prayer: "We thank You, God, for helping us to have so many ways to tell Your good news. Show us ways we can use these items. We love You and want others to love You, too. Amen."

Unit Thirteen: More Friends Tell the Good News

Bible Verse: Give thanks to him and praise his name. (Psalm 100:4, NIV)

Acts 27

Lesson 51

A TERRIBLE SHIPWRECK

AS THE CHILDREN ARRIVE: (See *As the Children Arrive* on p. 7) Greet each child warmly and direct him to one of the learning centers.

Attendance Check Center: (See Lesson 42, p. 118.) Help the children place Children-of-the-World stickers on the attendance chart.

Bible Words Center: (See Lesson 4, p. 21, for a suggested way of reviewing this verse.) Ask the children, "What does the Bible say about giving thanks?" Help them do the actions suggested in Lesson 4 as they say, "Give thanks to him and praise his name, Psalm 100:4."

Storms Center: Bring several children's raincoats, rainhats, umbrellas, and boots to class.

In class, talk about rain and wind storms, and act out a storm situation using the rain gear.

Ask the children, "Can a bear help you in a rain storm?" *No!* "Can a super hero help you in a rain storm?" *No!* "Can a strong cartoon man help you?" *No!* "Who can help you in a rain storm?" *God!*

At the sound of music from the cassette tape or piano, have the children go to the story area of the room for singing.

SINGING AND TALKING TO GOD: Have fun singing "Give Thanks" (p. 23, this book); "Paul and Silas" (p. 14, v. 2, *Songs for Preschool Children*); "Trust in the Lord" (p. 25, SPC); "Sing, Little Children, Sing" (p. 37, SPC); "God Is Good" (p. 38, SPC); "I Will Trust in God" (p. 38, SPC, change lines 2, 3 and 5 to read "Isaiah twelve, two").

Have a special time of talking to God. Thank God for helping us when we are in trouble.

Lead the children in a march around the room for exercise as you sing "Paul and Silas" again. Lead them back to the story area of the room.

READING ABOUT GOD'S WORD: Read or tell the Bible story.

Acts 27 CRp.190.

A Terrible Shipwreck

Paul was arrested and put in jail several times. He finally decided that he wanted the emperor who lived in Rome to decide whether he had done anything wrong. So Paul was put on a ship going to Italy so he could see Caesar, the emperor, in Rome.

There were many people on the ship with Paul—a Roman centurion, soldiers, sailors, other prisoners, and Paul's friends, Luke and Aristarchus.

The ship was carrying grain. And it was the fall of the year when the seas were rough, so the ship had to go very slowly. Paul told the captain and the other men running the ship, "This trip will end in trouble. The weather is bad this time of year. The grain, the ship, and our own lives could be lost."

The captain of the ship didn't believe Paul. And the Roman officer guarding him believed the captain and the ship's owner instead of Paul.

Paul's friend, Luke, wrote about what happened in the book of Acts in the Bible.

"A strong wind like a hurricane blew on our ship and pushed us. The sailors tied heavy ropes around the boat to keep the wind from tearing it apart. We were afraid of being driven onto quicksand.

"We worked hard fighting the storm," Luke said. "And on the second day, the sailors had to throw the grain overboard to make the boat lighter so it wouldn't sink. On the third day, they threw the ship's extra equipment into the sea. And for several days, the storm was so bad that we couldn't see the sun or the stars. There was no way to tell what direction we were going. And we hadn't eaten for several days. No one except Paul believed that we would live.

"Then Paul stood among this frightened group of people and said, 'Men, if you had listened to me and stayed in port when I told you, we would not have had these problems and lost our grain and gear from the ship. But be happy because no one will lose his life. Only the ship will be lost. I know this is true because an angel of God came to me tonight and said, 'Don't be afraid, Paul. You will make it to Rome to see the emperor, and God will save the lives of everyone on the ship with you.' And I believe that God will do what He said. We will be saved, but our ship will wreck on an island.''

Luke continued his story. ''After being tossed around the seas for two weeks, the sailors thought we were coming closer to land. They put four anchors down into the water to slow the ship and keep it from wrecking. Then the sailors tried to escape in a small boat, but Paul said, 'If these men don't stay on the ship, the rest of you can't be saved.'

''So the soldiers cut the ropes holding the small boat and let it fall into the sea. And when it was nearly daylight, the sailors saw land. They tried to guide the ship to a beach, but it ran aground. The front of it stuck and wouldn't move, and the waves broke the back of the ship.

''Then the soldiers wanted to kill the prisoners so they couldn't swim away and escape. But the centurion wanted to keep Paul alive, so he wouldn't let anyone be killed. The centurion said, 'Everyone who can swim, go ahead and swim to land. The rest of you float on planks of wood or whatever you can find from the ship.' And that is exactly what they did. Just as God had promised Paul, all two hundred and seventy-six people made it safely to land.''

From *A Child's First Book of Bible Stories* by Wanda Hayes. Standard Publishing, pp. 121, 122.

REMEMBERING GOD'S TRUTHS: Before class, remove the following picture cards from the *God's Care* section of your picture file. In class, be enthusiastic as you teach these concepts.
- God is the most powerful person in the universe. He is the one who takes care of us.
  Who takes care of you when you sleep?
  God takes care of me when I sleep.
  When you go far away, who will take care of you?
  God will take care of me.
- Super heroes are fun pretend friends, but only God can really help us. Can you answer these questions about God.

When you are alone and sad, what should you do?
I should ask God to help me.
Who can help you when you are afraid?
God can help me when I am afraid.

EXPERIENCING GOD'S TRUTHS: The truth that God really cares and helps is reinforced when the children are given an opportunity to role play the situation. Mark your copy of the *International Children's Version* so that you can easily read the verses appropriate to this lesson. Be sure to bring a small buttered roll for each child.

In class, turn a table upside down and put the chairs around the outside of the table to form a pretend boat whose sides are made of chairs. Let the children stand in the pretend boat and act out the story as you read it from the Bible

Read Acts 27:13-15a. Tell the children to pretend the strong wind is blowing, and they are frightened.

Then read verses 20 to the end of the first sentence of verse 26. Tell the children to look happy.

Read verses 34-36. Let the children eat a roll and butter as they sit in the pretend ship. Be sure to thank God for it first.

Now read the first sentence of verse 39. The children can cheer at the sight of land.

Read verse 41, and pull some of the chairs away from the upside-down table.

Read the end of verse 43. Have the children pretend to swim to land.

Read the end of verse 44. Let the children pray a thank-you prayer for their safety—as Paul surely must have done.

When you finish, turn the table upright and have the children sit at the tables. Give each child an activity sheet, ''God Really Cares'' (p. 12, *Through the Bible Activities for Preschoolers, Book 4*). Write each child's name on the back of his paper. Let each child trace the name of the person who can help them. Help each child read the word.

REVIEWING GOD'S TRUTHS: Paul went on a trip on a ship. Play ''Going On A Trip'' as described in the *Games* section on page 9.

Have the closing prayer, ''Thank You, God, for taking care of us all the time. We know You want only what is best for us. We love You. Amen.''

Unit 14—Heaven, Our Special Home

GETTING READY FOR UNIT FOURTEEN

Only one lesson makes up this unit. It's theme is the fact that Heaven is our special home. God and Jesus will be there. Heaven is a place we should want to go to, and in this unit, the children will learn important facts about Heaven. It is important not to frighten the children, but to present these truths in such a way that the children will be eager to learn more about Heaven.

Learning Objectives: Some things you should expect your children to accomplish in this unit:
The children should know (1) Heaven is a wonderful place; (2) God and Jesus are there; (3) All people who love and trust Jesus can go to Heaven.
The children should feel (1) Glad that God has planned Heaven for us; (2) Happy that we can learn about Heaven in God's Word.
The children should be able to (1) Tell the highlights of the Bible story; (2) Say the Bible verse by memory; (3) Tell two facts about Heaven.
Remember, because of the differences in age and maturity, some children will meet more of these objectives than others will.

Bible Verse: The Bible verse is a short one, and has been reviewed often in this curriculum. The children should know it from memory.

Books: Several books are suggested for reading or placing in the quiet, book corner of the room. *God Made Everything; Tell Me About God; What Is Faith?* and *God Loves You* are suitable for the ages of children and for the subject being studied.

Bulletin Board: Cut the letters for HEAVEN out of gold wrapping paper. Place them on the bulletin board. Add pictures that show what Heaven will be like.

THINGS TO DO for this lesson: You will need the Pict-O-Graph, Stories About John (#2261), or the twelve Bible figures used in Lessons 40 and 41. Write the names of the disciples on 1½" x 5" cards. Have a duplicate card for *John* and *James*. Find pictures to illustrate the characteristics of Heaven (see p. 143). Place these pictures in a large bag.

Unit Thirteen: Heaven, Our Special Home

Bible Verse: God is good. (Psalm 73:1, NIV)

Revelation 21

Lesson 52

JOHN SEES THE HEAVENLY CITY

AS THE CHILDREN ARRIVE: Greet each child warmly and direct him to one of the learning centers.

Attendance Check Center: (See Lesson 42, p. 118.) Help each child place a Children-of-the-World sticker on the attendance chart. State how glad you are that he came to class ____ times. Count the stickers.

Bible Words Center: (See Lesson 1, p. 12, for a suggested way of teaching this verse.) Use the word cards and let children place them in order. Ask, "What does the Bible tell us about God?" Answer with the children, "God is good, Psalm 73:1."

John, the Disciple Center: Use the Pict-O-Graph, **Stories about John** (#2261), or cut out figures from Bible pictures to represent the twelve disciples. (You can use the figures from Lesson 40, p. 114, **The Eleven Disciples Center**.) Write the names of each disciple on 1½" x 5" paper strips (cut 3" x 5" cards in half). Put the name with the figure.

Have a duplicate card with **John** written on it. Ask the children to match your card with the same card by a figure.

Pick up the figure and tell the children, "This is our pretend figure of John. He was a follower of Jesus. He had a brother, James. (Have a duplicate card with **James** written on it.) Ask the children to find the name card that matches this one. Explain that James and John were fishermen. They both left their fishing to follow Jesus.

After Jesus' death and resurrection, John wrote down what God told him to write so we would know about Jesus and God's plan for man. (Use the Pict-O-Graph story, "John Wrote About Jesus.") Show in your Bible the five books that John wrote—the Gospel of John; 1, 2 and 3 John; and Revelation. John loved Jesus very much.

At the sound of music from the cassette tape or piano, have the children go to the story area of the room for singing.

SINGING AND TALKING TO GOD: Have fun singing: "Please Him, Please Him" (p. 39, *Songs for Preschool Children*); "In His Bible Book" (p. 41, SPC); "Come to Me" (p. 51, SPC); "Clap, Clap Your Hands for Joy" (p. 54, SPC); "God Is Good" (p. 38, SPC, add second verse, "Psalm 73, one, God is good."); "Go To Heaven" (p. 90, this book); and "God's Family" (p. 90, this book).

Have a special time of talking to God. Prepare at home by reading the section in the front of this book called *Talking to God*. For this lesson, it would be appropriate to thank God for Heaven.

Lead the children in a march around the room for exercise as you sing "The Marching Song" (p. 11, SPC). Lead them back to the story area.

READING ABOUT GOD'S WORD: Read Revelation 1:1-3 from your copy of the *International Children's Version*. Show the children the top picture on the page after page 506 in this version. Use paper to cover the bottom picture so that your children do not ask questions about the complicated and possibly frightful subject depicted in that picture. On the back of that page, cover the top picture and show the bottom picture.

Now read or tell the Bible story.

Revelation 21

John Sees the Heavenly City

The Bible tells us about God and His Son, Jesus. It tells us why God put people on the earth.

A long time ago God had Moses write about the beginning of the world. Then later God had His servant, John, write about Heaven, because Heaven is the new world where the people who love and obey God will live someday.

John was an old man when he wrote about Heaven. He was a prisoner on an island called Patmos. John and many other followers of Jesus were arrested and punished for being Christians and teaching about Him. But John was glad he had done what he could for Jesus.

One special day God showed John in a vision

142

what Heaven would look like. John may have thought he was dreaming, but he knew that what he saw was true. And John wrote about what he saw that day because God told him to.

John wrote, "I saw a new Heaven and a new earth. The old Heaven and the old earth were gone. And I saw the holy city, the new Jerusalem, coming down out of Heaven from God. It was as beautiful as a bride coming to meet her husband.

"And I heard a loud voice say, 'God will be with His people and live with them. And they will not be sad anymore. God will wipe the tears from their eyes. No one will die anymore. No one will cry. No one will hurt.'"

And from the throne of Heaven, John heard the words, "I will make everything new."

In his vision, John was carried away to a high mountain where he could see the holy city. It shone as bright as crystal because God was there.

Heaven was like a great big square city, but it was more beautiful than any city on earth. The outside wall of the city was made of jasper. It shone bright and clear. The inside of the city was made of gold, and it was built on precious stones—red, green, blue, and every color of the rainbow. The twelve gates of the city were made of pearls, and the streets were pure gold. It was the most beautiful city anyone could imagine.

John said, "There was no temple in the new Jerusalem because God and Jesus themselves were there. The city did not need the sun or moon because God gave the people light. And nothing bad can ever go into the city.

"And I saw a river coming from the throne of God and Jesus. And on each side of the river were trees that grew fruit each month. They were called the tree of life."

John said, "I heard and saw these things I wrote about."

John wrote about the beautiful home that Jesus told Him to write about. Perhaps as he was writing, he remembered the words of Jesus before He was crucified. Jesus had said to His disciples, "Don't be worried or sad. You believe in God, and you believe in me. In Heaven where my Father is, there are many rooms. I am going back to Heaven to make a place for you so that someday you can come to Heaven and be with me. And one day I will come back for you."

Jesus told John, "Happy are the people who love and obey God. They will enter the Heavenly city. They will live there forever."

From *A Child's First Book of Bible Stories* by Wanda Hayes. Standard Publishing, pp. 126, 127.

REMEMBERING GOD'S TRUTHS: Remove the following picture cards from your picture file and be prepared to teach them in an enjoyable manner.

- The Bible tells us about Heaven.
  Who can go to Heaven?
  All people who love and trust Jesus can go to heaven. (*Heavenly Father* section) Be sure to explain to the children what it means to love and trust Jesus.
- One special day God showed John in a vision what Heaven was like.
  Who is God?
  God is our heavenly Father.
  Where is God?
  God is everywhere. (*Heavenly Father* section)
- There are people on earth who love Jesus, and all the people in Heaven love Jesus. All these people are the church.
  Who are the church?
  All people who love and trust Jesus are the church (*The Church* section) Be sure to explain to the children what it means to love and trust Jesus.

EXPERIENCING GOD'S TRUTHS: To help the children gain some understanding of what Heaven is like, you will need to read the following passages and find a picture to illustrate each characteristic of Heaven.

Mark the passages with a marker so that you can easily find them in class. Put the pictures into a large bag.

1) Jesus is there . . . . John 14:3
2) lots of rooms . . . . John 14:2a
3) no tears . . . . Revelation 7:17
4) no more nights . . . . Revelation 22:5
5) no pain . . . . Revelation 21:4
6) music . . . . Revelation 5:8-9

In class, ask the children, "Who can go to Heaven?" Say with them, "All people who love and trust Jesus can go to Heaven."

Show the pictures and talk about what Heaven is like, based on your study of the verses listed above. Use this method for teaching each characteristic:

1) Tell the children that we are going to be spies—peeping into Heaven to see what it is like. The Bible will help us peep. (Read John 14:3). So the first thing we learn about Heaven is that Jesus is there (place picture of Jesus on a chair).

2) Tell the children to stand up, move to another area of the room that you designate, and sit on the floor there. Open your Bible, read another passage from the list above, briefly explain, and show the picture to remind the children of that characteristic of Heaven. Leave the picture in that area of the room.

3) Follow this procedure for as many characteristics as the children can listen to. Keep each explanation very short, and read only the pertinent part of each verse. Always move between characteristics.

4) Then let the class walk back around the room and tell you what Heaven is like by looking at each picture. Compliment those who describe Heaven as it is described in the Bible. If children make up other possible characteristics (Example, ice cream everywhere), respond by saying, "Maybe that's right. I will be really happy when I get to Heaven. I'm going to see if there is lots of ice cream there."

Lead the children back to the tables and give each child an activity sheet, "What Is Heaven Like?" (p. 13, *Through the Bible Activities for Preschoolers, Book 4*).

Read the paper to the children. Tell the children to point to the first picture (sickness). Ask, "Is there going to be sickness in Heaven?" *No.* Then point to the second picture and *discuss* it. Do this for each picture. Give each child a pencil or crayon. Help each child name and *circle* things that are in Heaven, and put an 'X' on things not in Heaven. Put each child's name on the back of his paper.

REVIEWING GOD'S TRUTHS: Say, "We have learned that Heaven is a wonderful place. The Bible tells us so. What does the Bible tell us about God?" Help the children answer, "God is good, Psalm 73, verse 1."

Have a closing prayer: "Dear God, You are so good. You have planned a way for us to be in Heaven with You. Jesus came to save us. Thank You, God, for Jesus and Heaven. Amen."